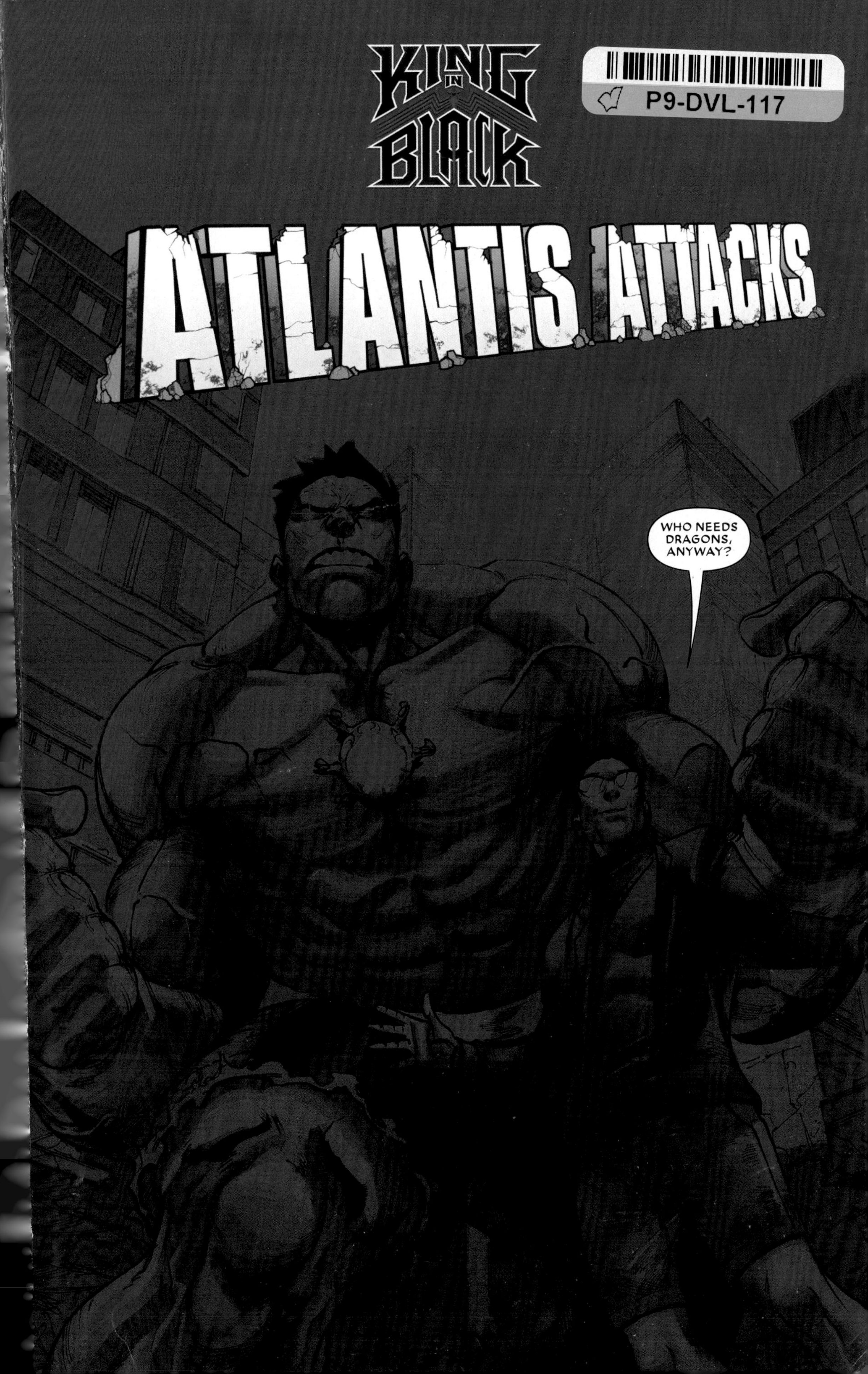
KING IN BLACK
ATLANTIS ATTACKS
WHO NEEDS DRAGONS, ANYWAY?

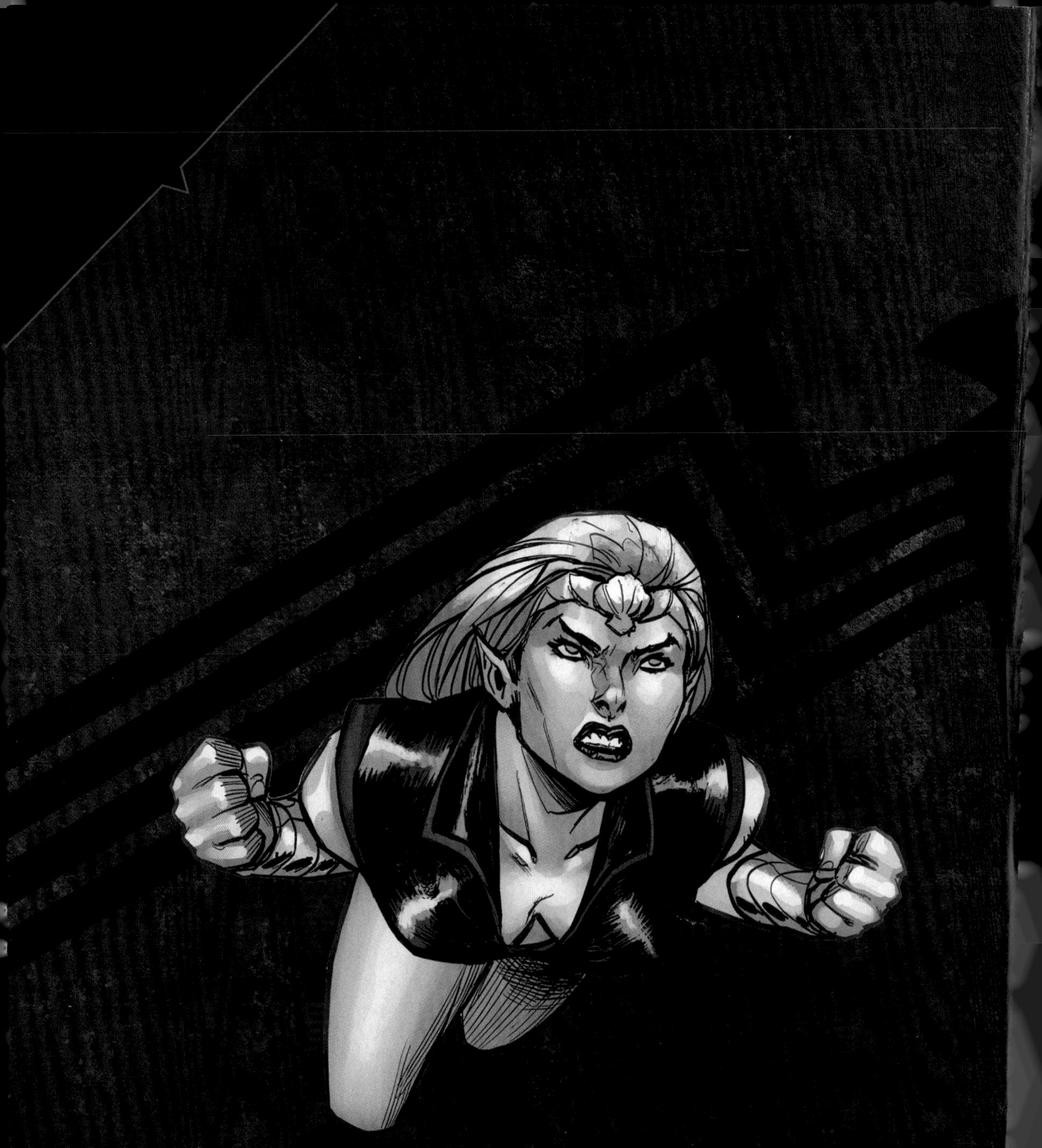

KING IN BLACK: ATLANTIS ATTACKS. Contains material originally published in magazine form as ATLANTIS ATTACKS (2020) #1-5. First printing 2021. ISBN 978-1-302-92456-0. Published by MARVEL WORLDWIDE, INC., a subsidiary of MARVEL ENTERTAINMENT, LLC. OFFICE OF PUBLICATION: 1290 Avenue of the Americas, New York, NY 10104. © 2021 MARVEL No similarity between any of the names, characters, persons, and/or institutions in this magazine with those of any living or dead person or institution is intended, and any such similarity which may exist is purely coincidental. Printed in Canada. KEVIN FEIGE, Chief Creative Officer; DAN BUCKLEY, President, Marvel Entertainment; JOE QUESADA, EVP & Creative Director; DAVID BOGART, Associate Publisher & SVP of Talent Affairs; TOM BREVOORT, VP, Executive Editor; NICK LOWE, Executive Editor, VP of Content, Digital Publishing; DAVID GABRIEL, VP of Print & Digital Publishing; JEFF YOUNGQUIST, VP of Production & Special Projects; ALEX MORALES, Director of Publishing Operations; DAN EDINGTON, Managing Editor; RICKEY PURDIN, Director of Talent Relations; JENNIFER GRÜNWALD, Senior Editor, Special Projects; SUSAN CRESPI, Production Manager; STAN LEE, Chairman Emeritus. For information regarding advertising in Marvel Comics or on Marvel.com, please contact Vit DeBellis, Custom Solutions & Integrated Advertising Manager, at vdebellis@marvel.com. For Marvel subscription inquiries, please call 888-511-5480. **Manufactured between 5/14/2021 and 6/15/2021 by SOLISCO PRINTERS, SCOTT, QC, CANADA.**

10 9 8 7 6 5 4 3 2 1

KNULL, THE PRIMORDIAL AND MALICIOUS GOD OF THE
SYMBIOTES, HAS ARRIVED ON EARTH WITH AN ARMY OF
SYMBIOTE DRAGONS. SO FAR, EARTH'S MIGHTIEST HEROES
HAVE BEEN HELPLESS TO STOP HIM – EVEN THE SENTRY,
ONE OF THE MOST POWERFUL SUPERHUMANS IN HISTORY.

ATLANTIS ATTACKS

YEARS AGO, FBI AGENT JIMMY WOO ASSUMED CONTROL OF THE ATLAS
FOUNDATION TO USE ITS INFLUENCE FOR GOOD. DURING THE WAR OF THE REALMS,
HE RECRUITED A NEW TEAM OF YOUNG HEROES LED BY AMADEUS CHO TO PROTECT
THE PACIFIC FROM DESTRUCTION. THEY BECAME THE NEW AGENTS OF ATLAS!

MIKE NGUYEN, C.E.O. OF THE BIG NGUYEN COMPANY, HAS FOUNDED THE
PAN-ASIAN PORTAL CITY OF PAN. NGUYEN CLAIMS TO HAVE BUILT PAN FOR
THE GREATER GOOD, BUT ATLAS IS NOT CONVINCED. AFTER THEY BROKE INTO
NGUYEN'S TOWER TO INVESTIGATE, THEY DISCOVERED THE DEADLY SECRET
POWERING ALL OF PAN'S AMAZING TECHNOLOGY. NGUYEN HAS WRONGED
ATLANTIS. NOW KING NAMOR IS COMING FOR NGUYEN, AND HIS FURY
THREATENS TO DESTROY ALL OF PAN ITSELF!

GREG PAK WRITER
ARIO ANINDITO (#1-5) & ROBERT GILL (#2-5) ARTISTS
RACHELLE ROSENBERG COLOR ARTIST

VC's JOE SABINO LETTERER
ROCK-HE KIM (#1, #3); MICO SUAYAN & FRANK D'ARMATA (#2);
AND CARLO PAGULAYAN, JASON PAZ & RAIN BEREDO (#4-5) COVER ART

TOM GRONEMAN ASSISTANT EDITOR
MARK PANICCIA EDITOR

JENNIFER GRÜNWALD COLLECTION EDITOR
DANIEL KIRCHHOFFER ASSISTANT EDITOR
MAIA LOY ASSISTANT MANAGING EDITOR
LISA MONTALBANO ASSISTANT MANAGING EDITOR
JEFF YOUNGQUIST VP PRODUCTION & SPECIAL PROJECTS
JAY BOWEN WITH ANTHONY GAMBINO BOOK DESIGNER
DAVID GABRIEL SVP PRINT, SALES & MARKETING
C.B. CEBULSKI EDITOR IN CHIEF

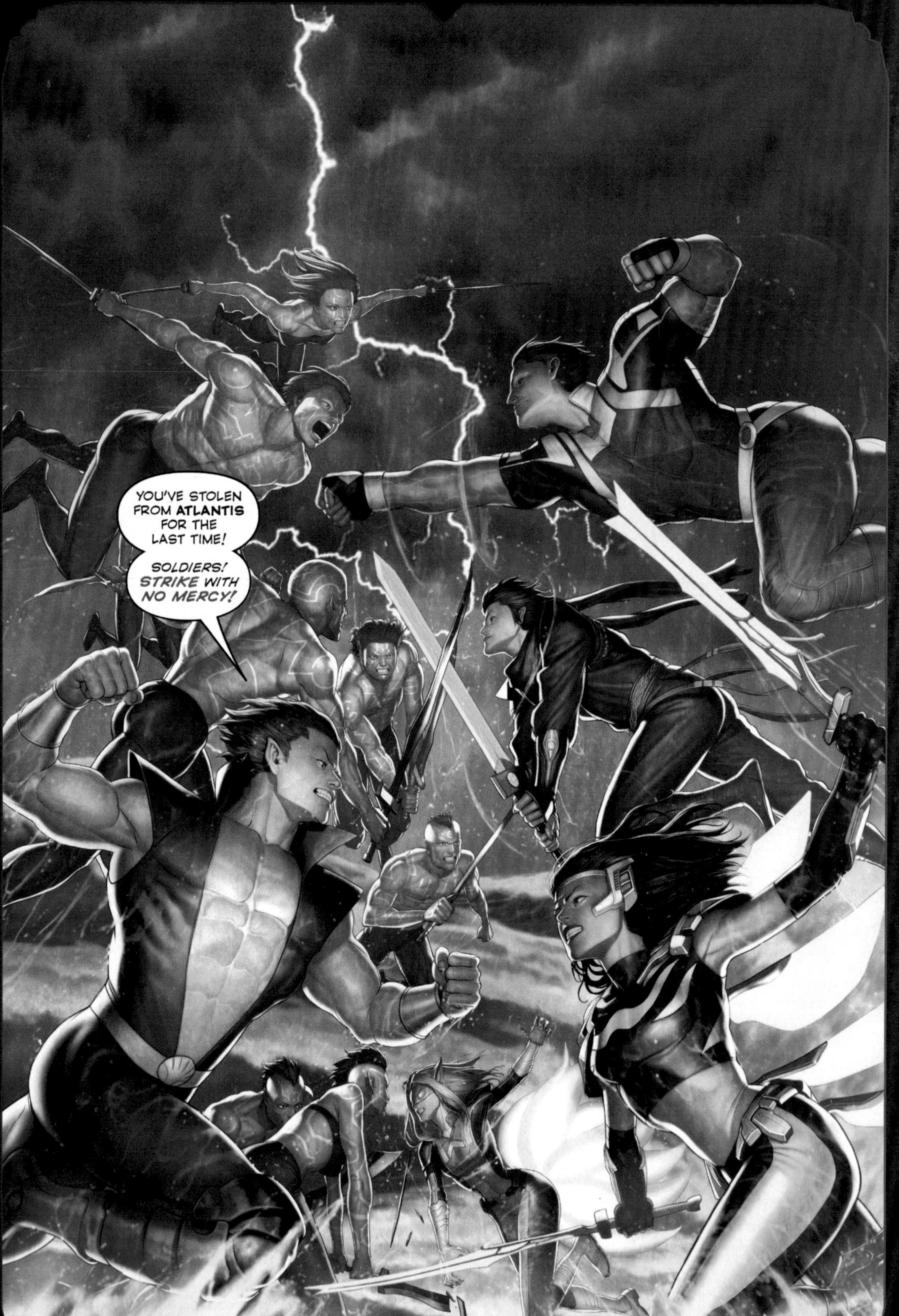
YOU'VE STOLEN FROM ATLANTIS FOR THE LAST TIME!
SOLDIERS! STRIKE WITH NO MERCY!

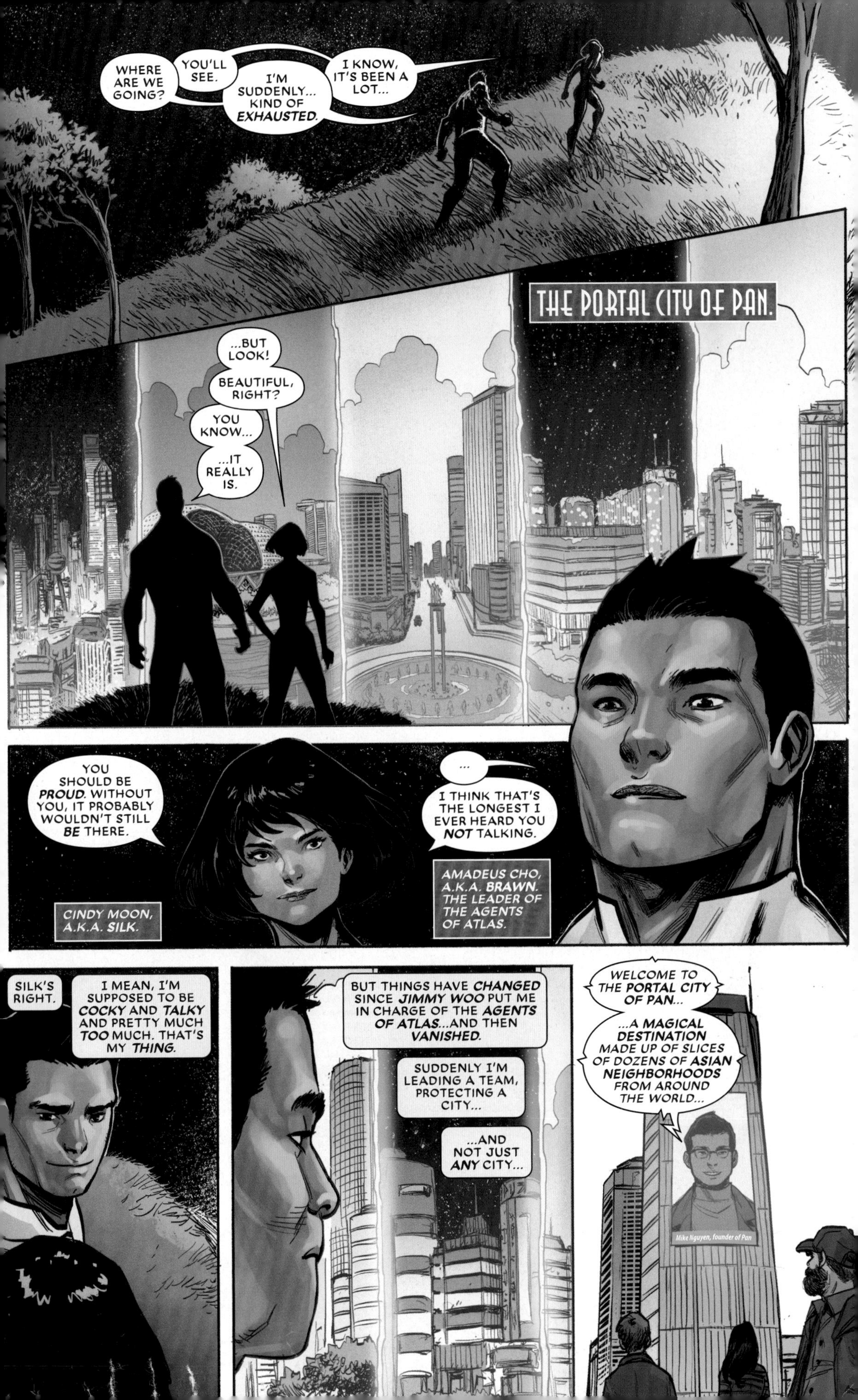

WHERE ARE WE GOING?
YOU'LL SEE.
I'M SUDDENLY... KIND OF EXHAUSTED.
I KNOW, IT'S BEEN A LOT...
THE PORTAL CITY OF PAN.
...BUT LOOK!
BEAUTIFUL, RIGHT?
YOU KNOW...
...IT REALLY IS.
YOU SHOULD BE PROUD. WITHOUT YOU, IT PROBABLY WOULDN'T STILL BE THERE.
CINDY MOON, A.K.A. SILK.
...
I THINK THAT'S THE LONGEST I EVER HEARD YOU NOT TALKING.
AMADEUS CHO, A.K.A. BRAWN. THE LEADER OF THE AGENTS OF ATLAS.
SILK'S RIGHT.
I MEAN, I'M SUPPOSED TO BE COCKY AND TALKY AND PRETTY MUCH TOO MUCH. THAT'S MY THING.
BUT THINGS HAVE CHANGED SINCE JIMMY WOO PUT ME IN CHARGE OF THE AGENTS OF ATLAS...AND THEN VANISHED.
SUDDENLY I'M LEADING A TEAM, PROTECTING A CITY...
...AND NOT JUST ANY CITY...
WELCOME TO THE PORTAL CITY OF PAN...
...A MAGICAL DESTINATION MADE UP OF SLICES OF DOZENS OF ASIAN NEIGHBORHOODS FROM AROUND THE WORLD...
Mike Nguyen, founder of Pan

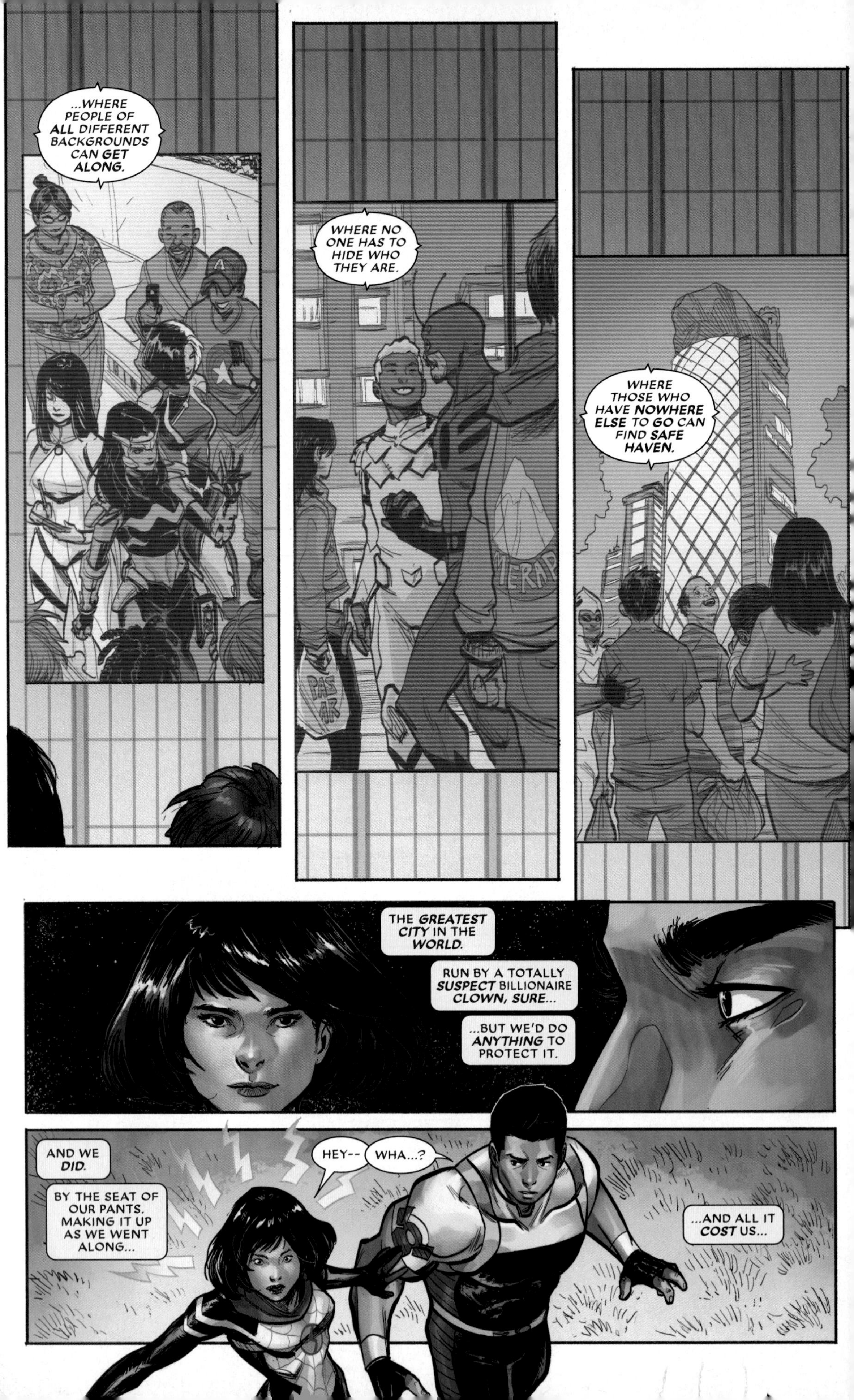
...WHERE PEOPLE OF ALL DIFFERENT BACKGROUNDS CAN GET ALONG.
WHERE NO ONE HAS TO HIDE WHO THEY ARE.
WHERE THOSE WHO HAVE NOWHERE ELSE TO GO CAN FIND SAFE HAVEN.
THE GREATEST CITY IN THE WORLD.
RUN BY A TOTALLY SUSPECT BILLIONAIRE CLOWN, SURE...
...BUT WE'D DO ANYTHING TO PROTECT IT.
AND WE DID.
BY THE SEAT OF OUR PANTS. MAKING IT UP AS WE WENT ALONG...
HEY--
WHA...?
...AND ALL IT COST US...

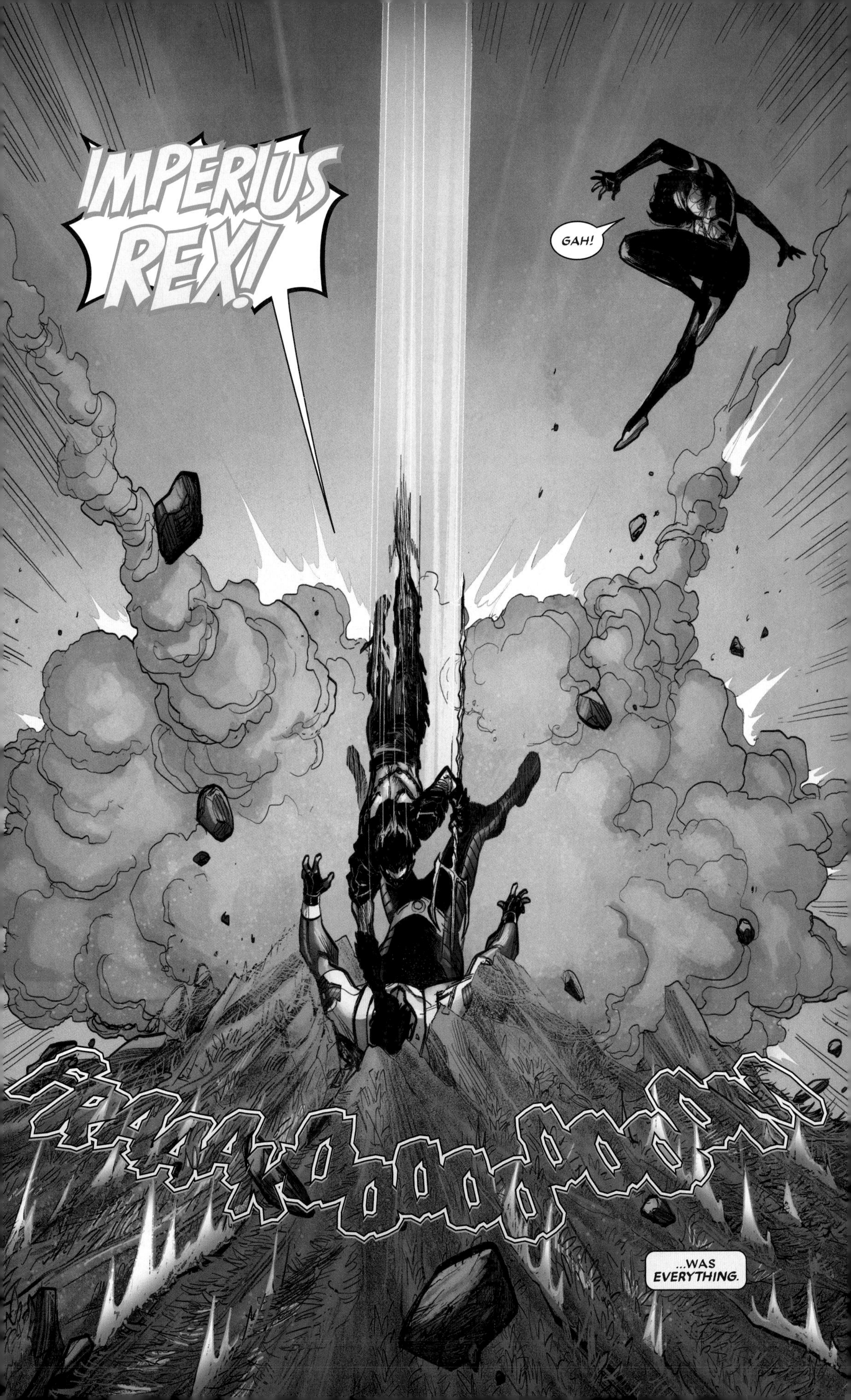
IMPERIUS REX!
GAH!
...WAS EVERYTHING.

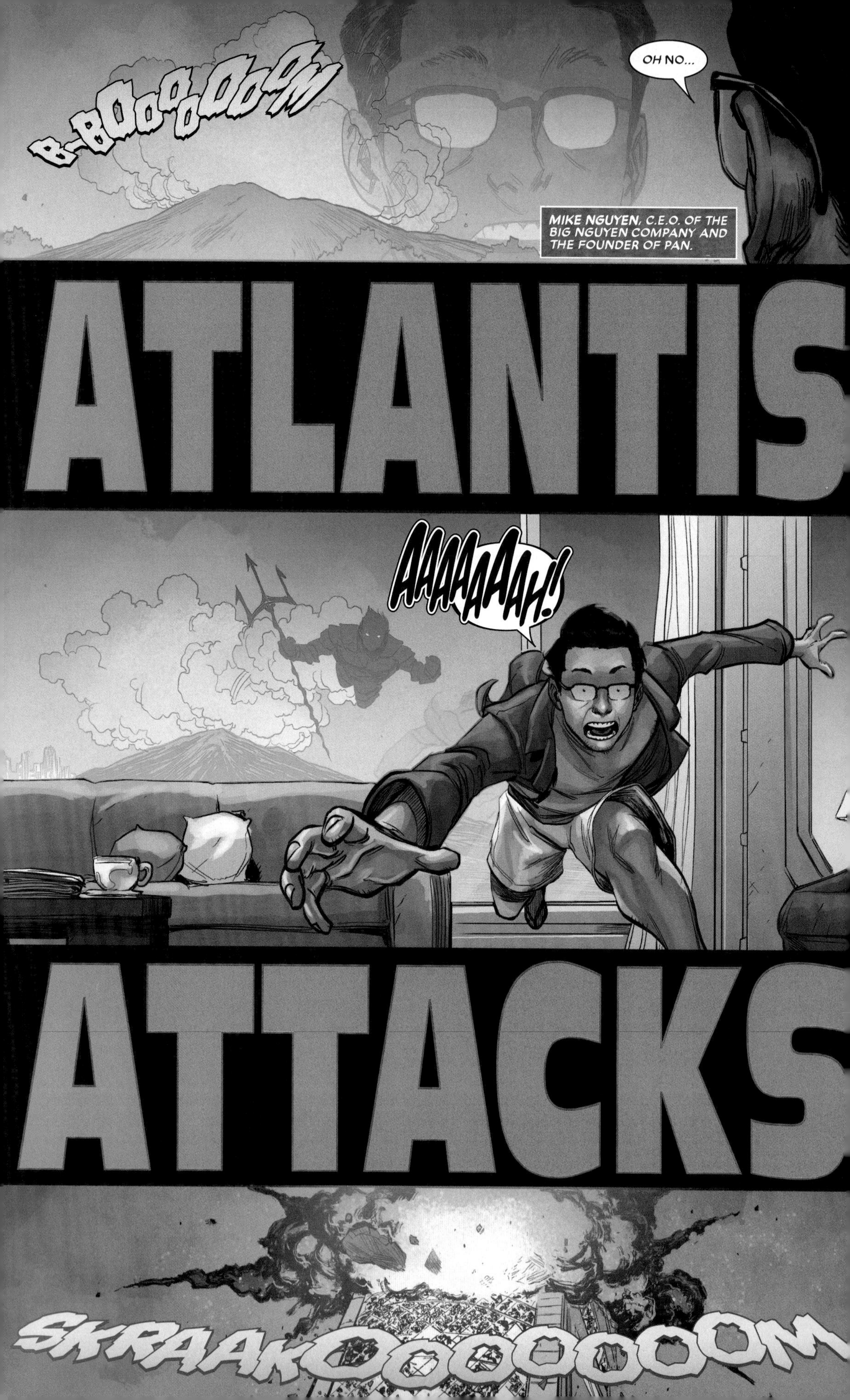
B-BOOOOOOOM
OH NO...
MIKE NGUYEN, C.E.O. OF THE BIG NGUYEN COMPANY AND THE FOUNDER OF PAN.
ATLANTIS
AAAAAAAH!!
ATTACKS
SKRAAKOOOOOOOOM

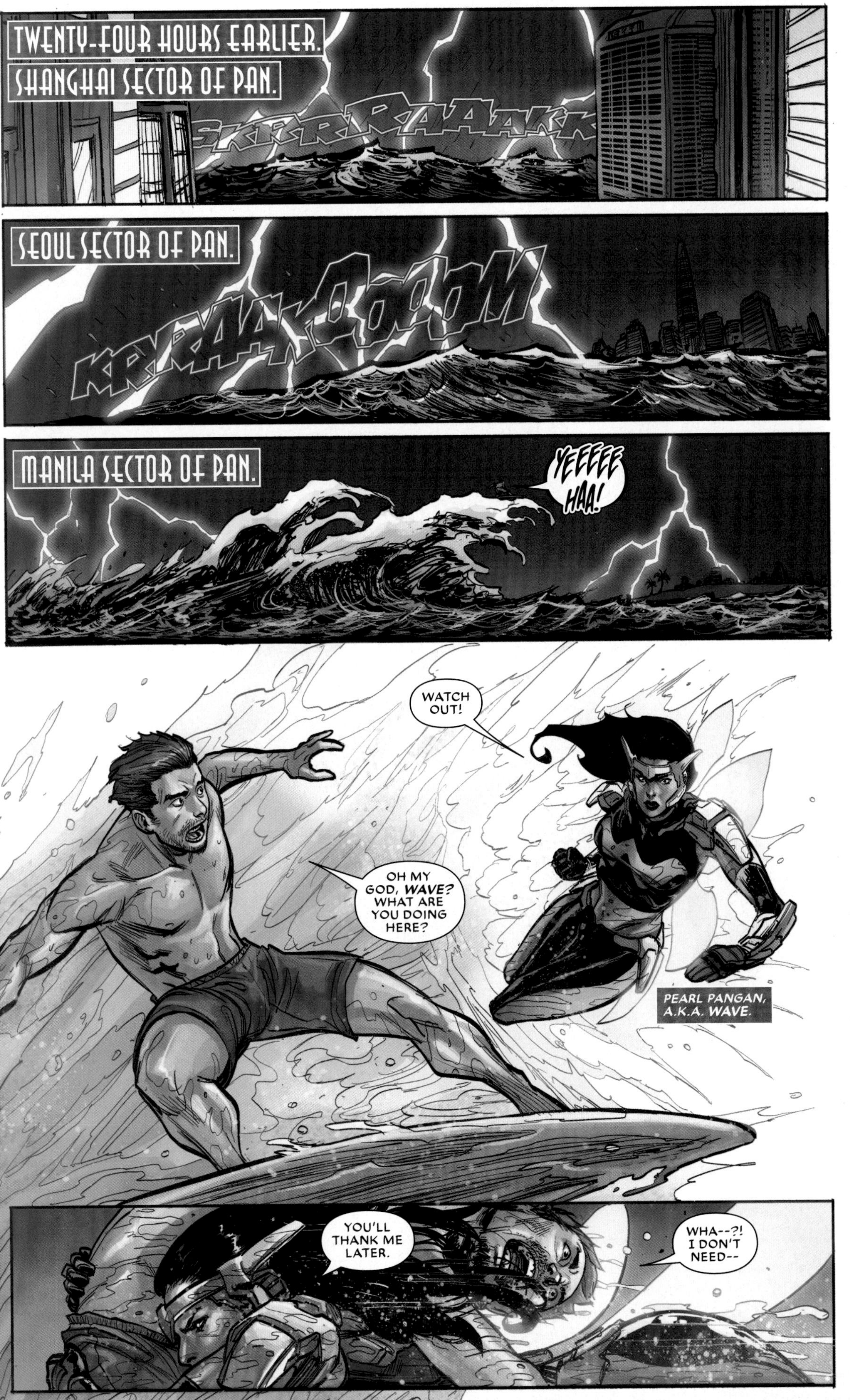
TWENTY-FOUR HOURS EARLIER.
SHANGHAI SECTOR OF PAN.
SKKRRAAAKK
SEOUL SECTOR OF PAN.
KRRAAKBOOOM
MANILA SECTOR OF PAN.
YEEEEE HAA!
WATCH OUT!
OH MY GOD, WAVE? WHAT ARE YOU DOING HERE?
PEARL PANGAN, A.K.A. WAVE.
YOU'LL THANK ME LATER.
WHA--?! I DON'T NEED--

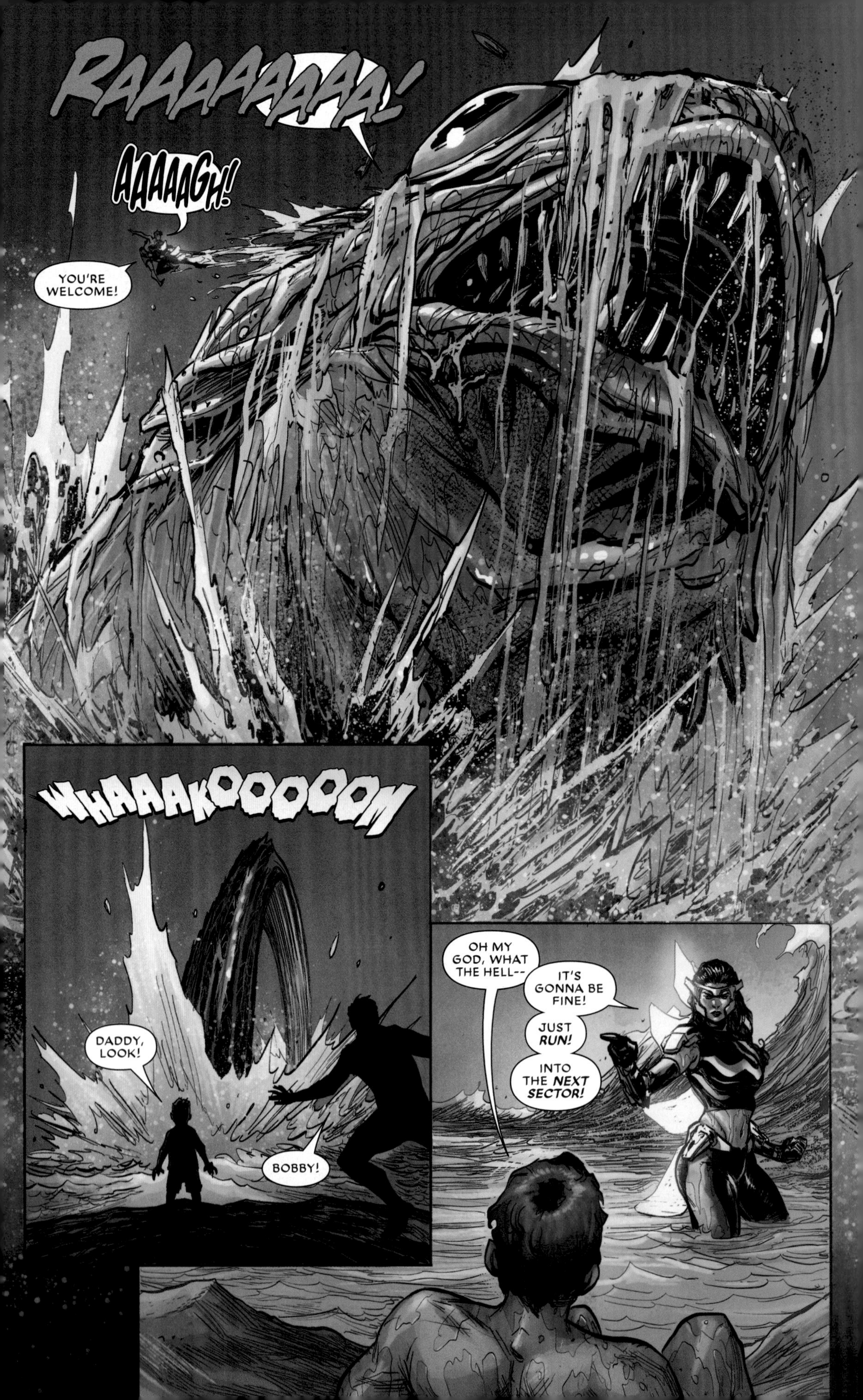
RAAAAAAAA!
AAAAAGH!
YOU'RE WELCOME!
WHAAAKOOOOOM
DADDY, LOOK!
BOBBY!
OH MY GOD, WHAT THE HELL--
IT'S GONNA BE FINE!
JUST *RUN!*
INTO THE *NEXT SECTOR!*

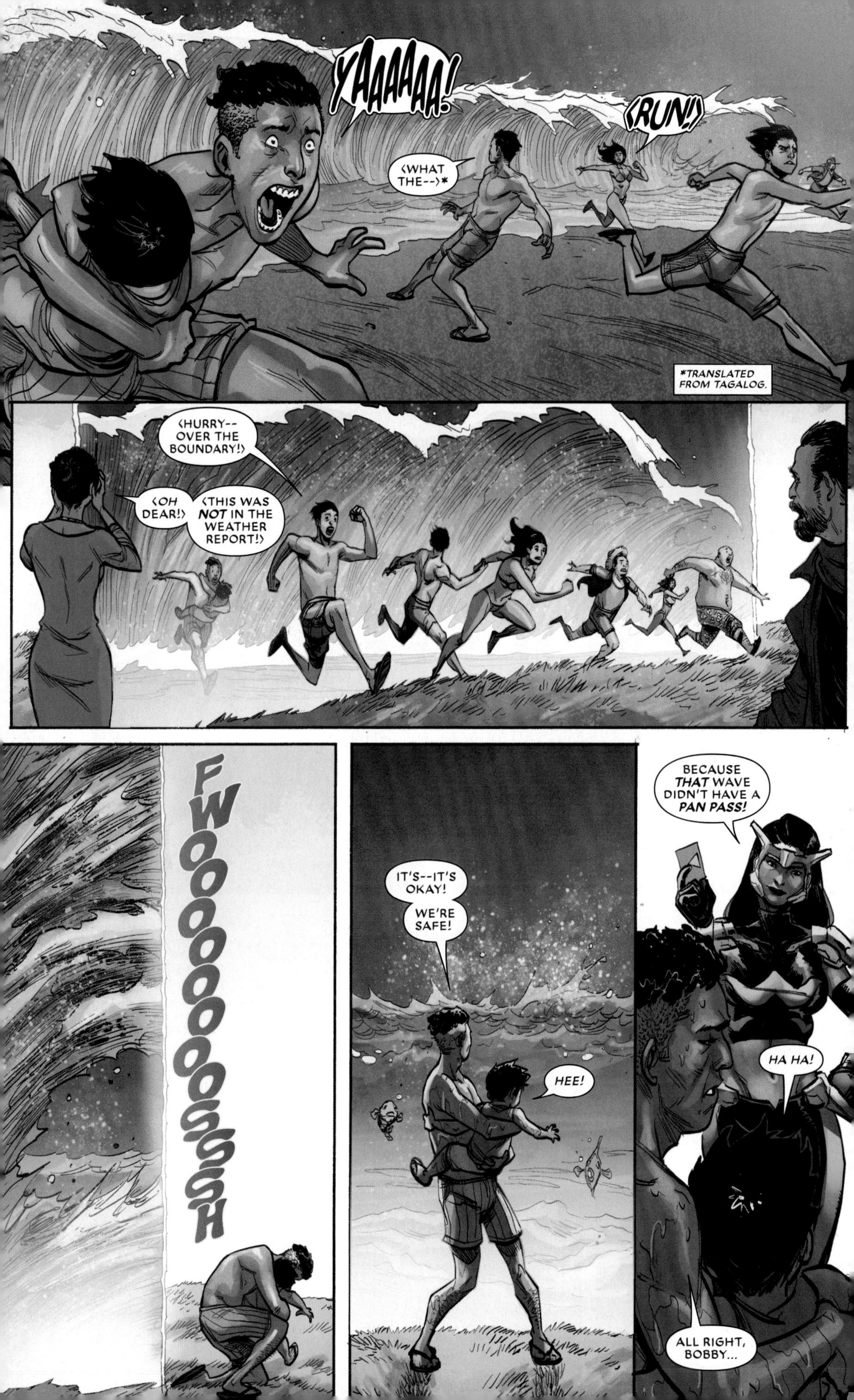
YAAAAAA!
⟨WHAT THE--⟩*
⟨RUN!⟩
*TRANSLATED FROM TAGALOG.
⟨HURRY-- OVER THE BOUNDARY!⟩
⟨OH DEAR!⟩
⟨THIS WAS NOT IN THE WEATHER REPORT!⟩
FWOOOOOOOOSSSH
IT'S--IT'S OKAY!
WE'RE SAFE!
HEE!
BECAUSE THAT WAVE DIDN'T HAVE A PAN PASS!
HA HA!
ALL RIGHT, BOBBY...

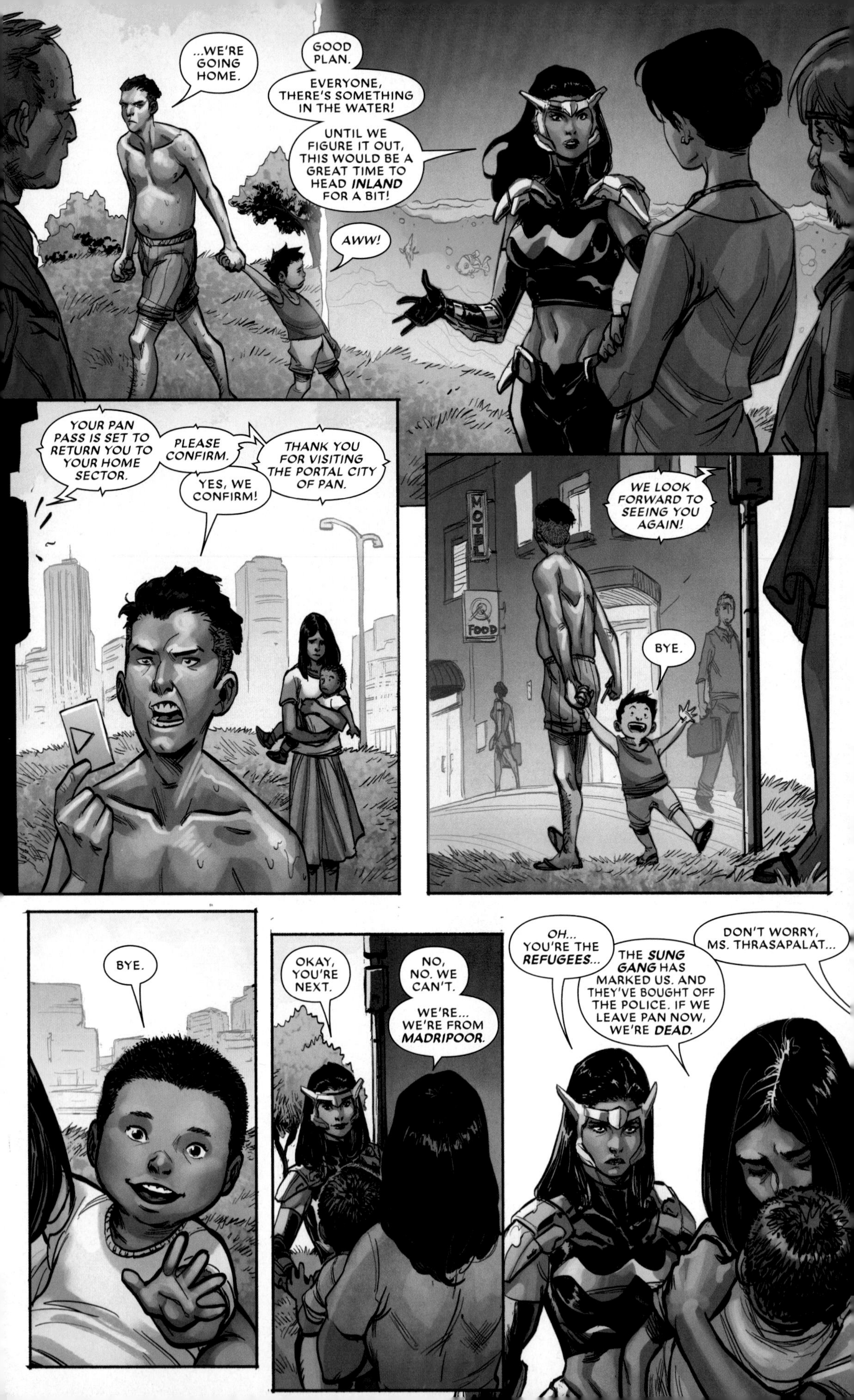

...WE'RE GOING HOME.
GOOD PLAN.
EVERYONE, THERE'S SOMETHING IN THE WATER!
UNTIL WE FIGURE IT OUT, THIS WOULD BE A GREAT TIME TO HEAD INLAND FOR A BIT!
AWW!
YOUR PAN PASS IS SET TO RETURN YOU TO YOUR HOME SECTOR.
PLEASE CONFIRM.
YES, WE CONFIRM!
THANK YOU FOR VISITING THE PORTAL CITY OF PAN.
WE LOOK FORWARD TO SEEING YOU AGAIN!
MOTEL
FOOD
BYE.
BYE.
OKAY, YOU'RE NEXT.
NO, NO. WE CAN'T.
WE'RE... WE'RE FROM MADRIPOOR.
OH... YOU'RE THE REFUGEES...
THE SUNG GANG HAS MARKED US. AND THEY'VE BOUGHT OFF THE POLICE. IF WE LEAVE PAN NOW, WE'RE DEAD.
DON'T WORRY, MS. THRASAPALAT...

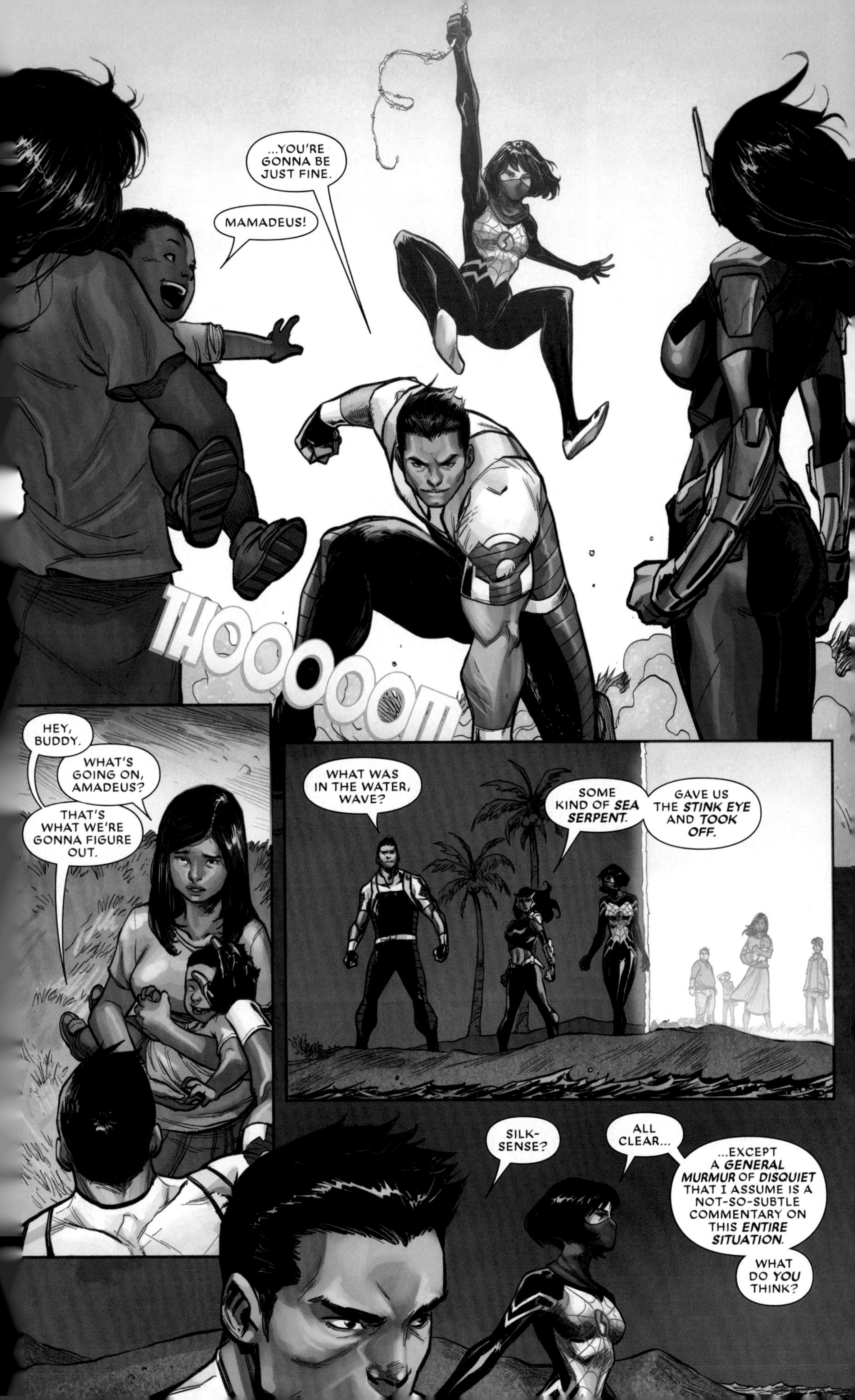

MAMADEUS!
...YOU'RE GONNA BE JUST FINE.
THOOOOOOM
HEY, BUDDY.
WHAT'S GOING ON, AMADEUS?
THAT'S WHAT WE'RE GONNA FIGURE OUT.
WHAT WAS IN THE WATER, WAVE?
SOME KIND OF SEA SERPENT.
GAVE US THE STINK EYE AND TOOK OFF.
SILK-SENSE?
ALL CLEAR...
...EXCEPT A GENERAL MURMUR OF DISQUIET THAT I ASSUME IS A NOT-SO-SUBTLE COMMENTARY ON THIS ENTIRE SITUATION.
WHAT DO YOU THINK?

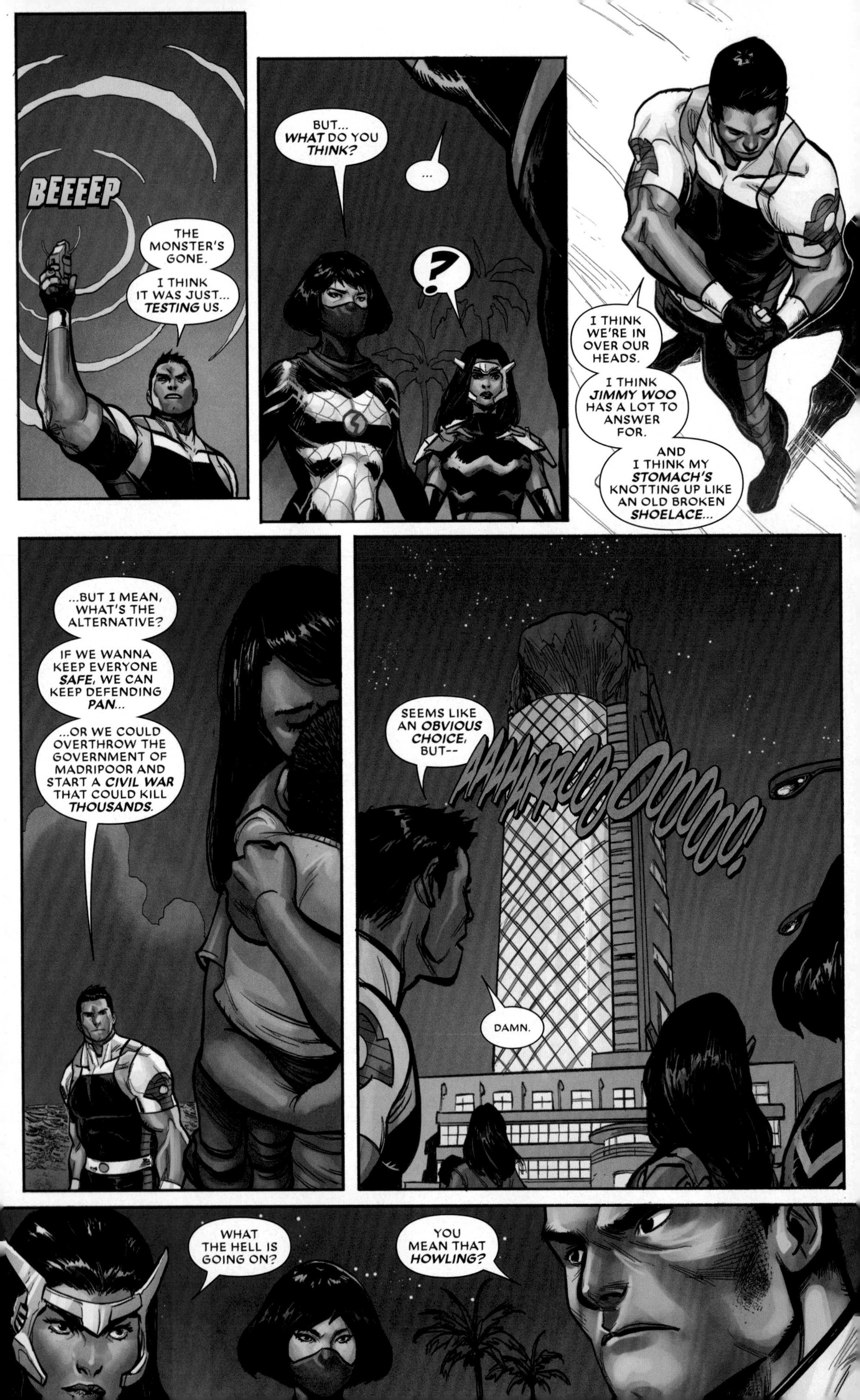

BEEEEP
THE MONSTER'S GONE.
I THINK IT WAS JUST... TESTING US.
BUT... WHAT DO YOU THINK?
...
?
I THINK WE'RE IN OVER OUR HEADS.
I THINK JIMMY WOO HAS A LOT TO ANSWER FOR.
AND I THINK MY STOMACH'S KNOTTING UP LIKE AN OLD BROKEN SHOELACE...
...BUT I MEAN, WHAT'S THE ALTERNATIVE?
IF WE WANNA KEEP EVERYONE SAFE, WE CAN KEEP DEFENDING PAN...
...OR WE COULD OVERTHROW THE GOVERNMENT OF MADRIPOOR AND START A CIVIL WAR THAT COULD KILL THOUSANDS.
SEEMS LIKE AN OBVIOUS CHOICE, BUT--
AAAAARROOOOOOOOO
DAMN.
WHAT THE HELL IS GOING ON?
YOU MEAN THAT HOWLING?

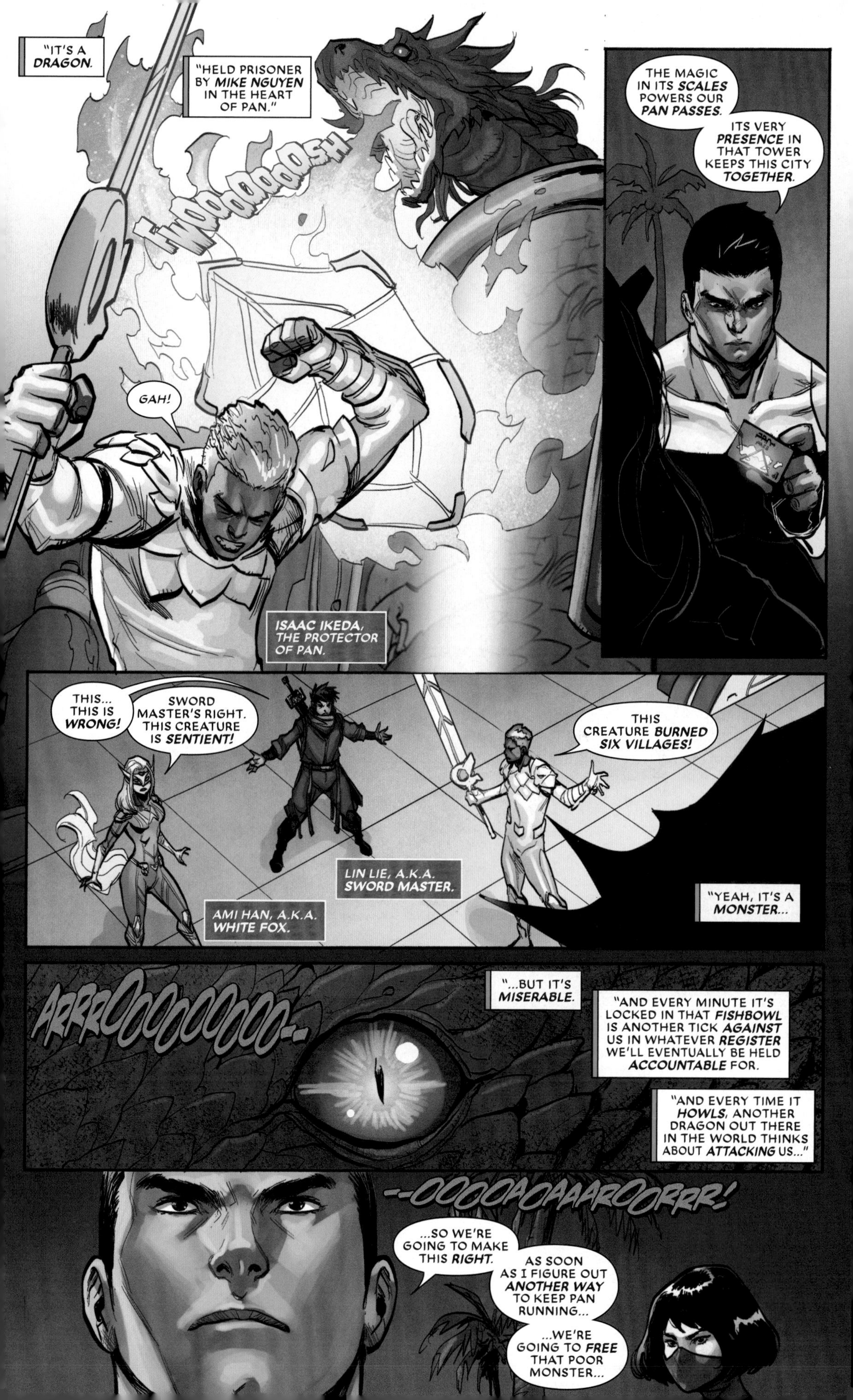
"IT'S A DRAGON.
"HELD PRISONER BY MIKE NGUYEN IN THE HEART OF PAN."
FWOOOOOOOSH
THE MAGIC IN ITS SCALES POWERS OUR PAN PASSES.
ITS VERY PRESENCE IN THAT TOWER KEEPS THIS CITY TOGETHER.
GAH!
ISAAC IKEDA, THE PROTECTOR OF PAN.
THIS... THIS IS WRONG!
SWORD MASTER'S RIGHT. THIS CREATURE IS SENTIENT!
THIS CREATURE BURNED SIX VILLAGES!
LIN LIE, A.K.A. SWORD MASTER.
AMI HAN, A.K.A. WHITE FOX.
"YEAH, IT'S A MONSTER...
ARRROOOOOOOOOO--
"...BUT IT'S MISERABLE.
"AND EVERY MINUTE IT'S LOCKED IN THAT FISHBOWL IS ANOTHER TICK AGAINST US IN WHATEVER REGISTER WE'LL EVENTUALLY BE HELD ACCOUNTABLE FOR.
"AND EVERY TIME IT HOWLS, ANOTHER DRAGON OUT THERE IN THE WORLD THINKS ABOUT ATTACKING US..."
--OOOOAOAAARROORRR!
...SO WE'RE GOING TO MAKE THIS RIGHT.
AS SOON AS I FIGURE OUT ANOTHER WAY TO KEEP PAN RUNNING...
...WE'RE GOING TO FREE THAT POOR MONSTER...

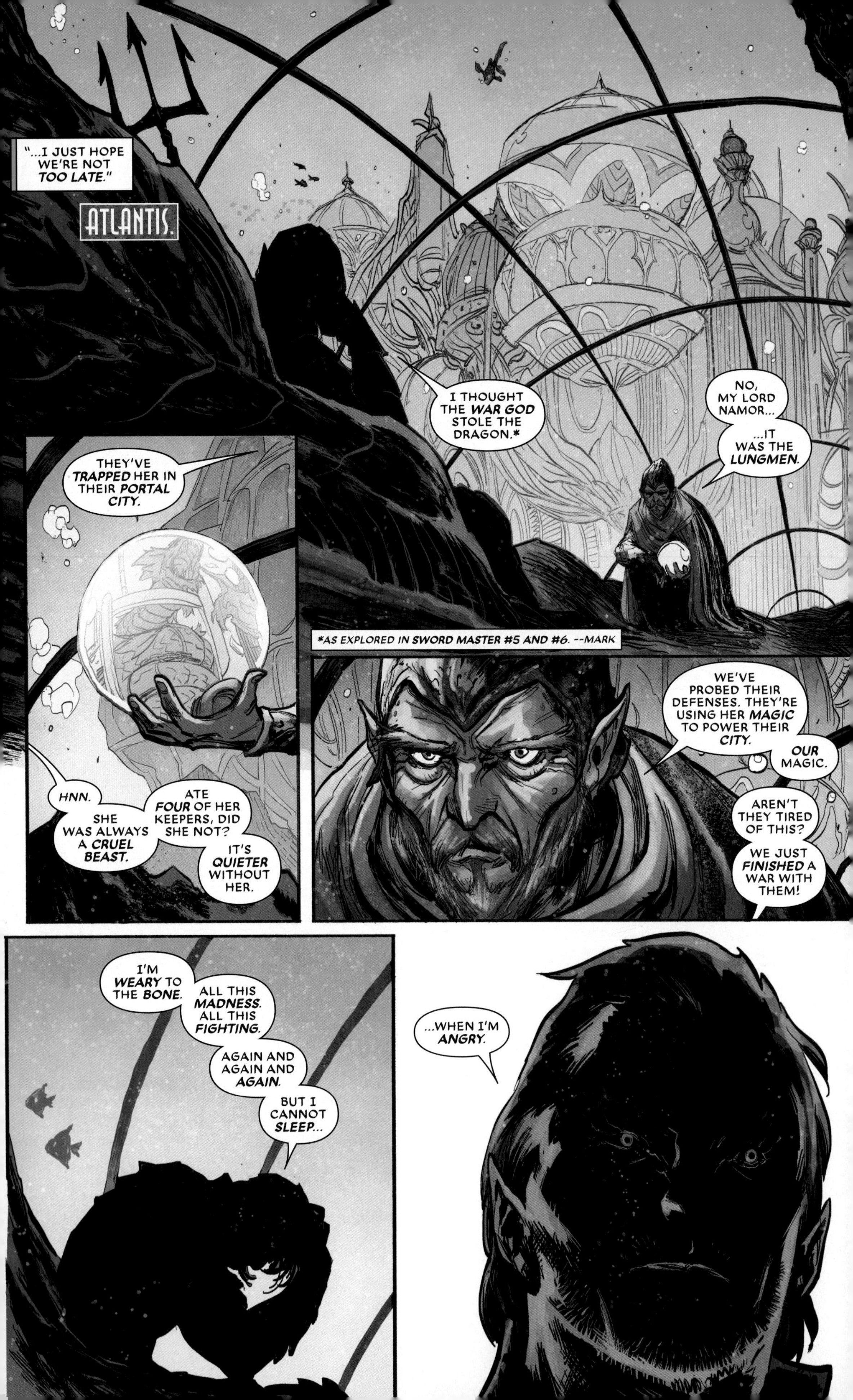
"...I JUST HOPE WE'RE NOT TOO LATE."
ATLANTIS.
I THOUGHT THE WAR GOD STOLE THE DRAGON.*
NO, MY LORD NAMOR...
...IT WAS THE LUNGMEN.
*AS EXPLORED IN SWORD MASTER #5 AND #6. --MARK
THEY'VE TRAPPED HER IN THEIR PORTAL CITY.
HNN.
SHE WAS ALWAYS A CRUEL BEAST.
ATE FOUR OF HER KEEPERS, DID SHE NOT?
IT'S QUIETER WITHOUT HER.
WE'VE PROBED THEIR DEFENSES. THEY'RE USING HER MAGIC TO POWER THEIR CITY.
OUR MAGIC.
AREN'T THEY TIRED OF THIS?
WE JUST FINISHED A WAR WITH THEM!
I'M WEARY TO THE BONE.
ALL THIS MADNESS. ALL THIS FIGHTING.
AGAIN AND AGAIN AND AGAIN.
BUT I CANNOT SLEEP...
...WHEN I'M ANGRY.

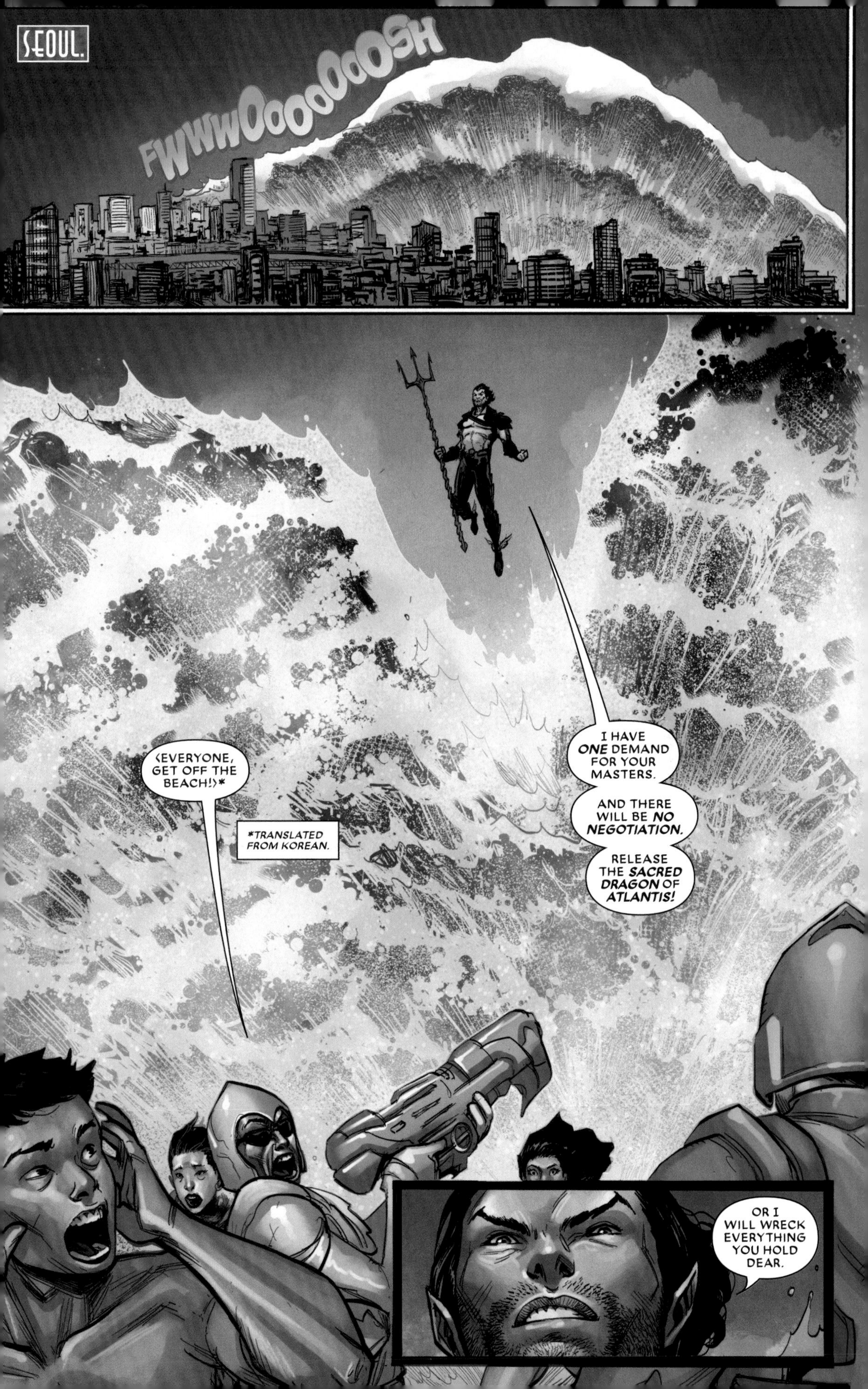
SEOUL.
FWWWOOOOOOOOSH
I HAVE ONE DEMAND FOR YOUR MASTERS.
AND THERE WILL BE NO NEGOTIATION.
RELEASE THE SACRED DRAGON OF ATLANTIS!
‹EVERYONE, GET OFF THE BEACH!›*
*TRANSLATED FROM KOREAN.
OR I WILL WRECK EVERYTHING YOU HOLD DEAR.

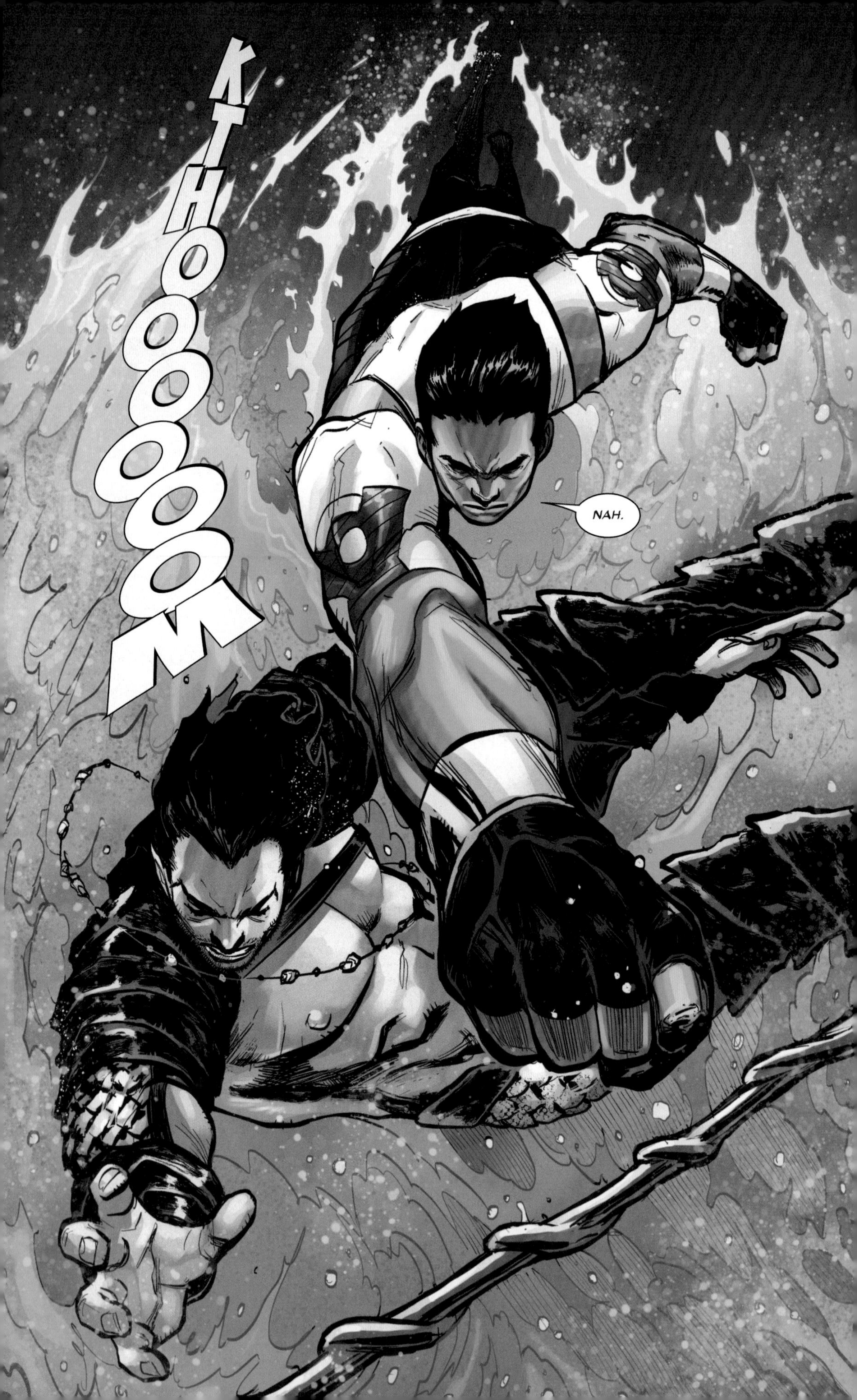
KTHOOOOOOOM
NAH.

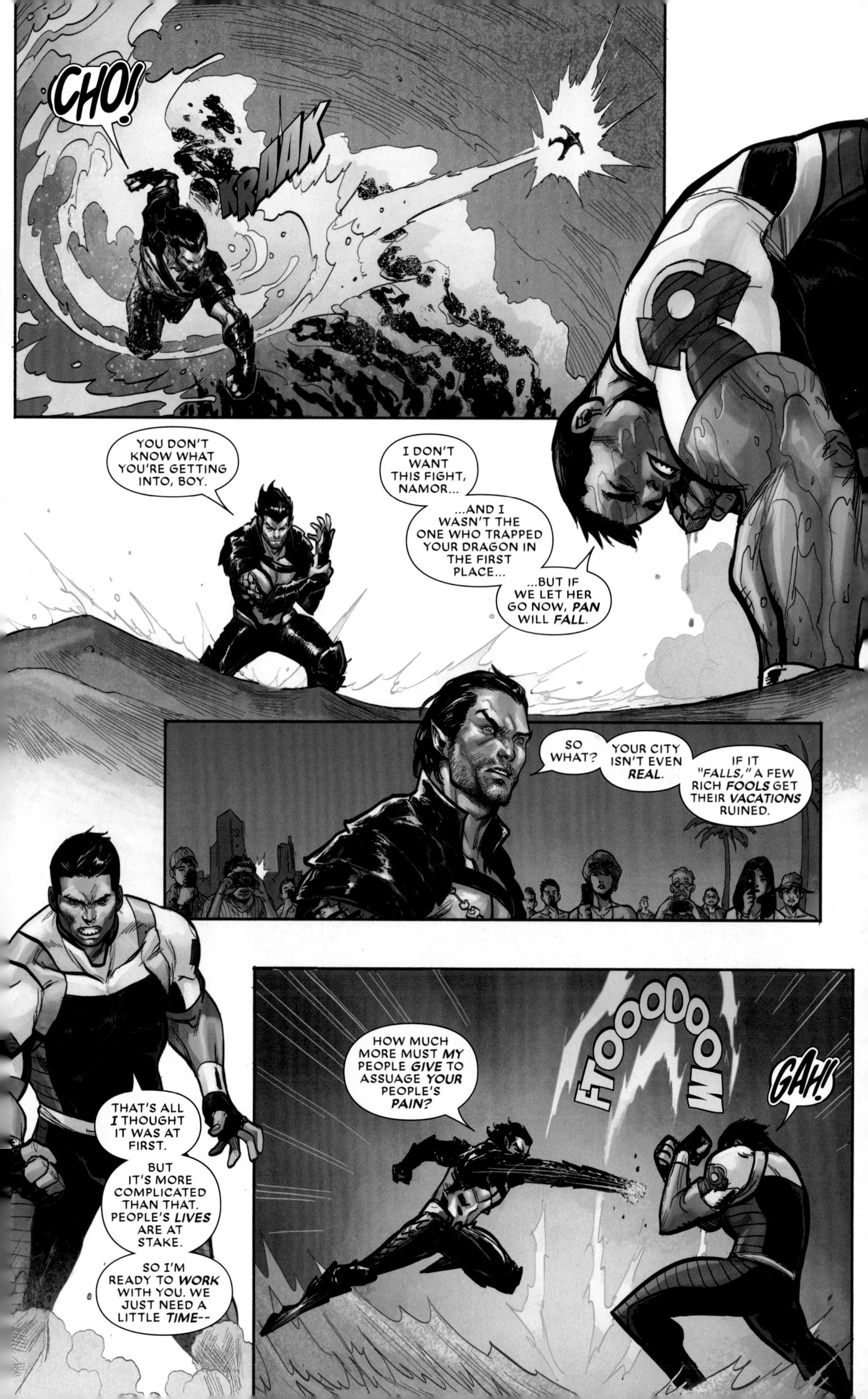
CHO!
KRAAAK
YOU DON'T KNOW WHAT YOU'RE GETTING INTO, BOY.
I DON'T WANT THIS FIGHT, NAMOR...
...AND I WASN'T THE ONE WHO TRAPPED YOUR DRAGON IN THE FIRST PLACE...
...BUT IF WE LET HER GO NOW, PAN WILL FALL.
SO WHAT?
YOUR CITY ISN'T EVEN REAL.
IF IT "FALLS," A FEW RICH FOOLS GET THEIR VACATIONS RUINED.
THAT'S ALL I THOUGHT IT WAS AT FIRST.
BUT IT'S MORE COMPLICATED THAN THAT. PEOPLE'S LIVES ARE AT STAKE.
SO I'M READY TO WORK WITH YOU. WE JUST NEED A LITTLE TIME--
HOW MUCH MORE MUST MY PEOPLE GIVE TO ASSUAGE YOUR PEOPLE'S PAIN?
FTOOOOOOOM
GAH!

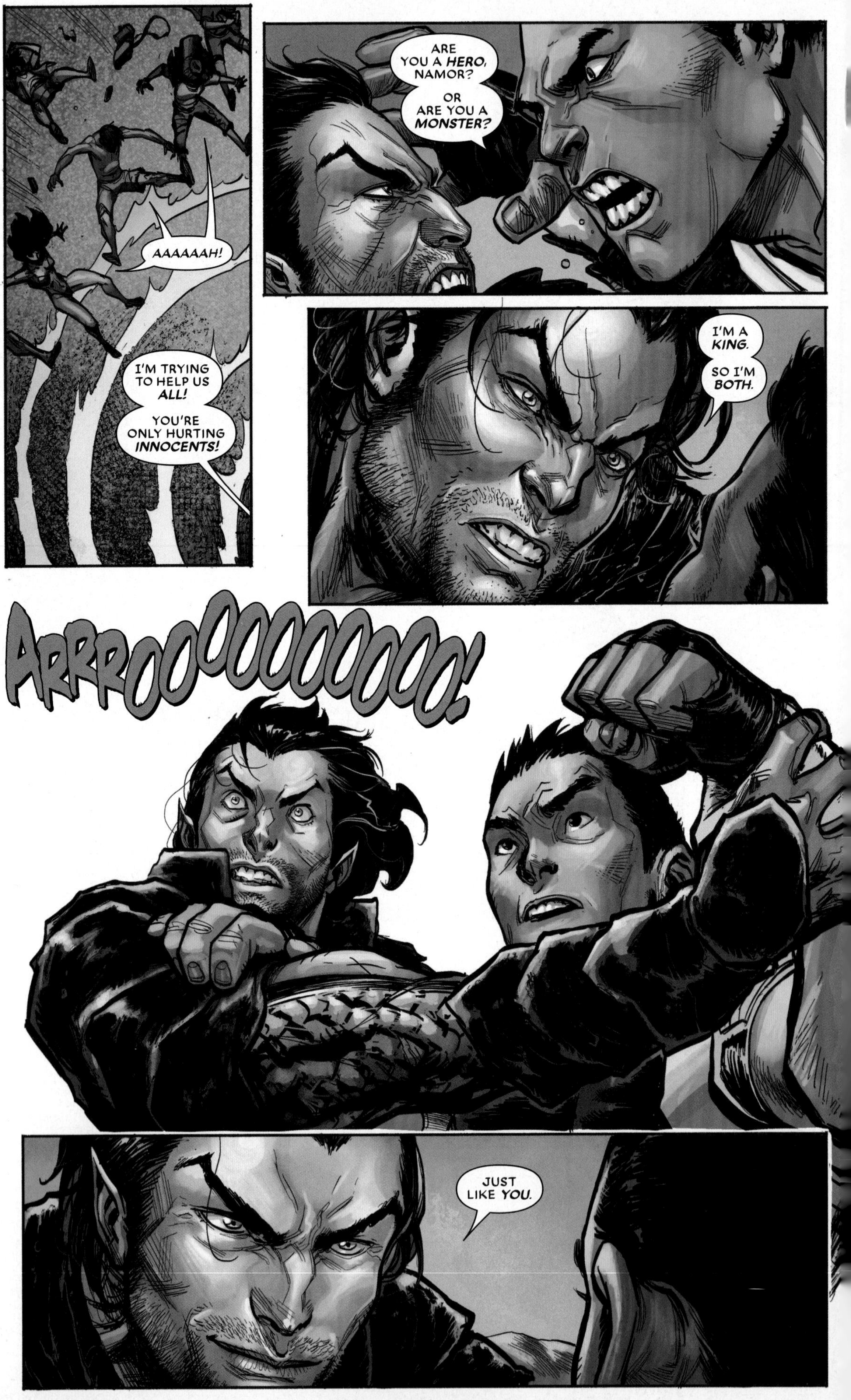
ARE YOU A HERO, NAMOR?
OR ARE YOU A MONSTER?
AAAAAAH!
I'M TRYING TO HELP US ALL!
YOU'RE ONLY HURTING INNOCENTS!
I'M A KING.
SO I'M BOTH.
ARRROOOOOOOOOO!
JUST LIKE YOU.

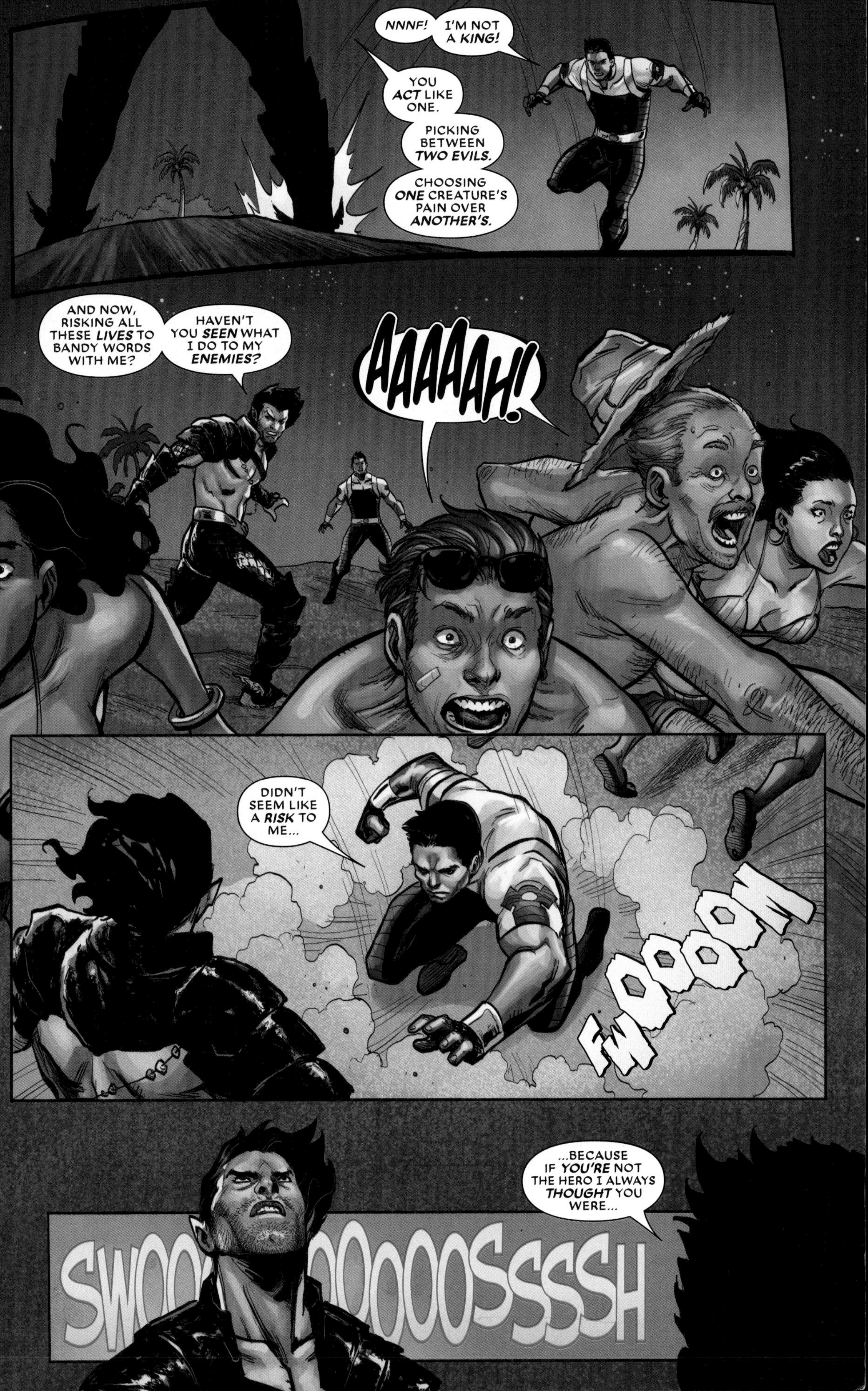
NNNF!
I'M NOT A KING!
YOU ACT LIKE ONE.
PICKING BETWEEN TWO EVILS.
CHOOSING ONE CREATURE'S PAIN OVER ANOTHER'S.
AND NOW, RISKING ALL THESE LIVES TO BANDY WORDS WITH ME?
HAVEN'T YOU SEEN WHAT I DO TO MY ENEMIES?
AAAAAH!
DIDN'T SEEM LIKE A RISK TO ME...
FWOOOOM
...BECAUSE IF YOU'RE NOT THE HERO I ALWAYS THOUGHT YOU WERE...

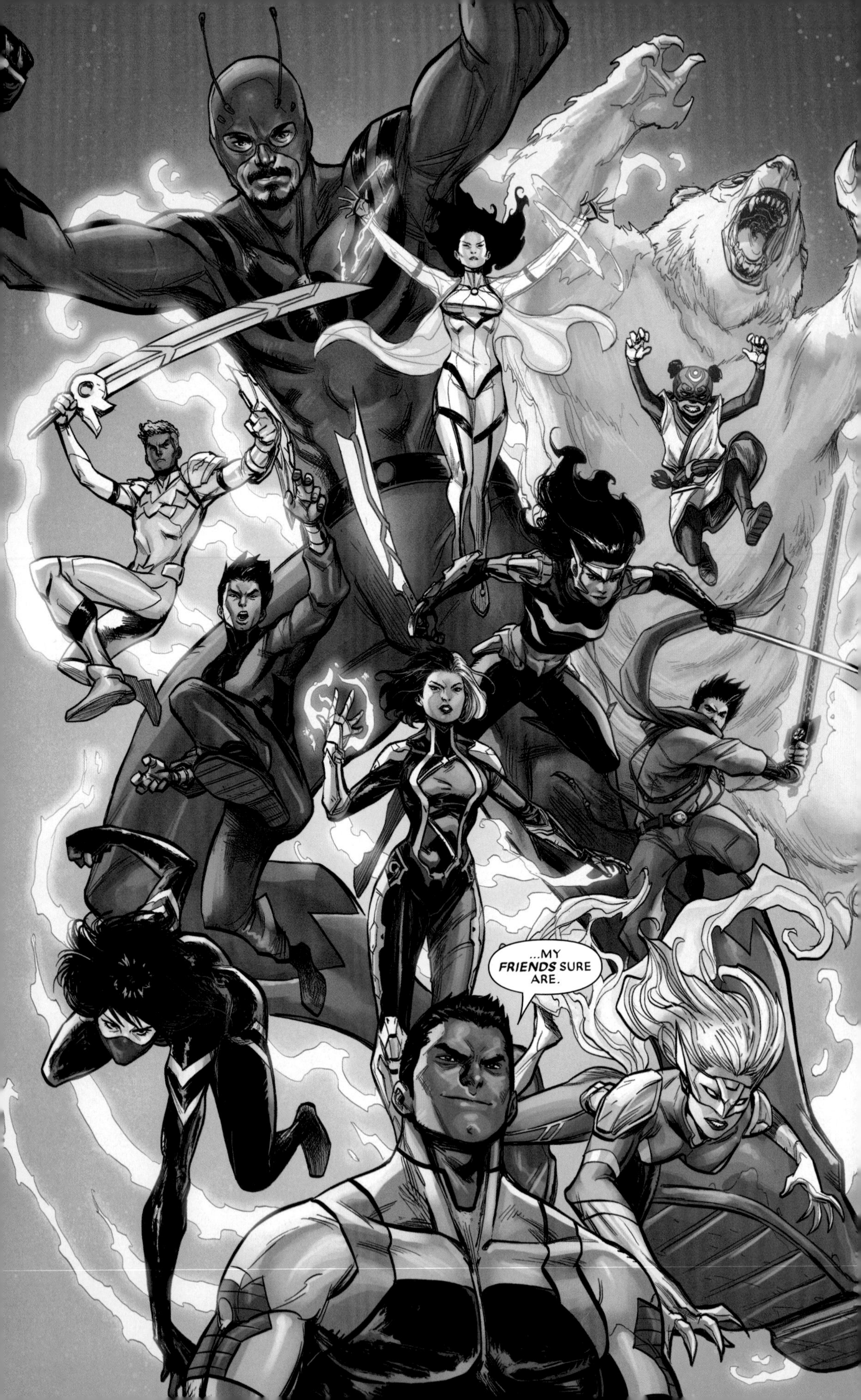
...MY *FRIENDS* SURE ARE.

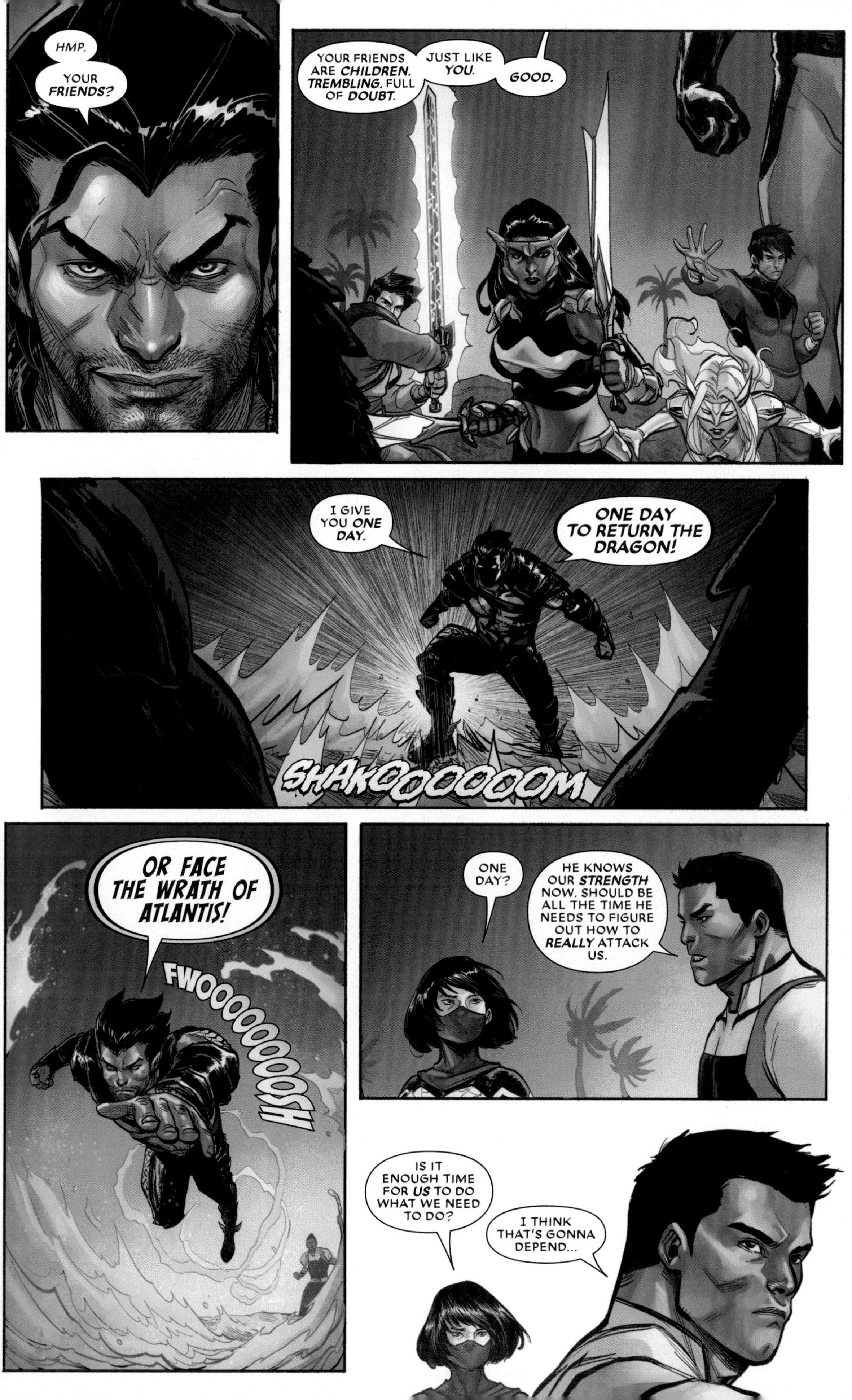
HMP.
YOUR FRIENDS?
YOUR FRIENDS ARE CHILDREN. TREMBLING. FULL OF DOUBT.
JUST LIKE YOU.
GOOD.
I GIVE YOU ONE DAY.
ONE DAY TO RETURN THE DRAGON!
SHAKOOOOOOOM
OR FACE THE WRATH OF ATLANTIS!
FWOOOOOOOOOSH
ONE DAY?
HE KNOWS OUR STRENGTH NOW. SHOULD BE ALL THE TIME HE NEEDS TO FIGURE OUT HOW TO REALLY ATTACK US.
IS IT ENOUGH TIME FOR US TO DO WHAT WE NEED TO DO?
I THINK THAT'S GONNA DEPEND...

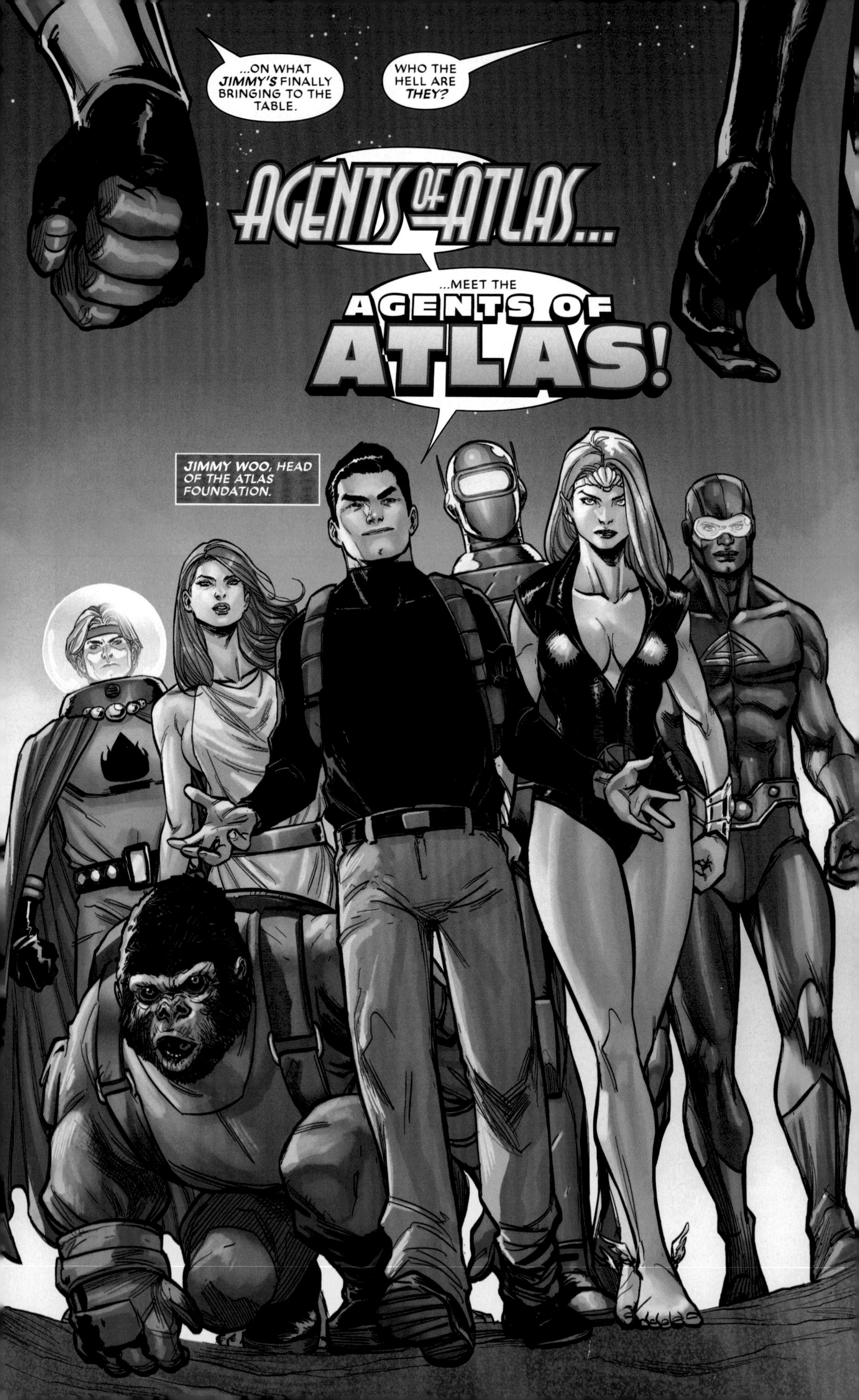
...ON WHAT JIMMY'S FINALLY BRINGING TO THE TABLE.
WHO THE HELL ARE THEY?
AGENTS OF ATLAS...
...MEET THE AGENTS OF ATLAS!
JIMMY WOO, HEAD OF THE ATLAS FOUNDATION.

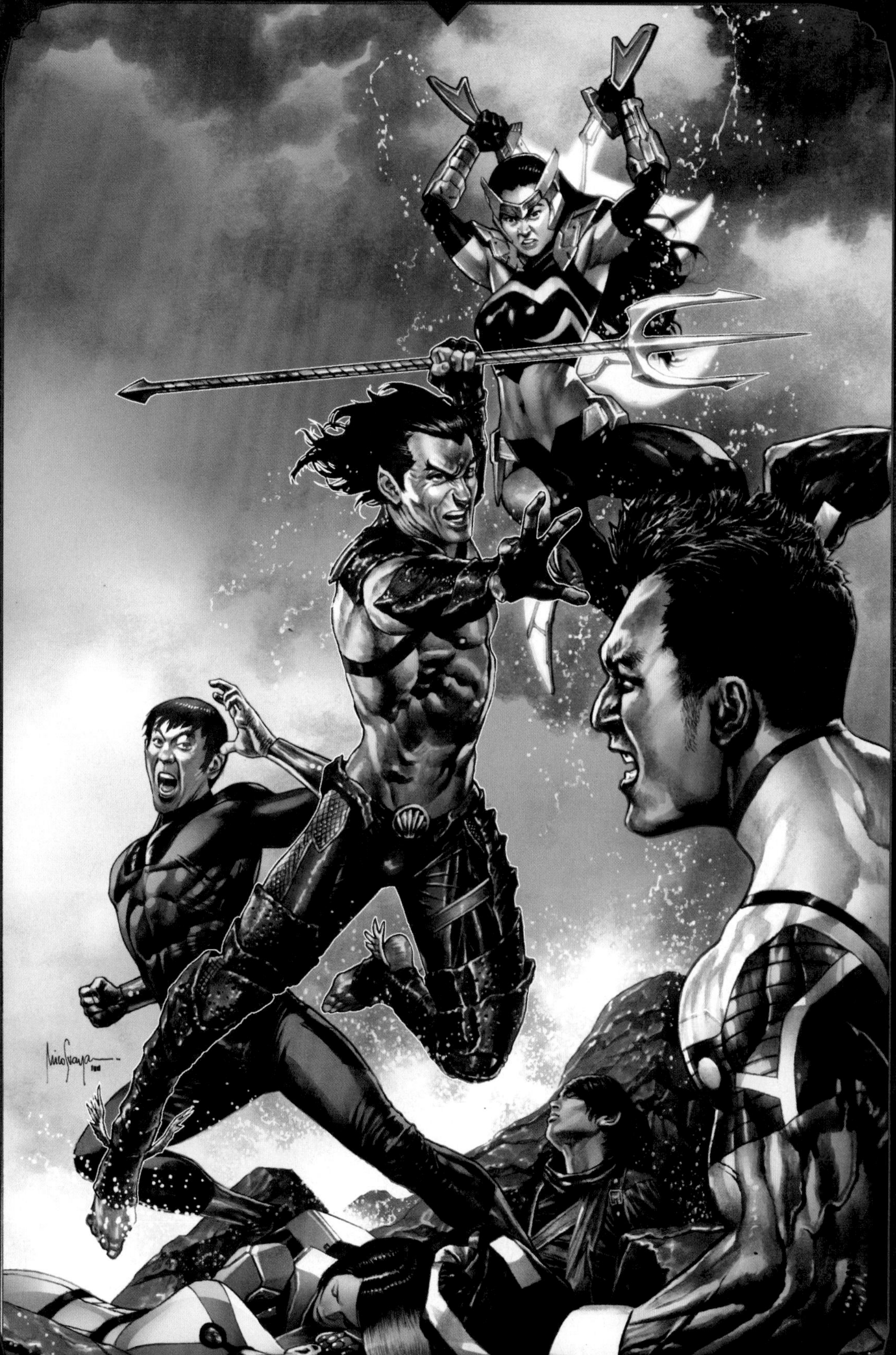

2

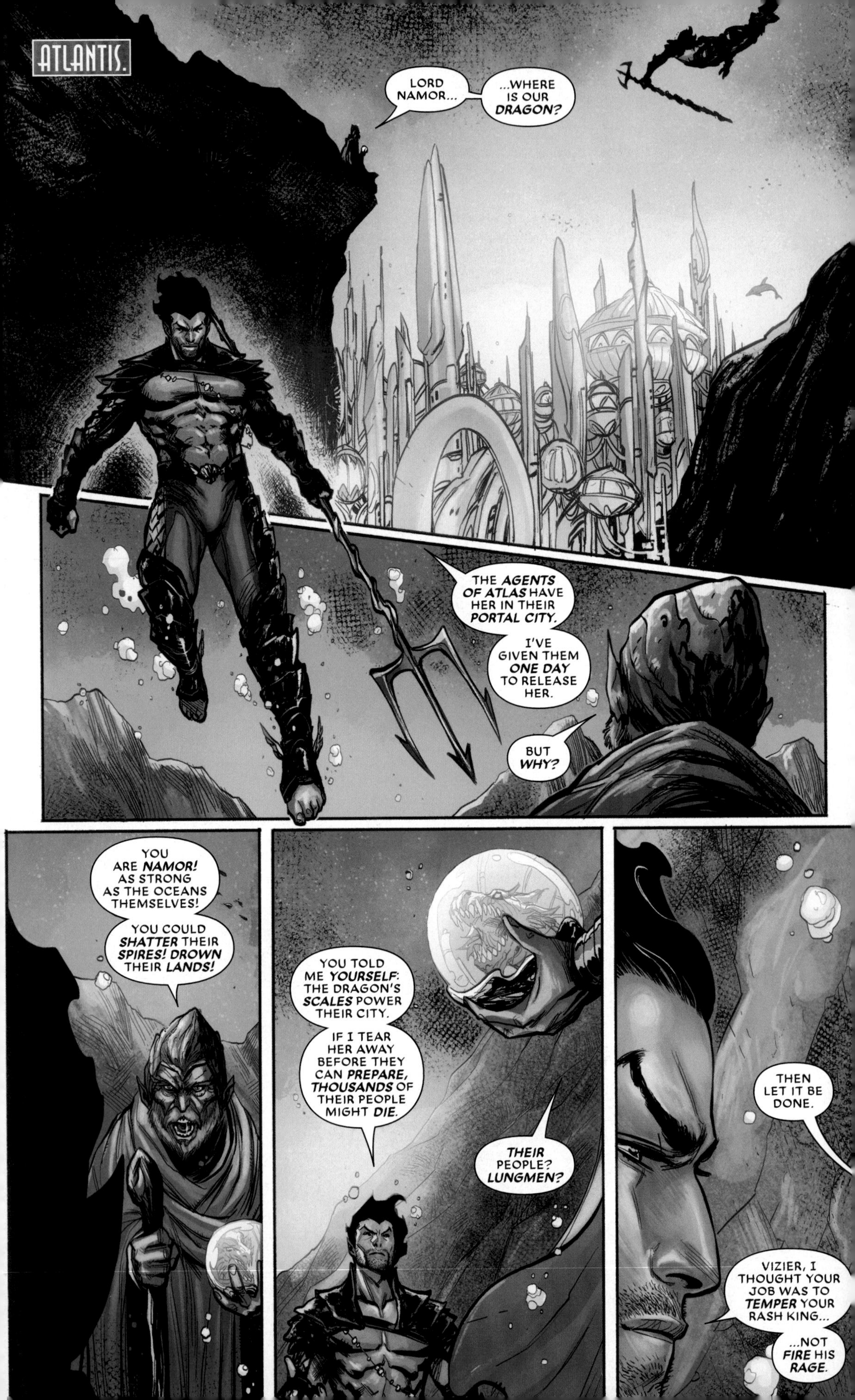
ATLANTIS.
LORD NAMOR...
...WHERE IS OUR DRAGON?
THE AGENTS OF ATLAS HAVE HER IN THEIR PORTAL CITY.
I'VE GIVEN THEM ONE DAY TO RELEASE HER.
BUT WHY?
YOU ARE NAMOR! AS STRONG AS THE OCEANS THEMSELVES!
YOU COULD SHATTER THEIR SPIRES! DROWN THEIR LANDS!
YOU TOLD ME YOURSELF: THE DRAGON'S SCALES POWER THEIR CITY.
IF I TEAR HER AWAY BEFORE THEY CAN PREPARE, THOUSANDS OF THEIR PEOPLE MIGHT DIE.
THEIR PEOPLE? LUNGMEN?
THEN LET IT BE DONE.
VIZIER, I THOUGHT YOUR JOB WAS TO TEMPER YOUR RASH KING...
...NOT FIRE HIS RAGE.

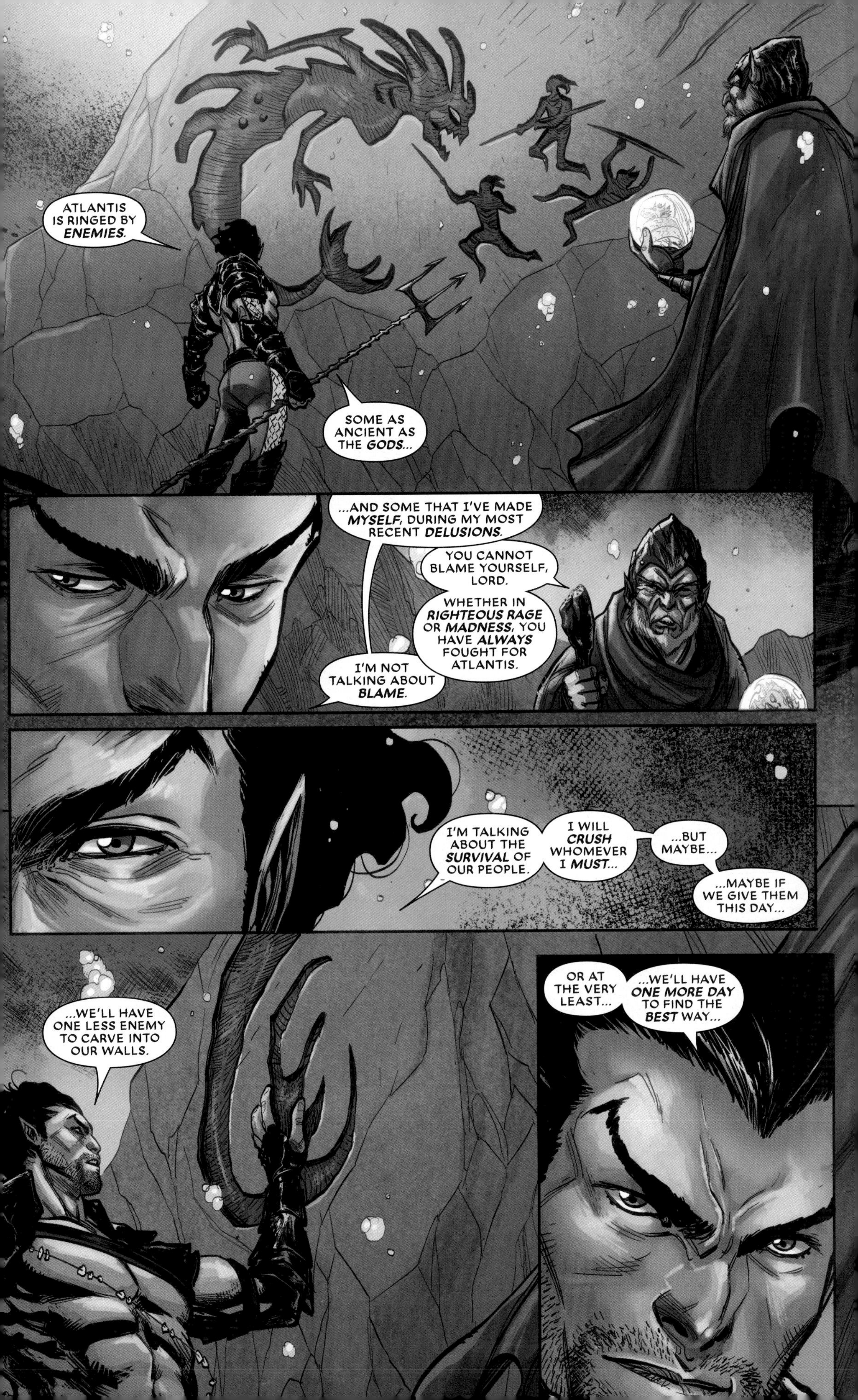
ATLANTIS IS RINGED BY ENEMIES.
SOME AS ANCIENT AS THE GODS...
...AND SOME THAT I'VE MADE MYSELF, DURING MY MOST RECENT DELUSIONS.
YOU CANNOT BLAME YOURSELF, LORD.
WHETHER IN RIGHTEOUS RAGE OR MADNESS, YOU HAVE ALWAYS FOUGHT FOR ATLANTIS.
I'M NOT TALKING ABOUT BLAME.
I'M TALKING ABOUT THE SURVIVAL OF OUR PEOPLE.
I WILL CRUSH WHOMEVER I MUST...
...BUT MAYBE...
...MAYBE IF WE GIVE THEM THIS DAY...
...WE'LL HAVE ONE LESS ENEMY TO CARVE INTO OUR WALLS.
OR AT THE VERY LEAST...
...WE'LL HAVE ONE MORE DAY TO FIND THE BEST WAY...

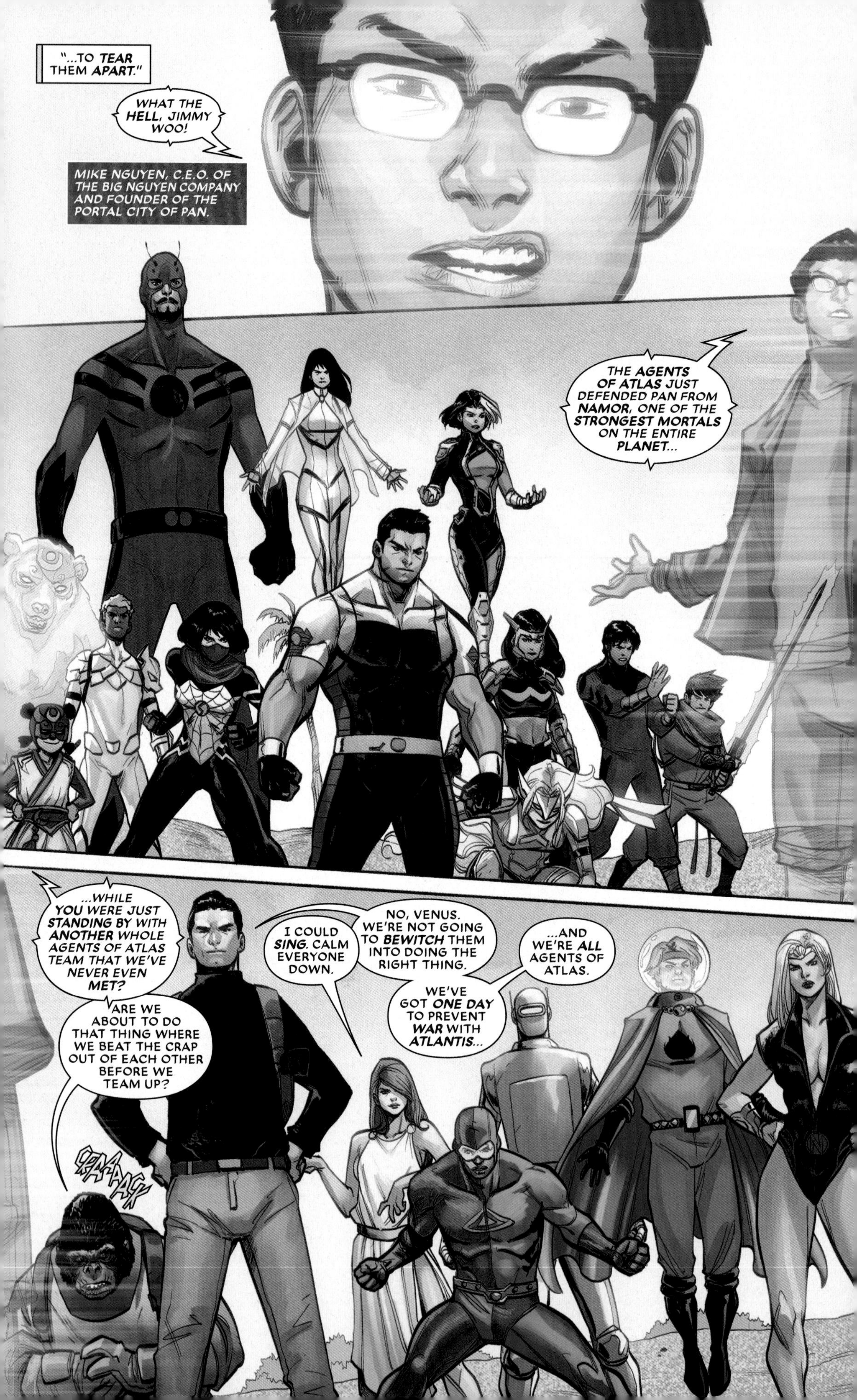

"...TO TEAR THEM APART."
WHAT THE HELL, JIMMY WOO!
MIKE NGUYEN, C.E.O. OF THE BIG NGUYEN COMPANY AND FOUNDER OF THE PORTAL CITY OF PAN.
THE AGENTS OF ATLAS JUST DEFENDED PAN FROM NAMOR, ONE OF THE STRONGEST MORTALS ON THE ENTIRE PLANET...
...WHILE YOU WERE JUST STANDING BY WITH ANOTHER WHOLE AGENTS OF ATLAS TEAM THAT WE'VE NEVER EVEN MET?
ARE WE ABOUT TO DO THAT THING WHERE WE BEAT THE CRAP OUT OF EACH OTHER BEFORE WE TEAM UP?
I COULD SING. CALM EVERYONE DOWN.
NO, VENUS. WE'RE NOT GOING TO BEWITCH THEM INTO DOING THE RIGHT THING.
WE'VE GOT ONE DAY TO PREVENT WAR WITH ATLANTIS...
...AND WE'RE ALL AGENTS OF ATLAS.
CRAAAAK

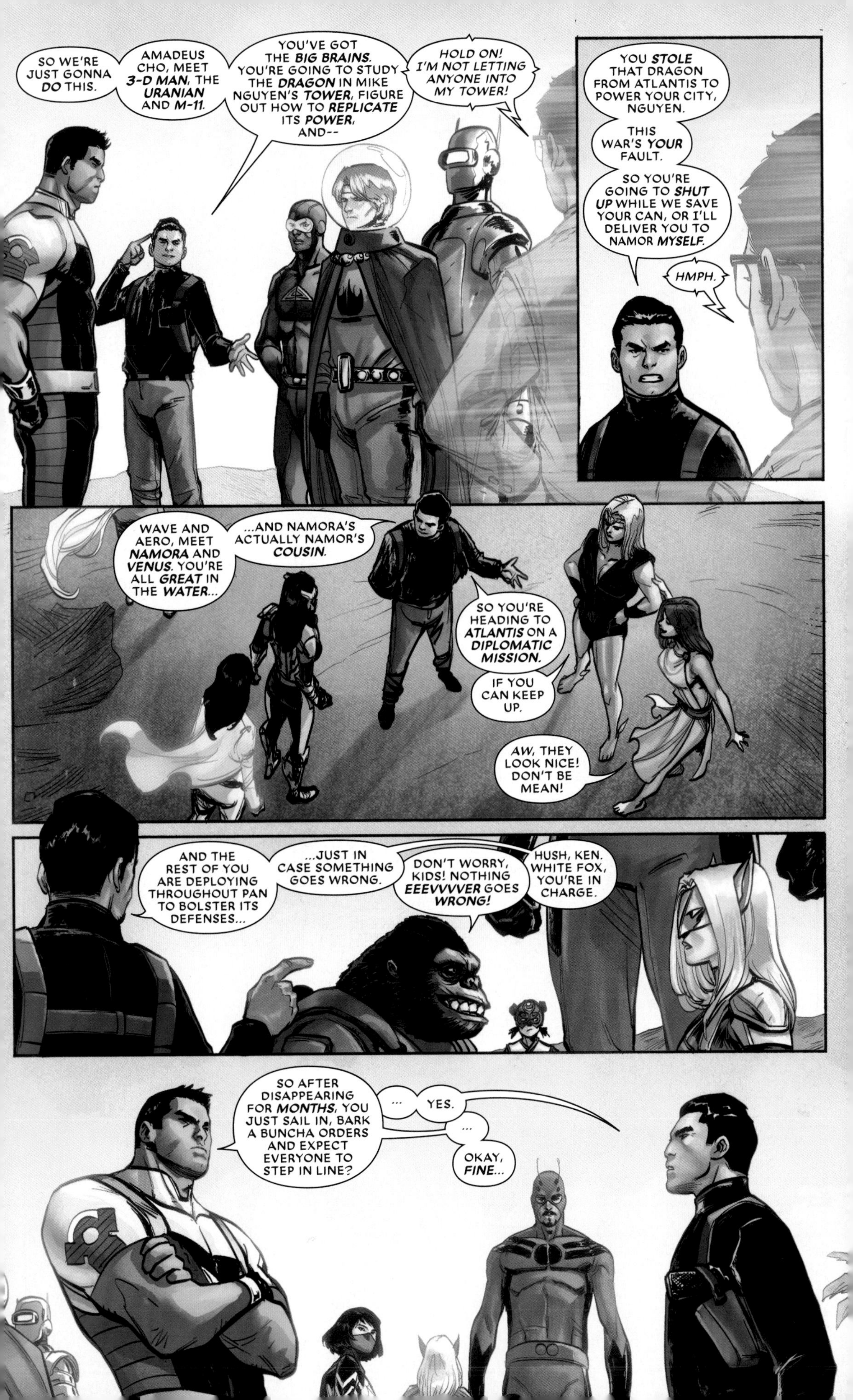
SO WE'RE JUST GONNA DO THIS.
AMADEUS CHO, MEET 3-D MAN, THE URANIAN AND M-11.
YOU'VE GOT THE BIG BRAINS. YOU'RE GOING TO STUDY THE DRAGON IN MIKE NGUYEN'S TOWER, FIGURE OUT HOW TO REPLICATE ITS POWER, AND--
HOLD ON! I'M NOT LETTING ANYONE INTO MY TOWER!
YOU STOLE THAT DRAGON FROM ATLANTIS TO POWER YOUR CITY, NGUYEN.
THIS WAR'S YOUR FAULT.
SO YOU'RE GOING TO SHUT UP WHILE WE SAVE YOUR CAN, OR I'LL DELIVER YOU TO NAMOR MYSELF.
HMPH.
WAVE AND AERO, MEET NAMORA AND VENUS. YOU'RE ALL GREAT IN THE WATER...
...AND NAMORA'S ACTUALLY NAMOR'S COUSIN.
SO YOU'RE HEADING TO ATLANTIS ON A DIPLOMATIC MISSION.
IF YOU CAN KEEP UP.
AW, THEY LOOK NICE! DON'T BE MEAN!
AND THE REST OF YOU ARE DEPLOYING THROUGHOUT PAN TO BOLSTER ITS DEFENSES...
...JUST IN CASE SOMETHING GOES WRONG.
DON'T WORRY, KIDS! NOTHING EEEVVVVER GOES WRONG!
HUSH, KEN. WHITE FOX, YOU'RE IN CHARGE.
SO AFTER DISAPPEARING FOR MONTHS, YOU JUST SAIL IN, BARK A BUNCHA ORDERS AND EXPECT EVERYONE TO STEP IN LINE?
...
YES.
...
OKAY, FINE...

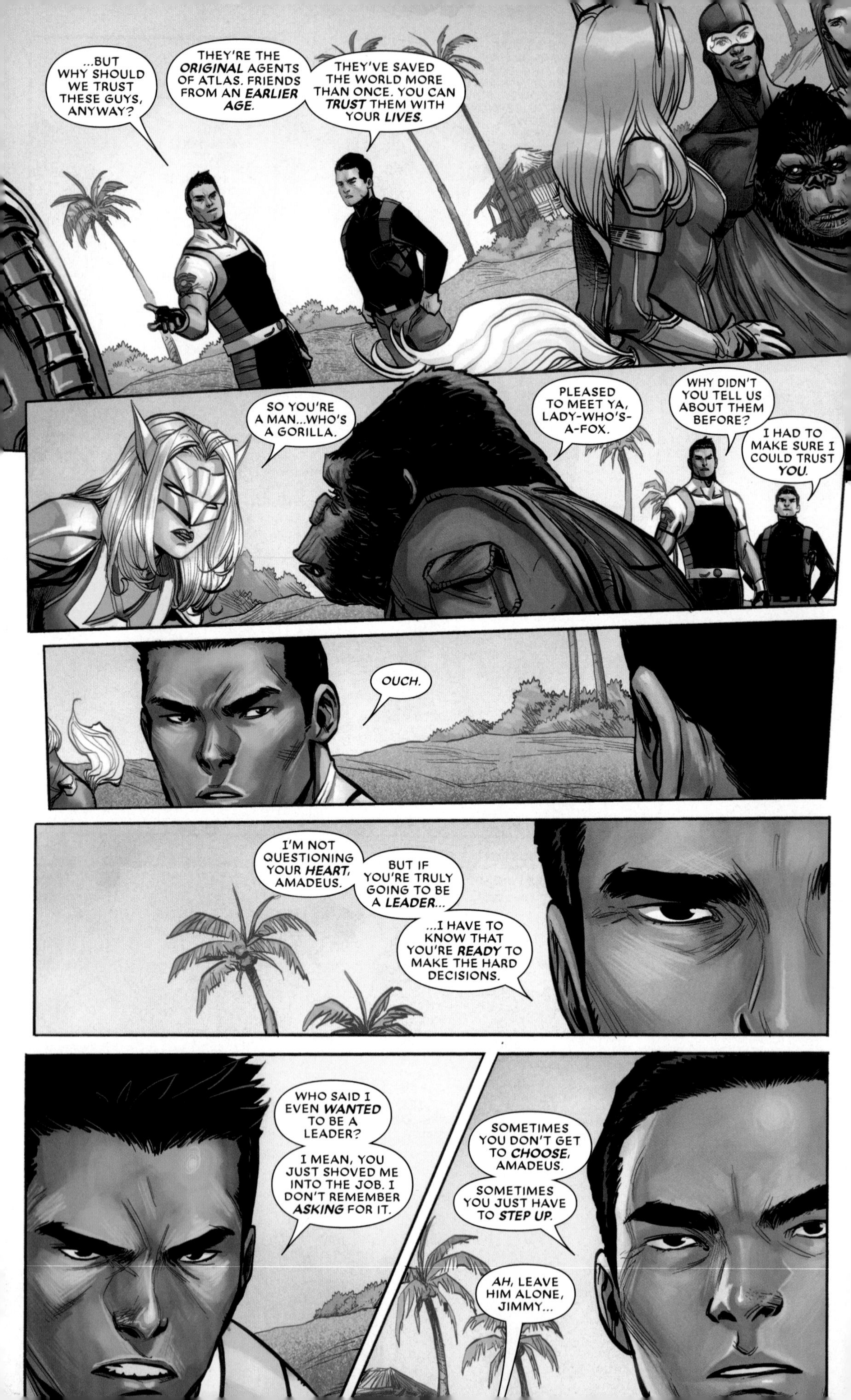
...BUT WHY SHOULD WE TRUST THESE GUYS, ANYWAY?
THEY'RE THE ORIGINAL AGENTS OF ATLAS. FRIENDS FROM AN EARLIER AGE.
THEY'VE SAVED THE WORLD MORE THAN ONCE. YOU CAN TRUST THEM WITH YOUR LIVES.
SO YOU'RE A MAN...WHO'S A GORILLA.
PLEASED TO MEET YA, LADY-WHO'S-A-FOX.
WHY DIDN'T YOU TELL US ABOUT THEM BEFORE?
I HAD TO MAKE SURE I COULD TRUST YOU.
OUCH.
I'M NOT QUESTIONING YOUR HEART, AMADEUS.
BUT IF YOU'RE TRULY GOING TO BE A LEADER...
...I HAVE TO KNOW THAT YOU'RE READY TO MAKE THE HARD DECISIONS.
WHO SAID I EVEN WANTED TO BE A LEADER?
I MEAN, YOU JUST SHOVED ME INTO THE JOB. I DON'T REMEMBER ASKING FOR IT.
SOMETIMES YOU DON'T GET TO CHOOSE, AMADEUS.
SOMETIMES YOU JUST HAVE TO STEP UP.
AH, LEAVE HIM ALONE, JIMMY...

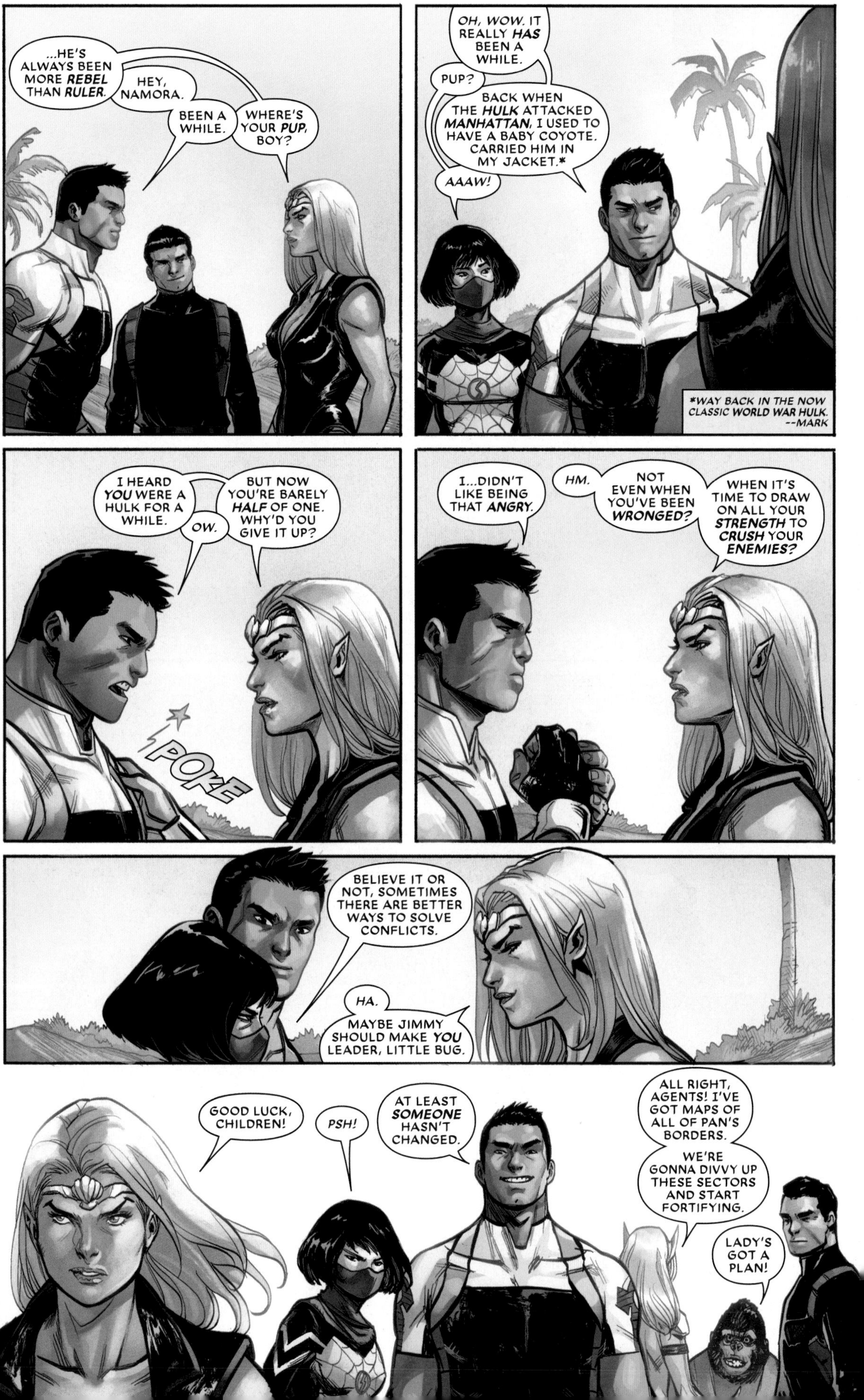
...HE'S ALWAYS BEEN MORE *REBEL* THAN *RULER*.
HEY, NAMORA.
BEEN A WHILE.
WHERE'S YOUR *PUP*, BOY?
OH, WOW. IT REALLY *HAS* BEEN A WHILE.
PUP?
BACK WHEN THE *HULK* ATTACKED *MANHATTAN*, I USED TO HAVE A BABY COYOTE. CARRIED HIM IN MY JACKET.*
AAAW!
*WAY BACK IN THE NOW CLASSIC *WORLD WAR HULK*. --MARK
I HEARD *YOU* WERE A HULK FOR A WHILE.
OW.
BUT NOW YOU'RE BARELY *HALF* OF ONE. WHY'D YOU GIVE IT UP?
POKE
I...DIDN'T LIKE BEING THAT *ANGRY*.
HM.
NOT EVEN WHEN YOU'VE BEEN *WRONGED?*
WHEN IT'S TIME TO DRAW ON ALL YOUR *STRENGTH* TO *CRUSH* YOUR *ENEMIES?*
BELIEVE IT OR NOT, SOMETIMES THERE ARE BETTER WAYS TO SOLVE CONFLICTS.
HA.
MAYBE JIMMY SHOULD MAKE *YOU* LEADER, LITTLE BUG.
GOOD LUCK, CHILDREN!
PSH!
AT LEAST *SOMEONE* HASN'T CHANGED.
ALL RIGHT, AGENTS! I'VE GOT MAPS OF ALL OF PAN'S BORDERS.
WE'RE GONNA DIVVY UP THESE SECTORS AND START FORTIFYING.
LADY'S GOT A PLAN!

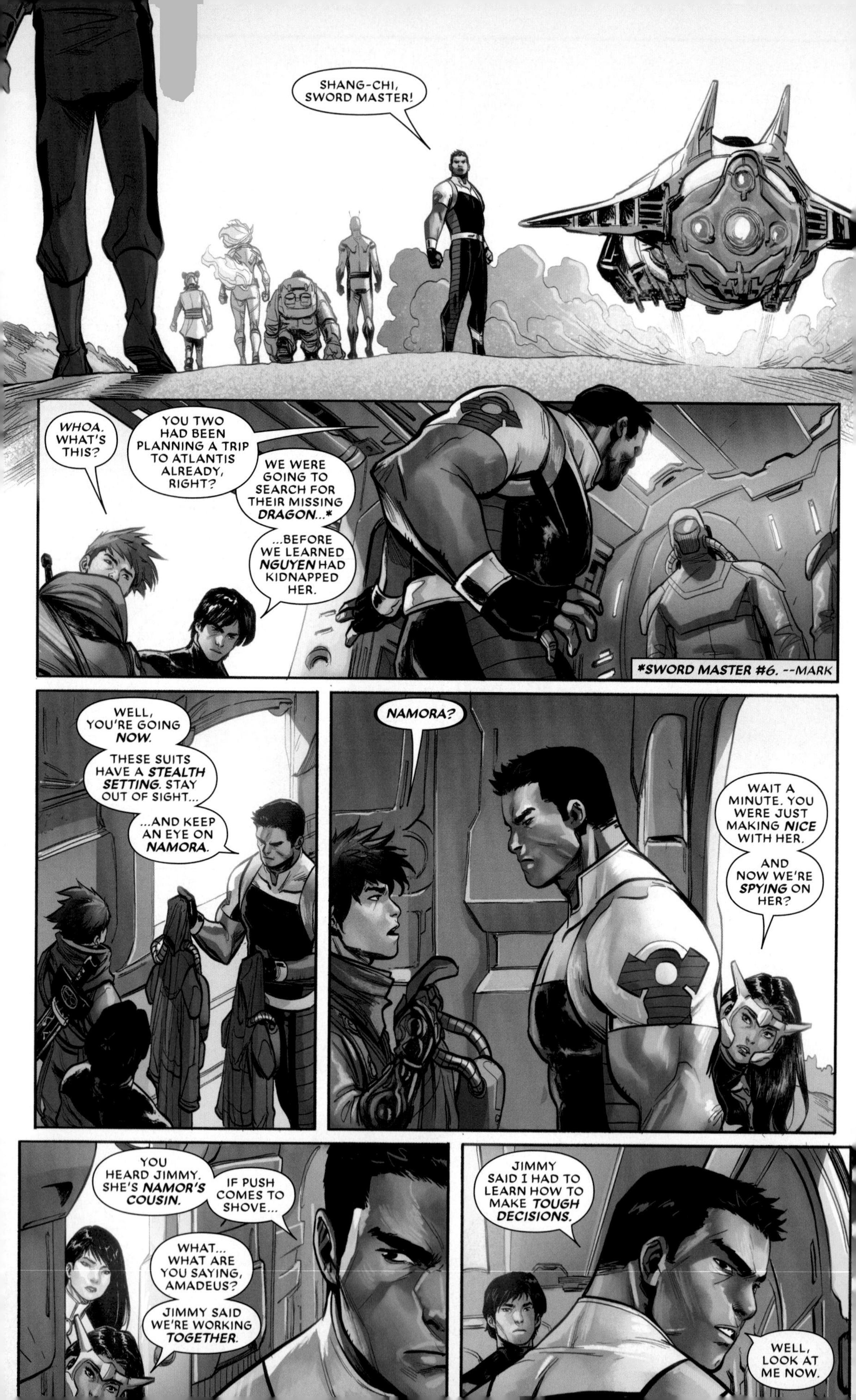
SHANG-CHI, SWORD MASTER!
WHOA. WHAT'S THIS?
YOU TWO HAD BEEN PLANNING A TRIP TO ATLANTIS ALREADY, RIGHT?
WE WERE GOING TO SEARCH FOR THEIR MISSING DRAGON...*
...BEFORE WE LEARNED NGUYEN HAD KIDNAPPED HER.
*SWORD MASTER #6. --MARK
WELL, YOU'RE GOING NOW.
THESE SUITS HAVE A STEALTH SETTING. STAY OUT OF SIGHT...
...AND KEEP AN EYE ON NAMORA.
NAMORA?
WAIT A MINUTE. YOU WERE JUST MAKING NICE WITH HER.
AND NOW WE'RE SPYING ON HER?
YOU HEARD JIMMY. SHE'S NAMOR'S COUSIN.
IF PUSH COMES TO SHOVE...
WHAT... WHAT ARE YOU SAYING, AMADEUS?
JIMMY SAID WE'RE WORKING TOGETHER.
JIMMY SAID I HAD TO LEARN HOW TO MAKE TOUGH DECISIONS.
WELL, LOOK AT ME NOW.

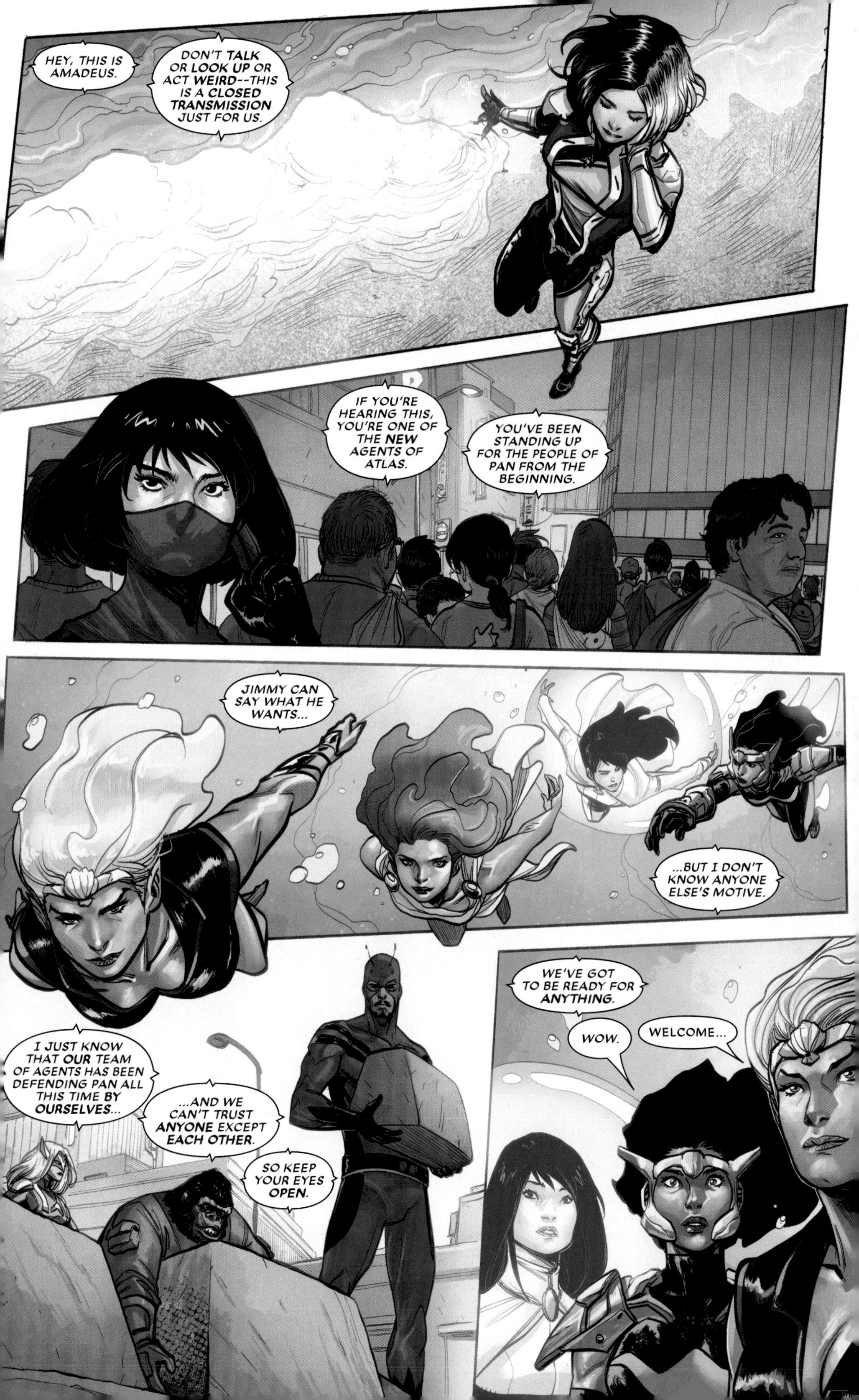

HEY, THIS IS AMADEUS.
DON'T TALK OR LOOK UP OR ACT WEIRD--THIS IS A CLOSED TRANSMISSION JUST FOR US.
IF YOU'RE HEARING THIS, YOU'RE ONE OF THE NEW AGENTS OF ATLAS.
YOU'VE BEEN STANDING UP FOR THE PEOPLE OF PAN FROM THE BEGINNING.
JIMMY CAN SAY WHAT HE WANTS...
...BUT I DON'T KNOW ANYONE ELSE'S MOTIVE.
I JUST KNOW THAT OUR TEAM OF AGENTS HAS BEEN DEFENDING PAN ALL THIS TIME BY OURSELVES...
...AND WE CAN'T TRUST ANYONE EXCEPT EACH OTHER.
SO KEEP YOUR EYES OPEN.
WE'VE GOT TO BE READY FOR ANYTHING.
WOW.
WELCOME...

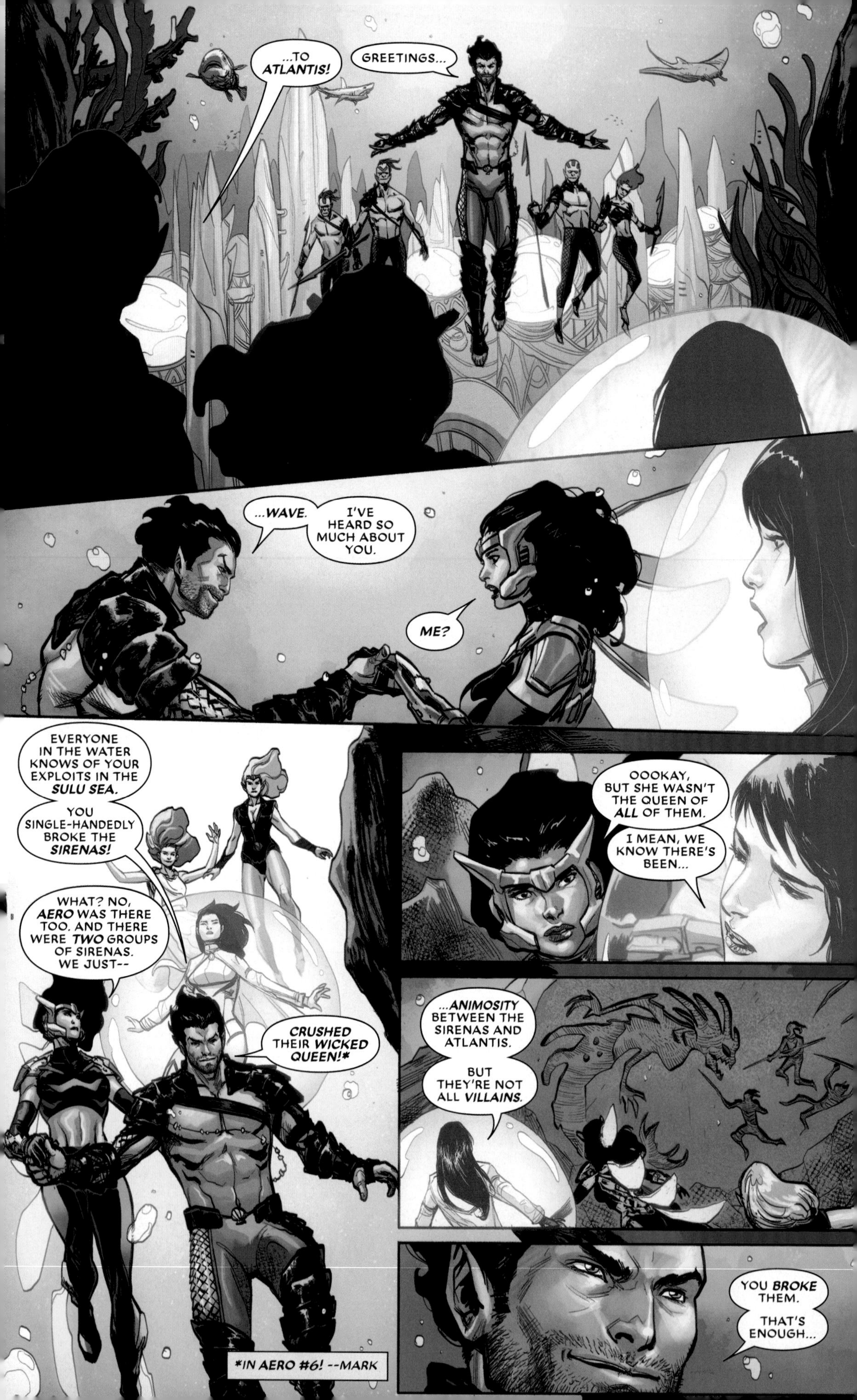
GREETINGS...
...TO ATLANTIS!
...WAVE. I'VE HEARD SO MUCH ABOUT YOU.
ME?
EVERYONE IN THE WATER KNOWS OF YOUR EXPLOITS IN THE SULU SEA.
YOU SINGLE-HANDEDLY BROKE THE SIRENAS!
WHAT? NO, AERO WAS THERE TOO. AND THERE WERE TWO GROUPS OF SIRENAS. WE JUST--
CRUSHED THEIR WICKED QUEEN!*
*IN AERO #6! --MARK
OOOKAY, BUT SHE WASN'T THE QUEEN OF ALL OF THEM.
I MEAN, WE KNOW THERE'S BEEN...
...ANIMOSITY BETWEEN THE SIRENAS AND ATLANTIS.
BUT THEY'RE NOT ALL VILLAINS.
YOU BROKE THEM.
THAT'S ENOUGH...

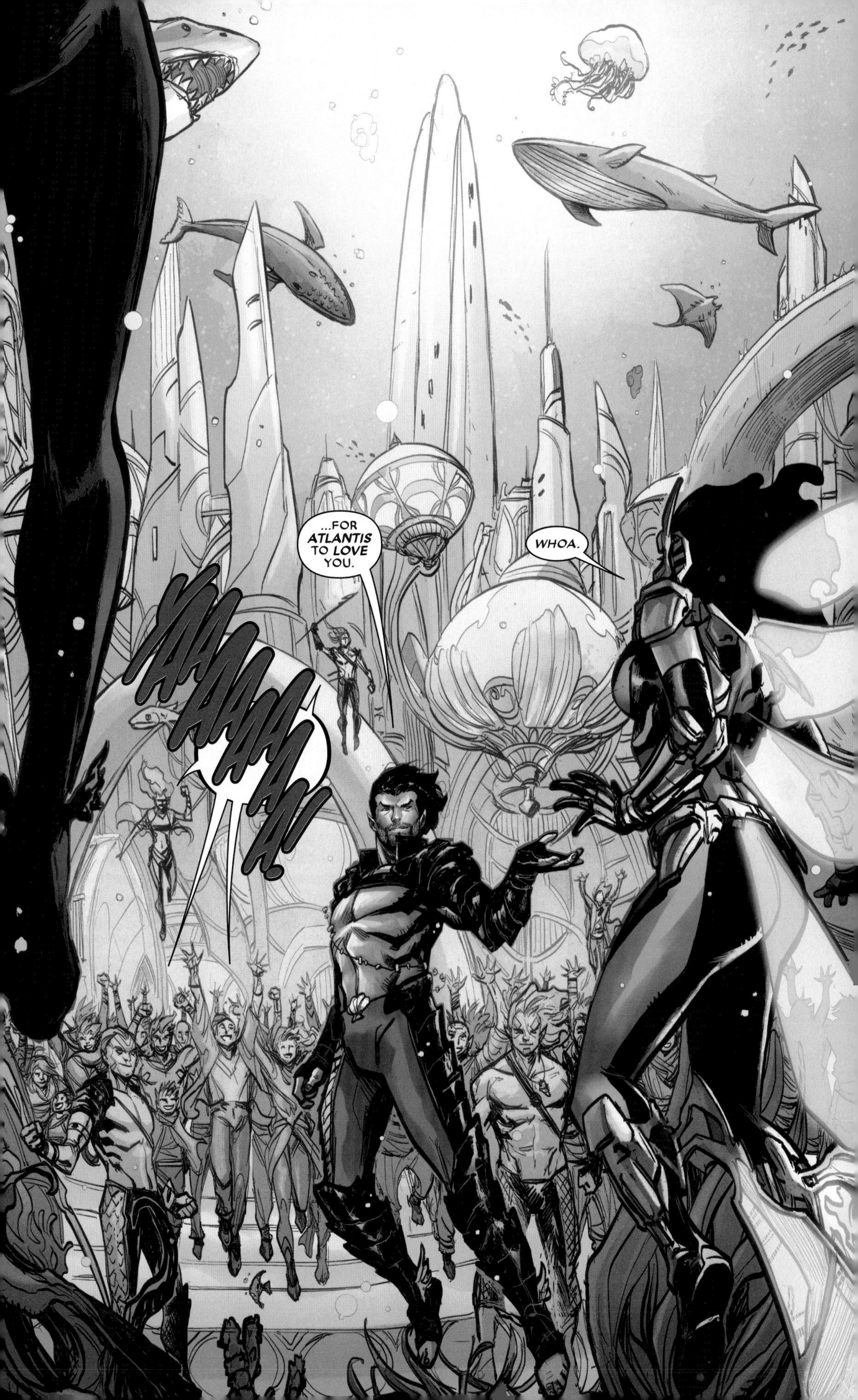

...FOR ATLANTIS TO LOVE YOU.
WHOA.
YAAAAAAAAAA!

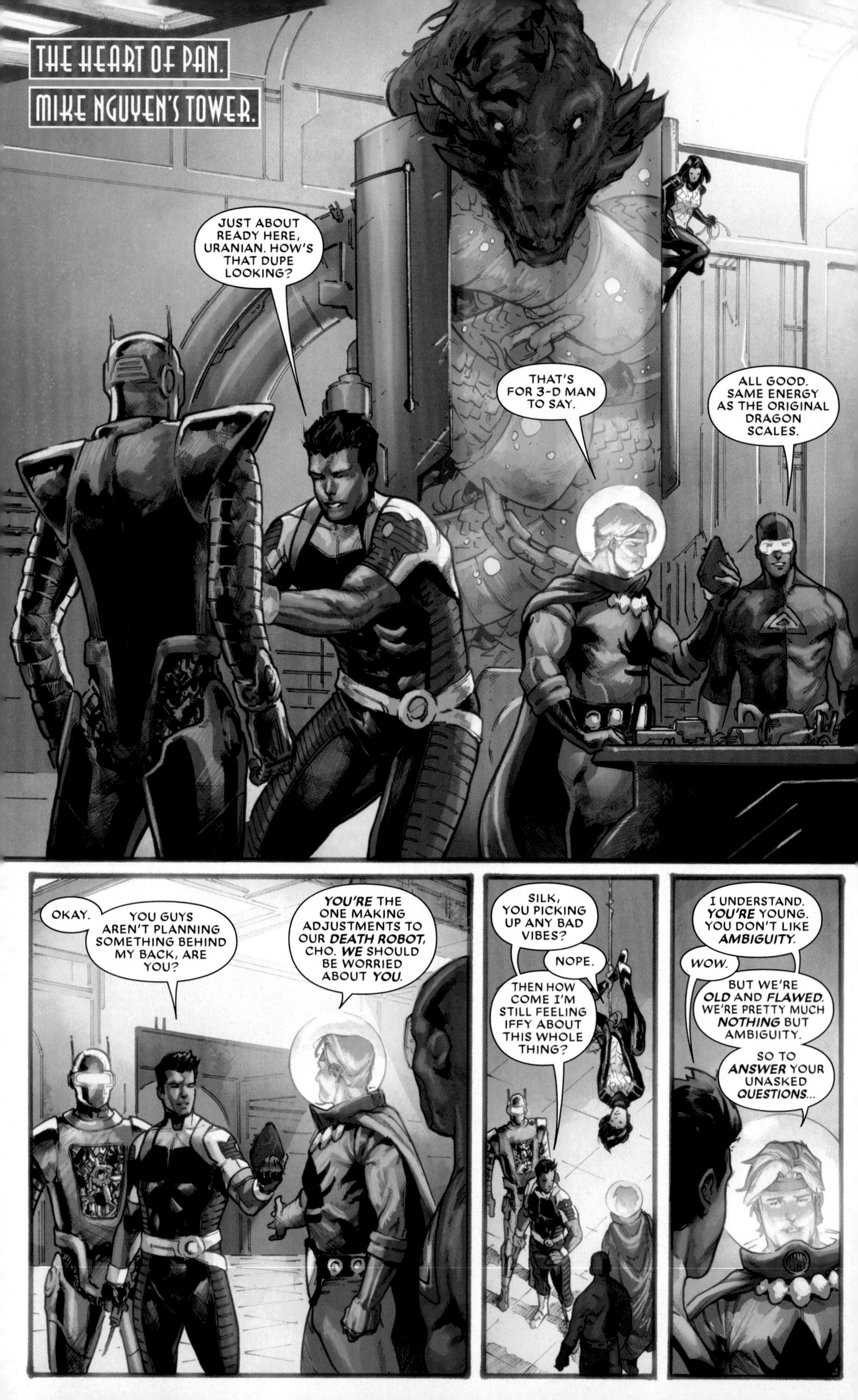
THE HEART OF PAN.
MIKE NGUYEN'S TOWER.
JUST ABOUT READY HERE, URANIAN. HOW'S THAT DUPE LOOKING?
THAT'S FOR 3-D MAN TO SAY.
ALL GOOD. SAME ENERGY AS THE ORIGINAL DRAGON SCALES.
OKAY.
YOU GUYS AREN'T PLANNING SOMETHING BEHIND MY BACK, ARE YOU?
YOU'RE THE ONE MAKING ADJUSTMENTS TO OUR *DEATH ROBOT,* CHO. *WE* SHOULD BE WORRIED ABOUT *YOU.*
SILK, YOU PICKING UP ANY BAD VIBES?
NOPE.
THEN HOW COME I'M STILL FEELING IFFY ABOUT THIS WHOLE THING?
I UNDERSTAND. *YOU'RE* YOUNG. YOU DON'T LIKE *AMBIGUITY.*
WOW.
BUT WE'RE *OLD* AND *FLAWED.* WE'RE PRETTY MUCH *NOTHING* BUT AMBIGUITY.
SO TO *ANSWER* YOUR UNASKED *QUESTIONS...*

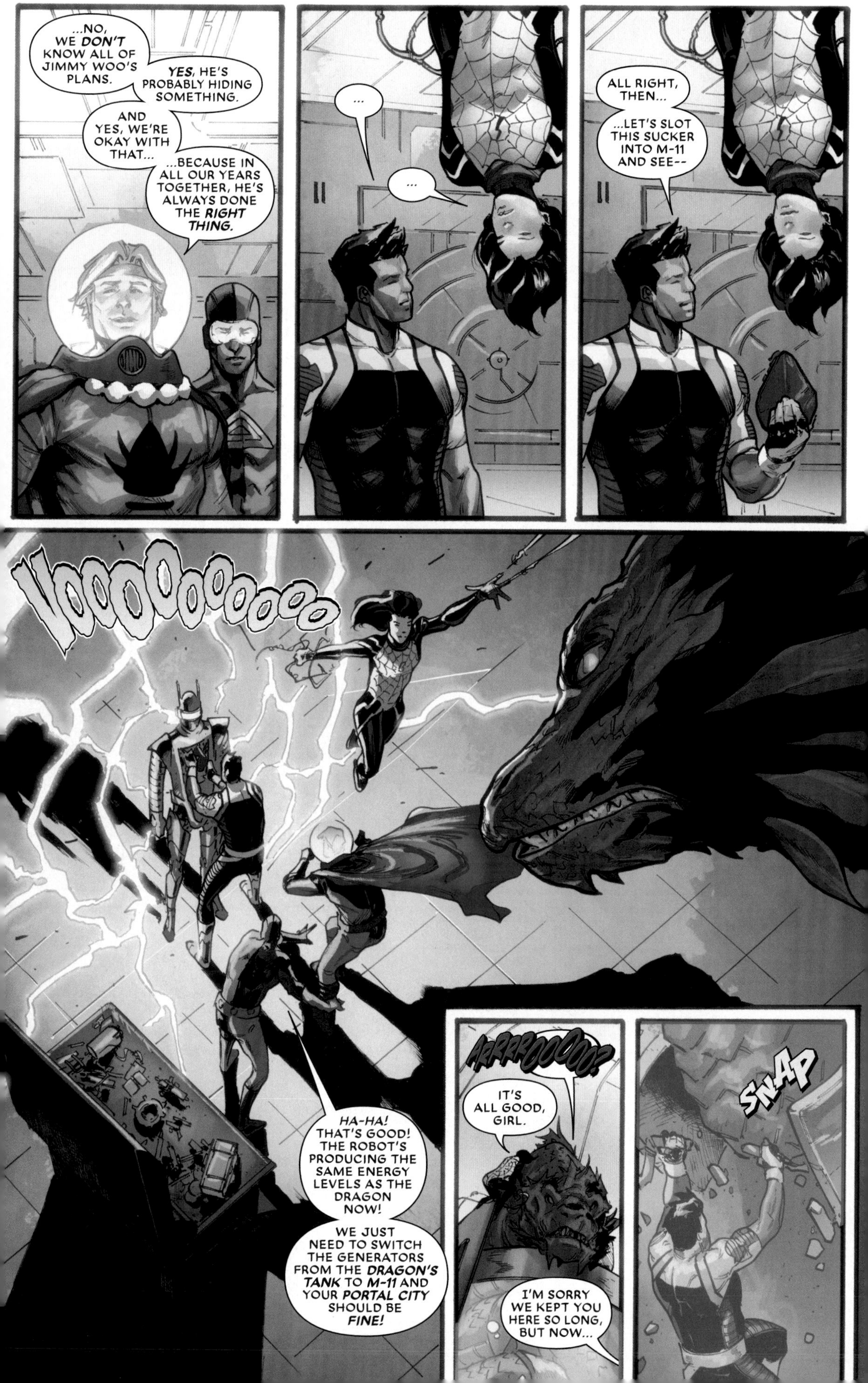

...NO, WE DON'T KNOW ALL OF JIMMY WOO'S PLANS.
YES, HE'S PROBABLY HIDING SOMETHING.
AND YES, WE'RE OKAY WITH THAT...
...BECAUSE IN ALL OUR YEARS TOGETHER, HE'S ALWAYS DONE THE RIGHT THING.
...
...
ALL RIGHT, THEN...
...LET'S SLOT THIS SUCKER INTO M-11 AND SEE--
VOOOOOOOOOOO
HA-HA! THAT'S GOOD! THE ROBOT'S PRODUCING THE SAME ENERGY LEVELS AS THE DRAGON NOW!
WE JUST NEED TO SWITCH THE GENERATORS FROM THE DRAGON'S TANK TO M-11 AND YOUR PORTAL CITY SHOULD BE FINE!
ARRRROOOOO?
IT'S ALL GOOD, GIRL.
I'M SORRY WE KEPT YOU HERE SO LONG, BUT NOW...
SNAP

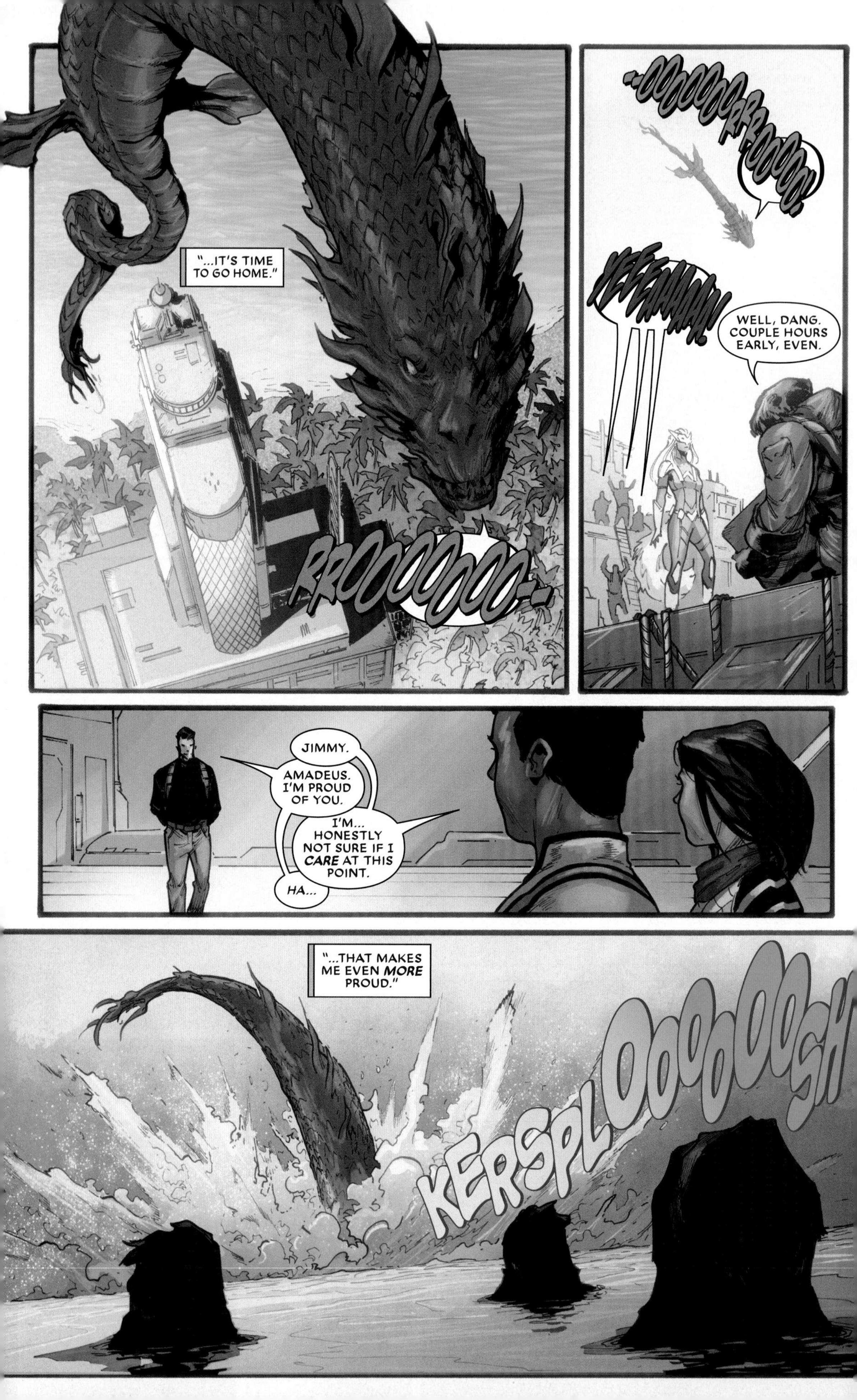
"...IT'S TIME TO GO HOME."
RROOOOOOO--
--OOOOOOOOORROOOOO!
YEEEAAAAAAA!
WELL, DANG. COUPLE HOURS EARLY, EVEN.
JIMMY.
AMADEUS. I'M PROUD OF YOU.
I'M... HONESTLY NOT SURE IF I CARE AT THIS POINT.
HA...
"...THAT MAKES ME EVEN MORE PROUD."
KERSPLOOOOOOOSH

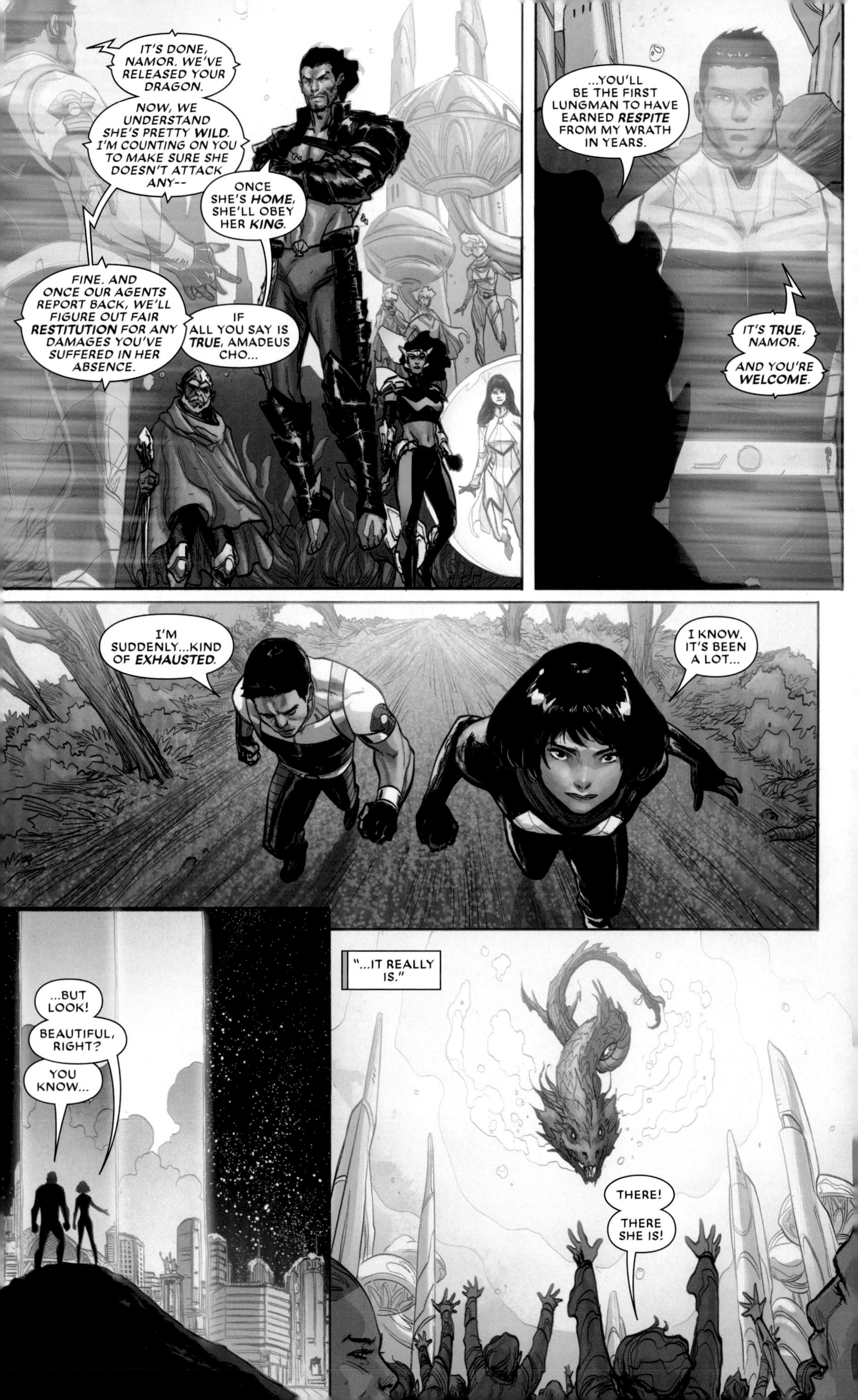
IT'S DONE, NAMOR. WE'VE RELEASED YOUR DRAGON.
NOW, WE UNDERSTAND SHE'S PRETTY WILD. I'M COUNTING ON YOU TO MAKE SURE SHE DOESN'T ATTACK ANY--
ONCE SHE'S HOME, SHE'LL OBEY HER KING.
FINE. AND ONCE OUR AGENTS REPORT BACK, WE'LL FIGURE OUT FAIR RESTITUTION FOR ANY DAMAGES YOU'VE SUFFERED IN HER ABSENCE.
IF ALL YOU SAY IS TRUE, AMADEUS CHO...
...YOU'LL BE THE FIRST LUNGMAN TO HAVE EARNED RESPITE FROM MY WRATH IN YEARS.
IT'S TRUE, NAMOR.
AND YOU'RE WELCOME.
I'M SUDDENLY...KIND OF EXHAUSTED.
I KNOW. IT'S BEEN A LOT...
...BUT LOOK!
BEAUTIFUL, RIGHT?
YOU KNOW...
"...IT REALLY IS."
THERE!
THERE SHE IS!

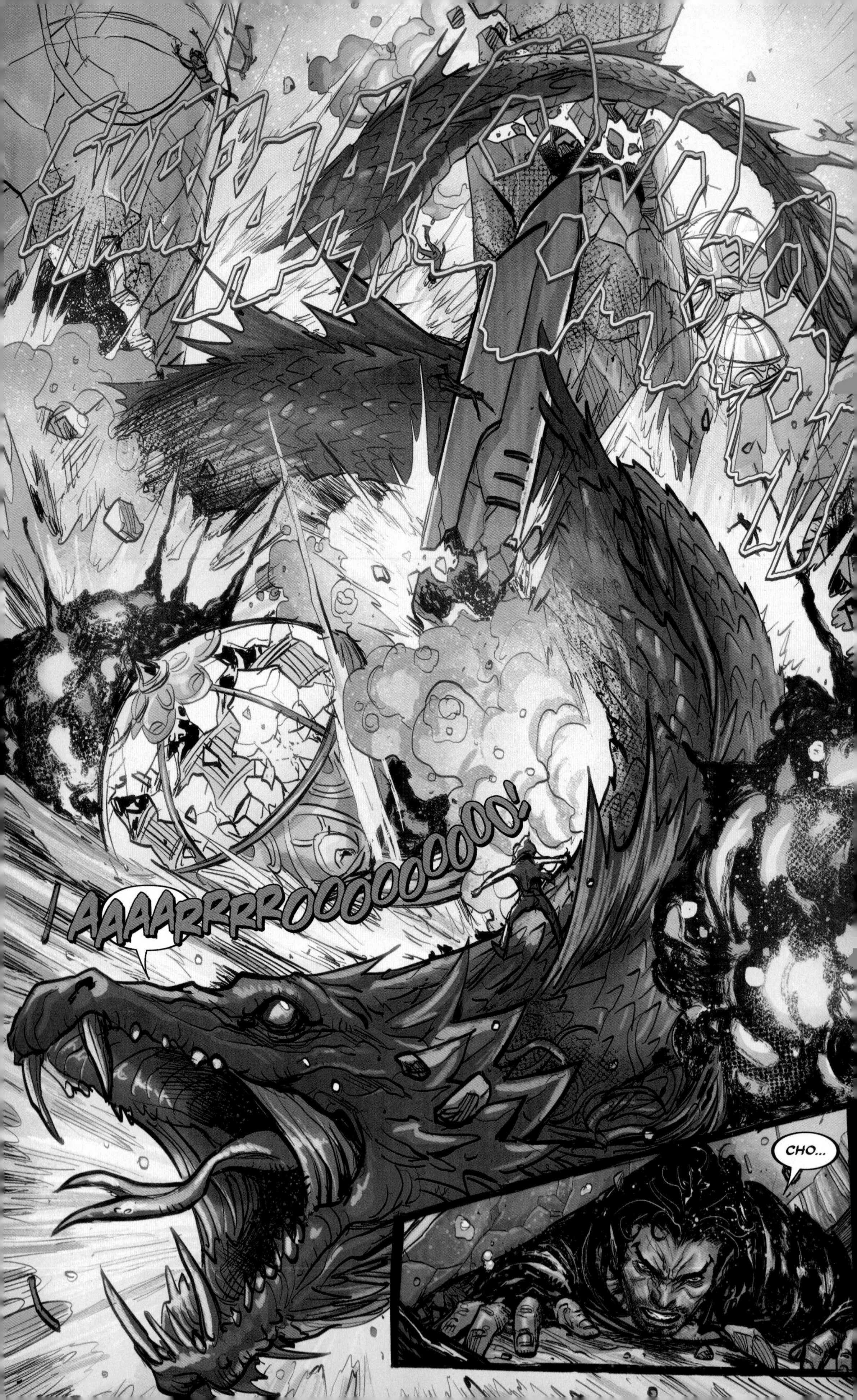
AAAARRROOOOOOOOOO!
CHO...

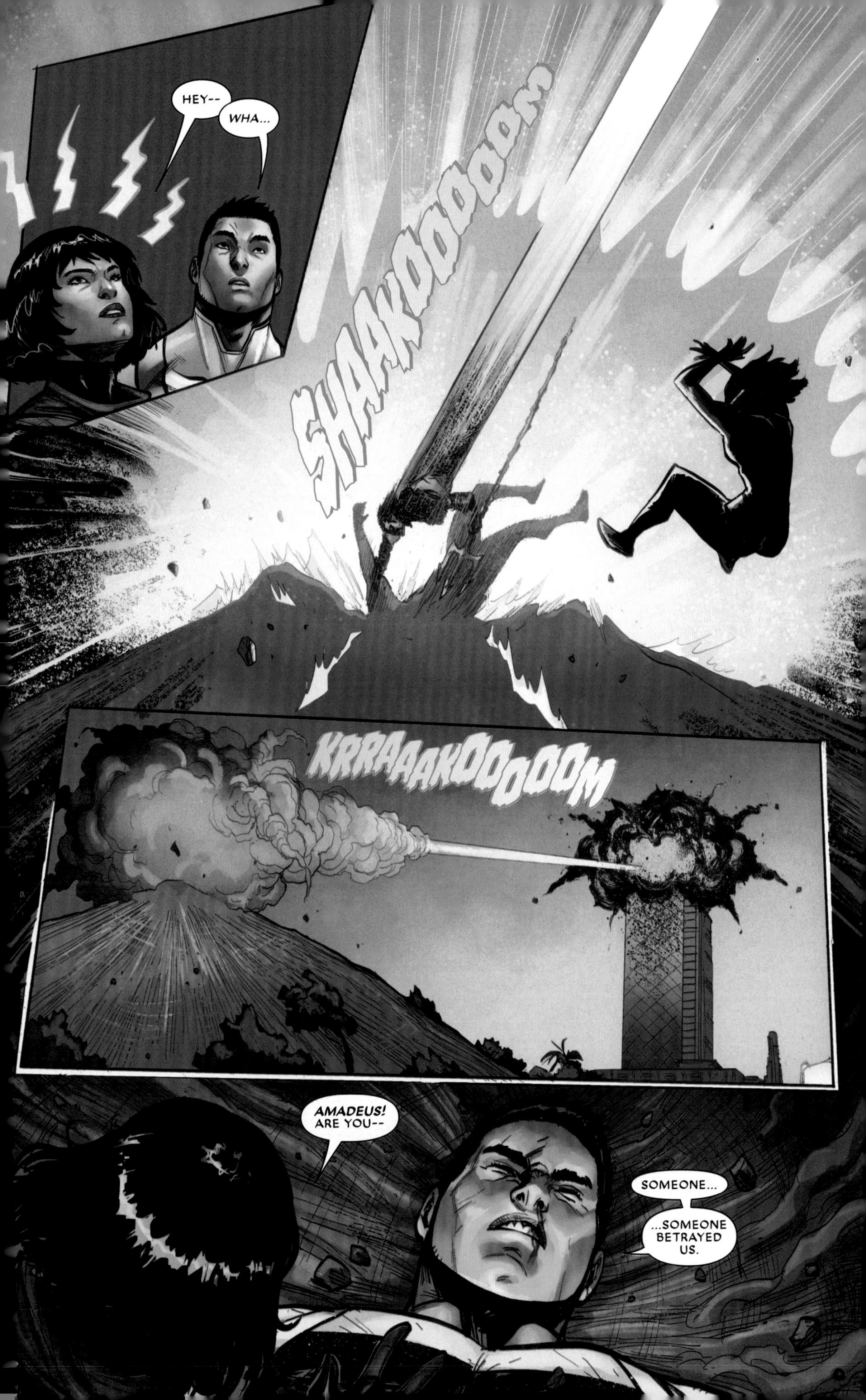
HEY--
WHA...
SHAAKOOOOOOM
KRRAAAKOOOOOOM
AMADEUS! ARE YOU--
SOMEONE...
...SOMEONE BETRAYED US.

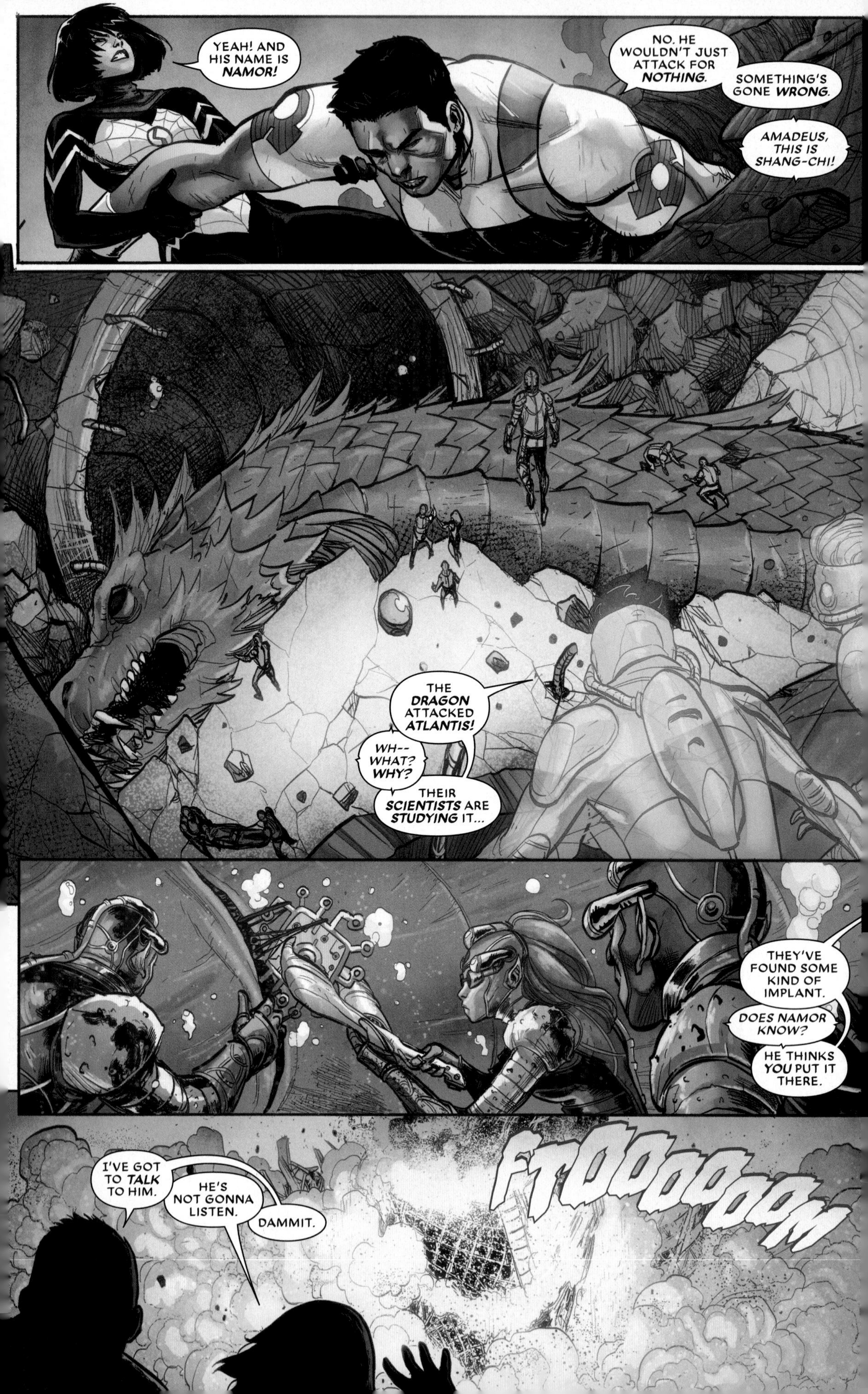
YEAH! AND HIS NAME IS NAMOR!
NO, HE WOULDN'T JUST ATTACK FOR NOTHING.
SOMETHING'S GONE WRONG.
AMADEUS, THIS IS SHANG-CHI!
THE DRAGON ATTACKED ATLANTIS!
WH-- WHAT? WHY?
THEIR SCIENTISTS ARE STUDYING IT...
THEY'VE FOUND SOME KIND OF IMPLANT.
DOES NAMOR KNOW?
HE THINKS YOU PUT IT THERE.
I'VE GOT TO TALK TO HIM.
HE'S NOT GONNA LISTEN.
DAMMIT.
FTOOOOOOOM

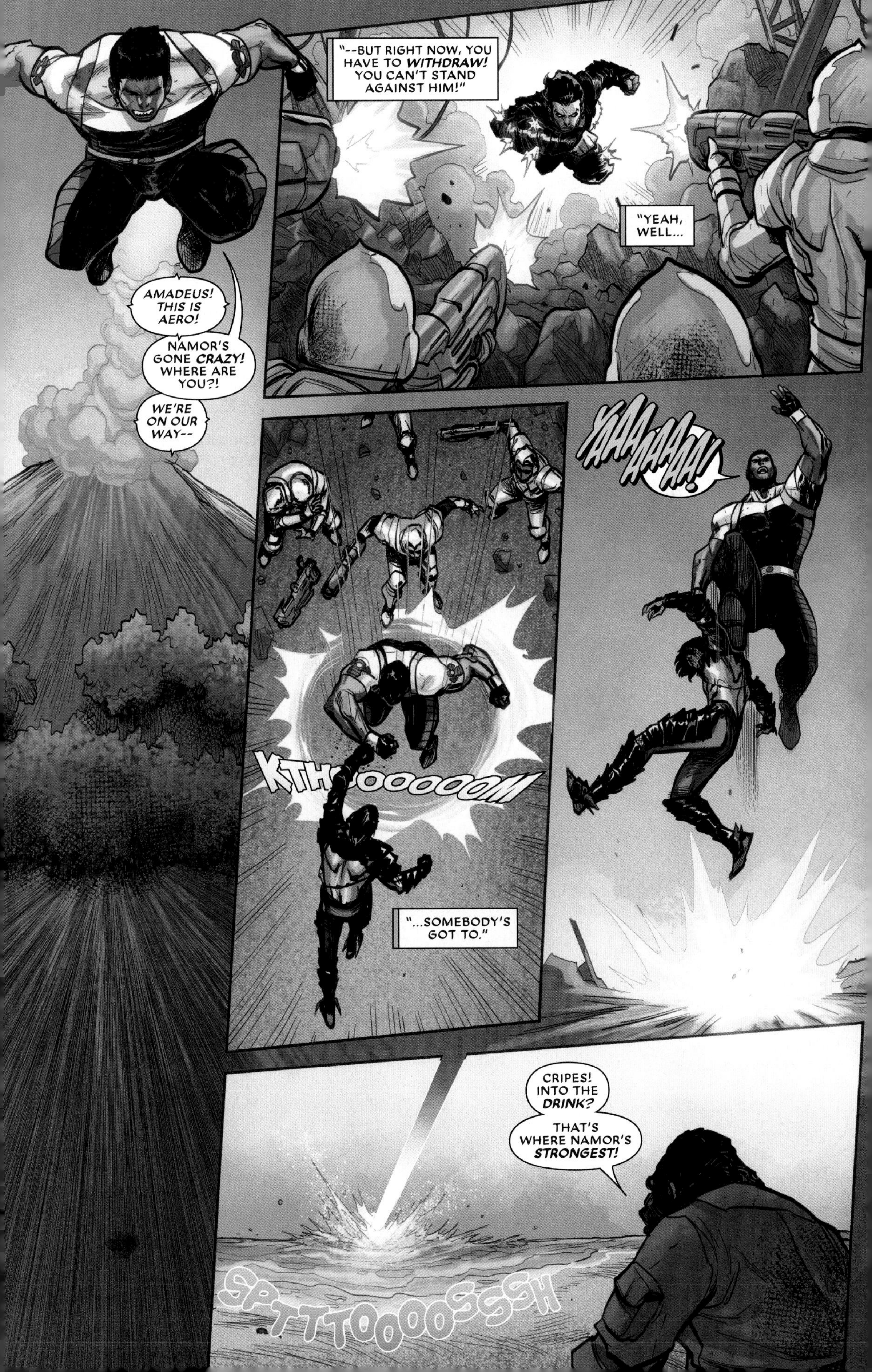
"--BUT RIGHT NOW, YOU HAVE TO WITHDRAW! YOU CAN'T STAND AGAINST HIM!"
"YEAH, WELL...
AMADEUS! THIS IS AERO!
NAMOR'S GONE CRAZY! WHERE ARE YOU?!
WE'RE ON OUR WAY--
YAAAAAAAA!
KTHOOOOOOOM
"...SOMEBODY'S GOT TO."
CRIPES! INTO THE DRINK?
THAT'S WHERE NAMOR'S STRONGEST!
SPTTTOOOOSSSH

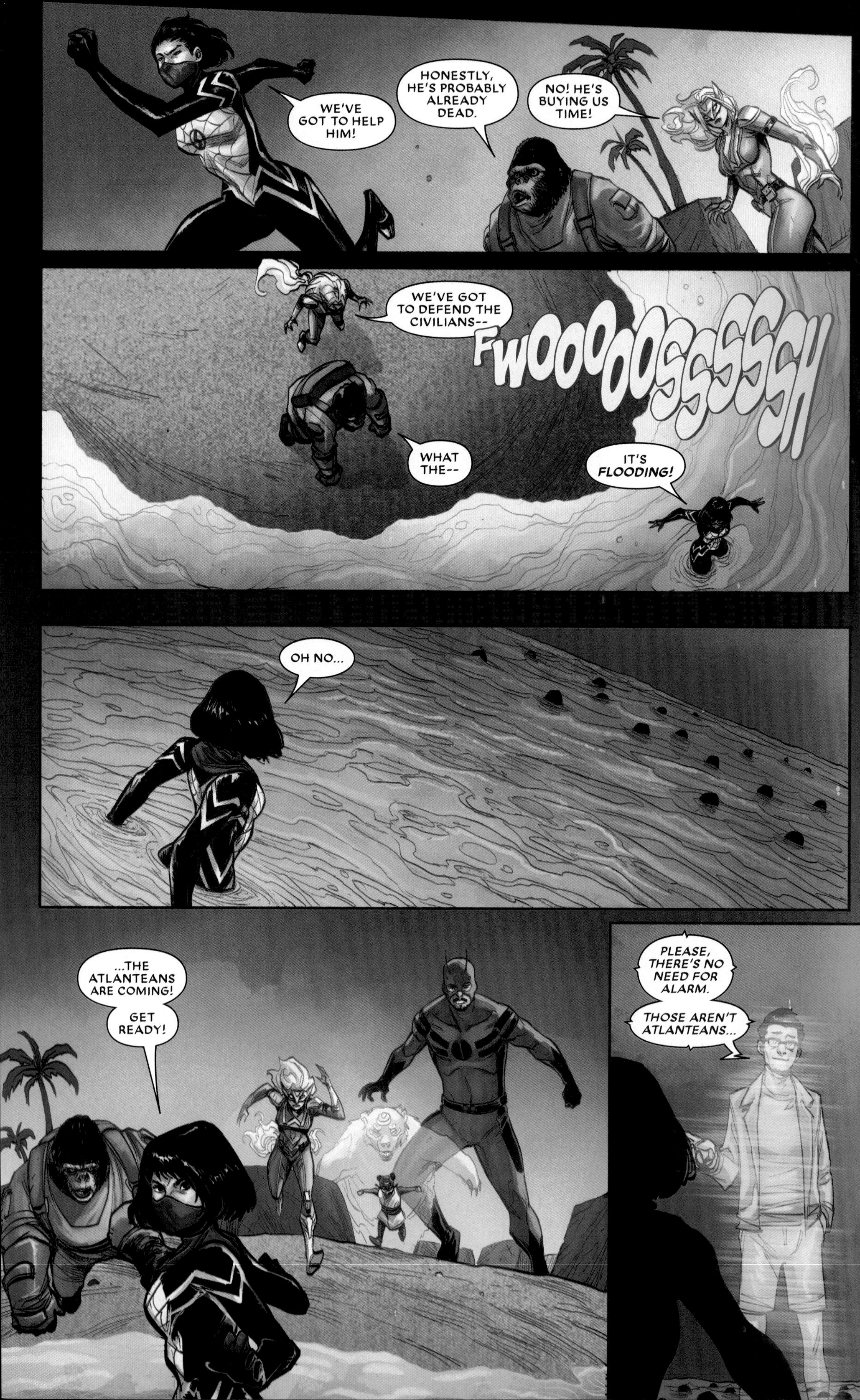
WE'VE GOT TO HELP HIM!
HONESTLY, HE'S PROBABLY ALREADY DEAD.
NO! HE'S BUYING US TIME!
WE'VE GOT TO DEFEND THE CIVILIANS--
FWOOOOOSSSSSH
WHAT THE--
IT'S FLOODING!
OH NO...
...THE ATLANTEANS ARE COMING!
GET READY!
PLEASE, THERE'S NO NEED FOR ALARM.
THOSE AREN'T ATLANTEANS...

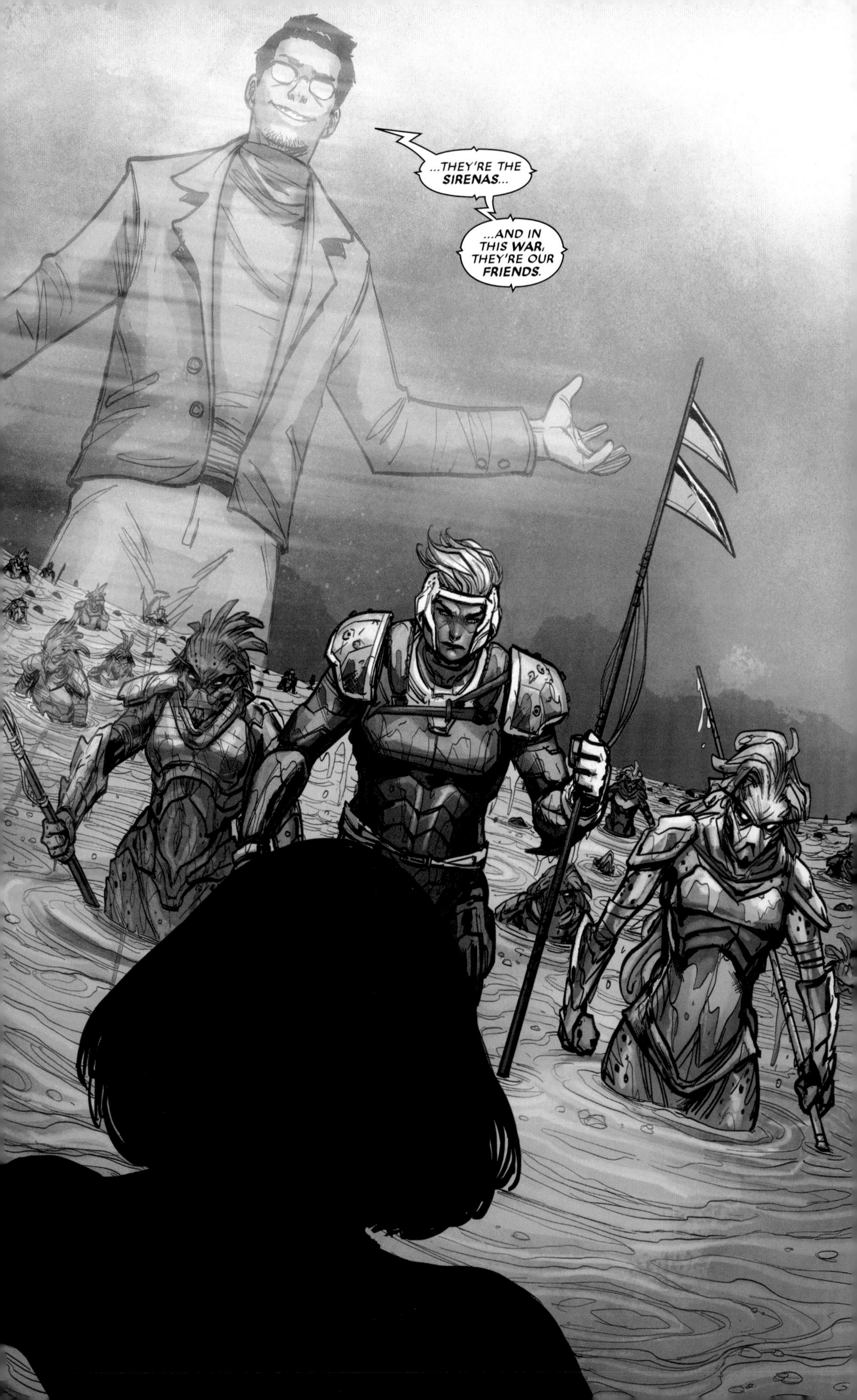
...THEY'RE THE SIRENAS...
...AND IN THIS WAR, THEY'RE OUR FRIENDS.

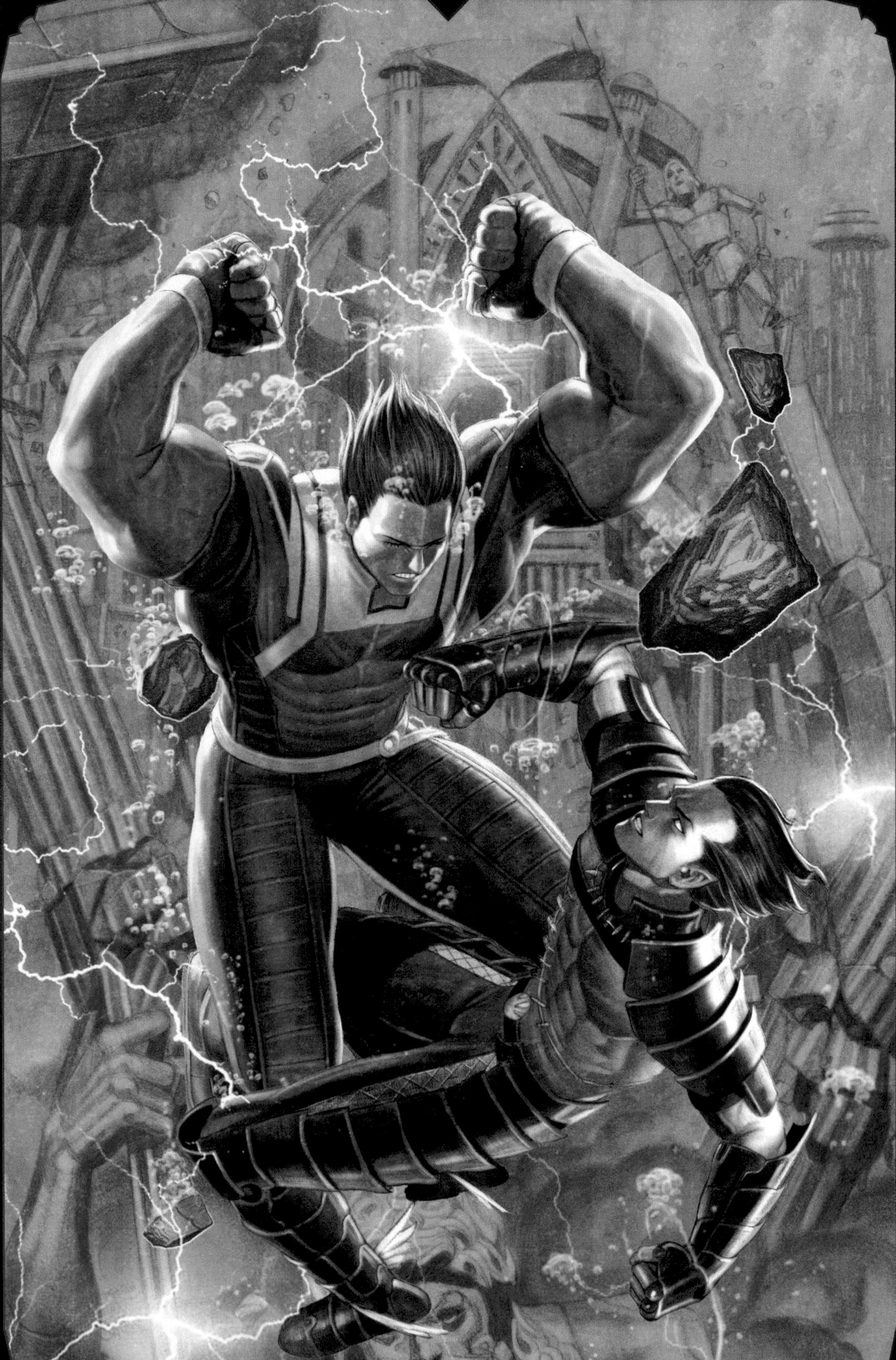

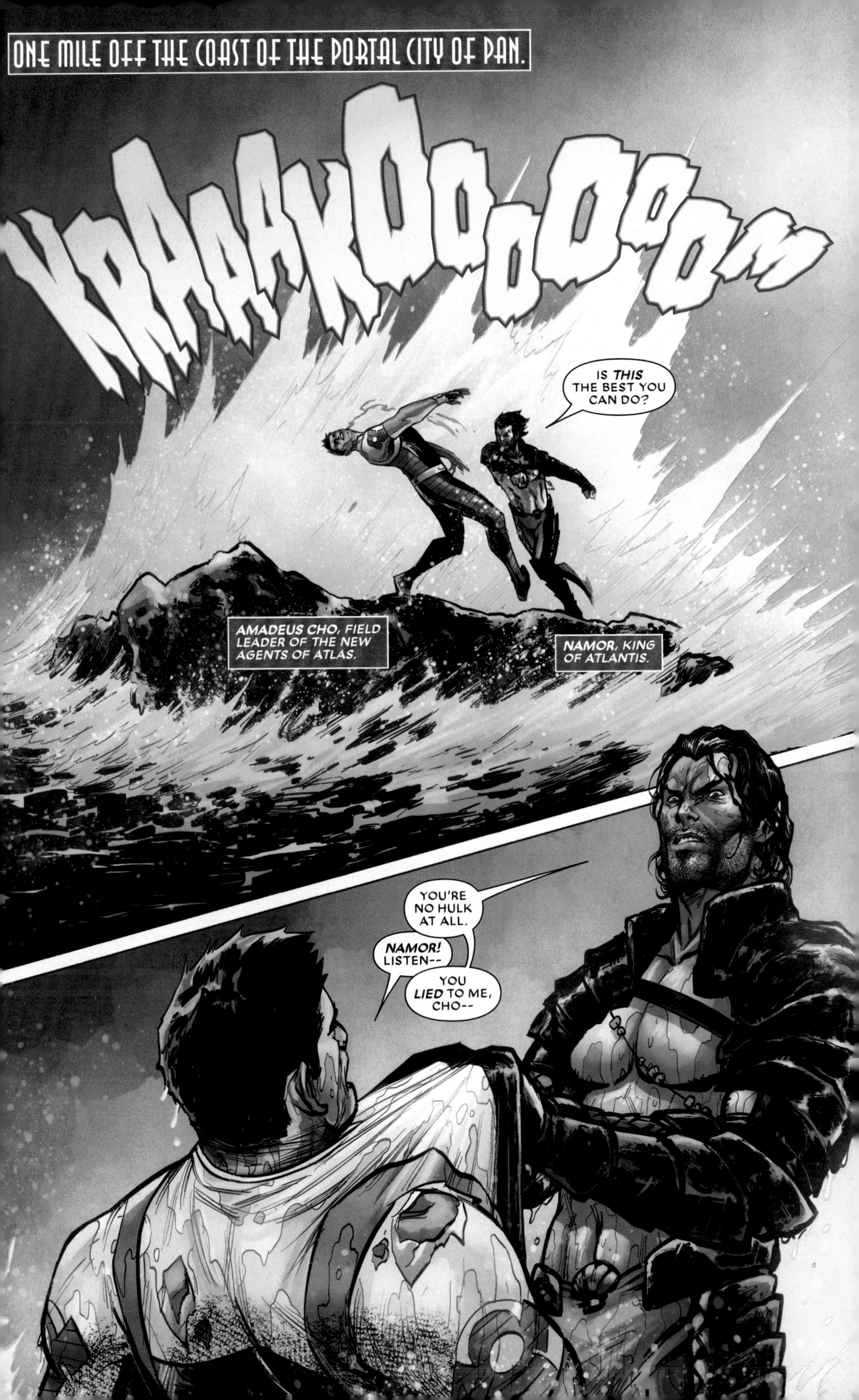
ONE MILE OFF THE COAST OF THE PORTAL CITY OF PAN.
KRAAAKOOOOOOOOM
IS THIS THE BEST YOU CAN DO?
AMADEUS CHO, FIELD LEADER OF THE NEW AGENTS OF ATLAS.
NAMOR, KING OF ATLANTIS.
YOU'RE NO HULK AT ALL.
NAMOR! LISTEN--
YOU LIED TO ME, CHO--

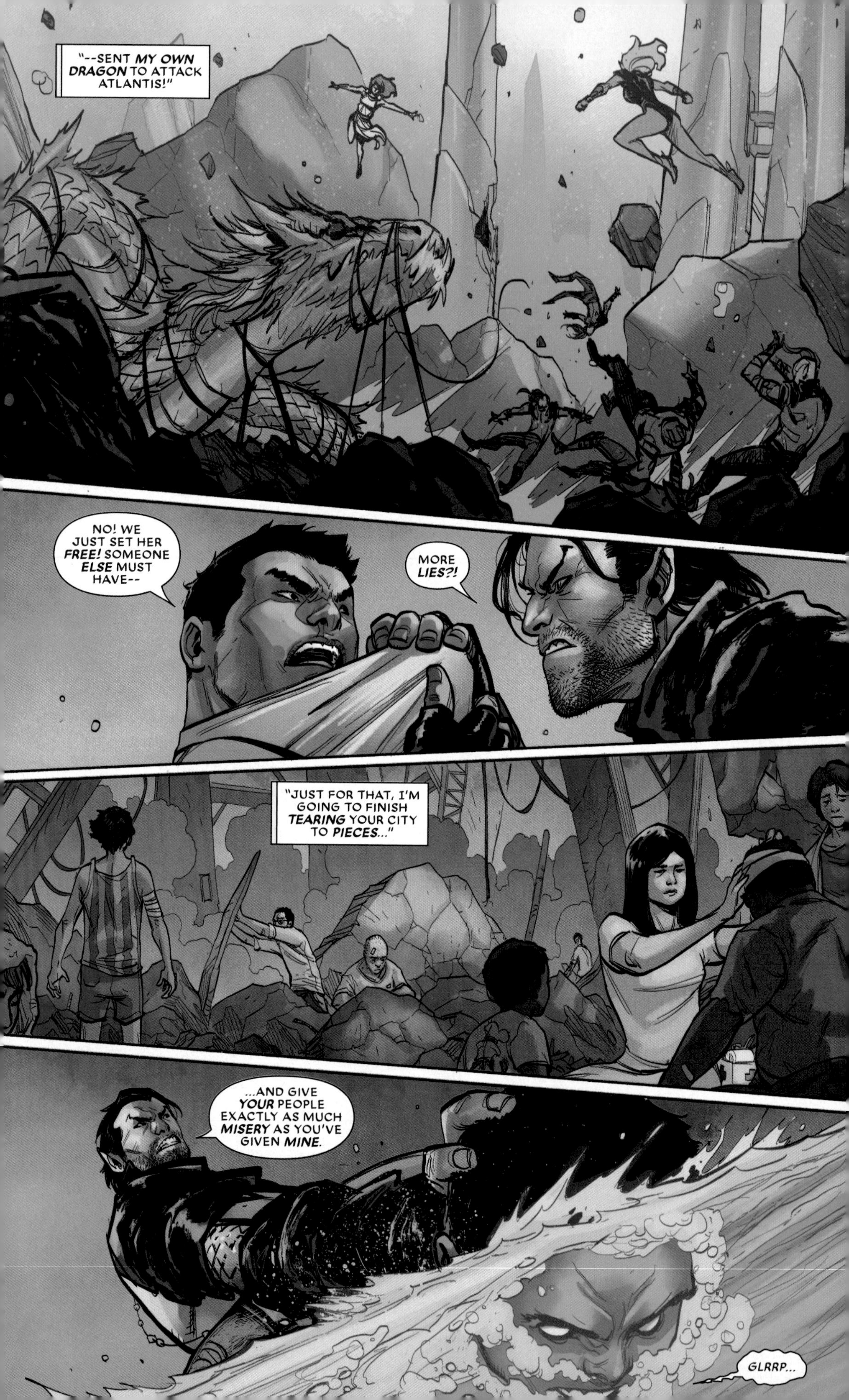
"--SENT MY OWN DRAGON TO ATTACK ATLANTIS!"
NO! WE JUST SET HER FREE! SOMEONE ELSE MUST HAVE--
MORE LIES?!
"JUST FOR THAT, I'M GOING TO FINISH TEARING YOUR CITY TO PIECES..."
...AND GIVE YOUR PEOPLE EXACTLY AS MUCH MISERY AS YOU'VE GIVEN MINE.
GLRRP...

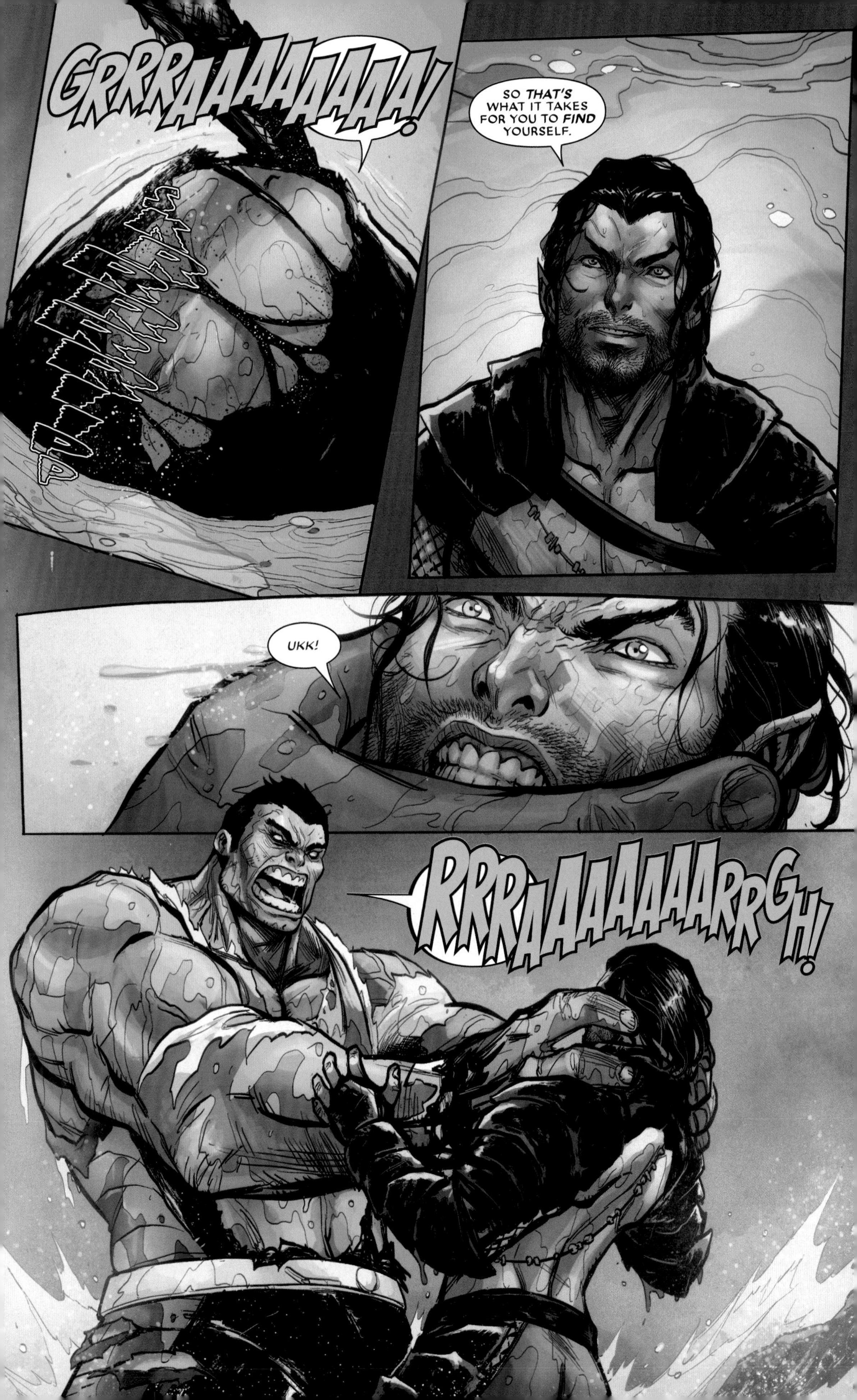
GRRRAAAAAAAAA!
SO THAT'S WHAT IT TAKES FOR YOU TO FIND YOURSELF.
UKK!
RRRAAAAAAARRGH!

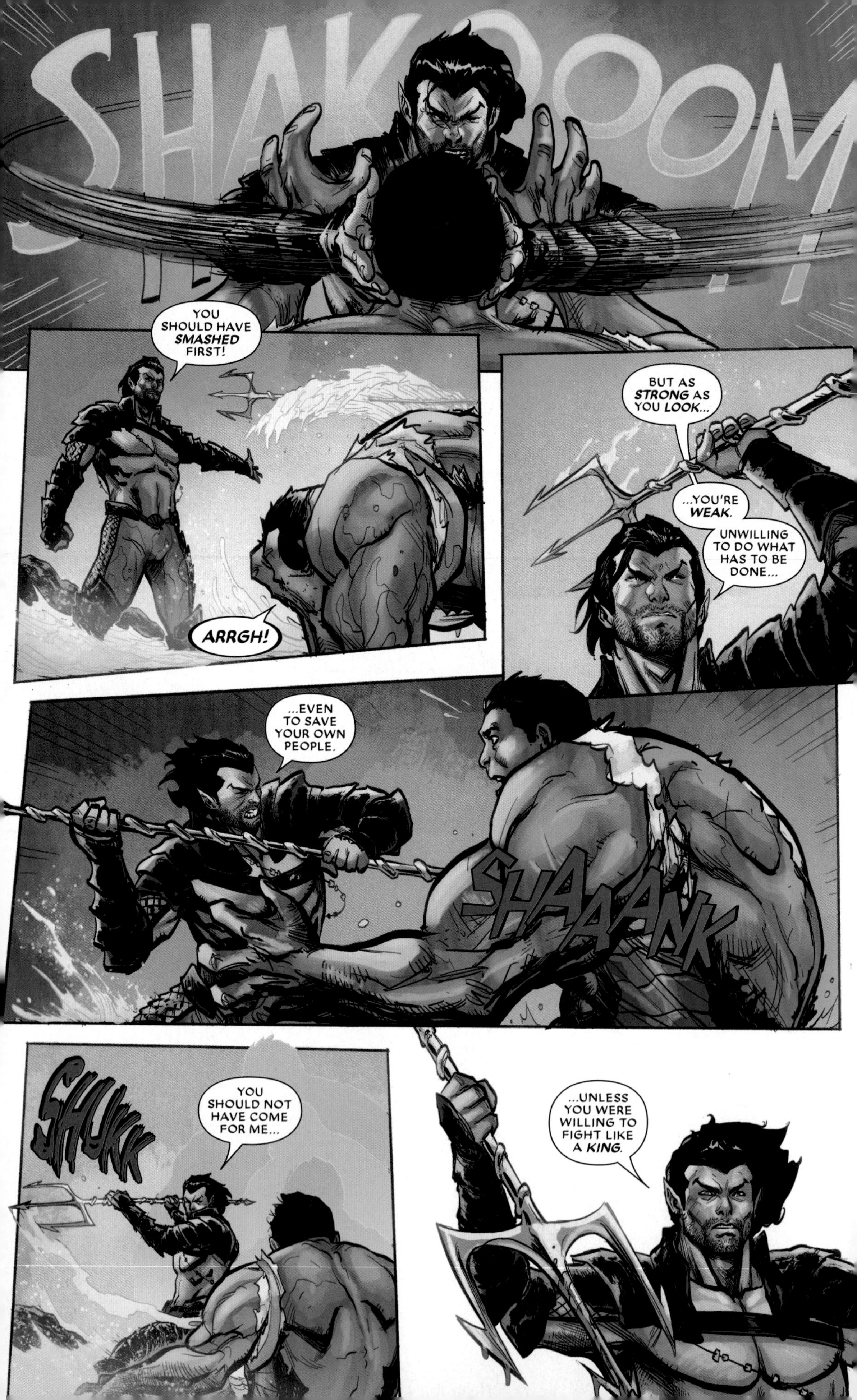
SHAKOOOM!
YOU SHOULD HAVE SMASHED FIRST!
ARRGH!
BUT AS STRONG AS YOU LOOK...
...YOU'RE WEAK.
UNWILLING TO DO WHAT HAS TO BE DONE...
...EVEN TO SAVE YOUR OWN PEOPLE.
SHAAANK
SHUKK
YOU SHOULD NOT HAVE COME FOR ME...
...UNLESS YOU WERE WILLING TO FIGHT LIKE A KING.

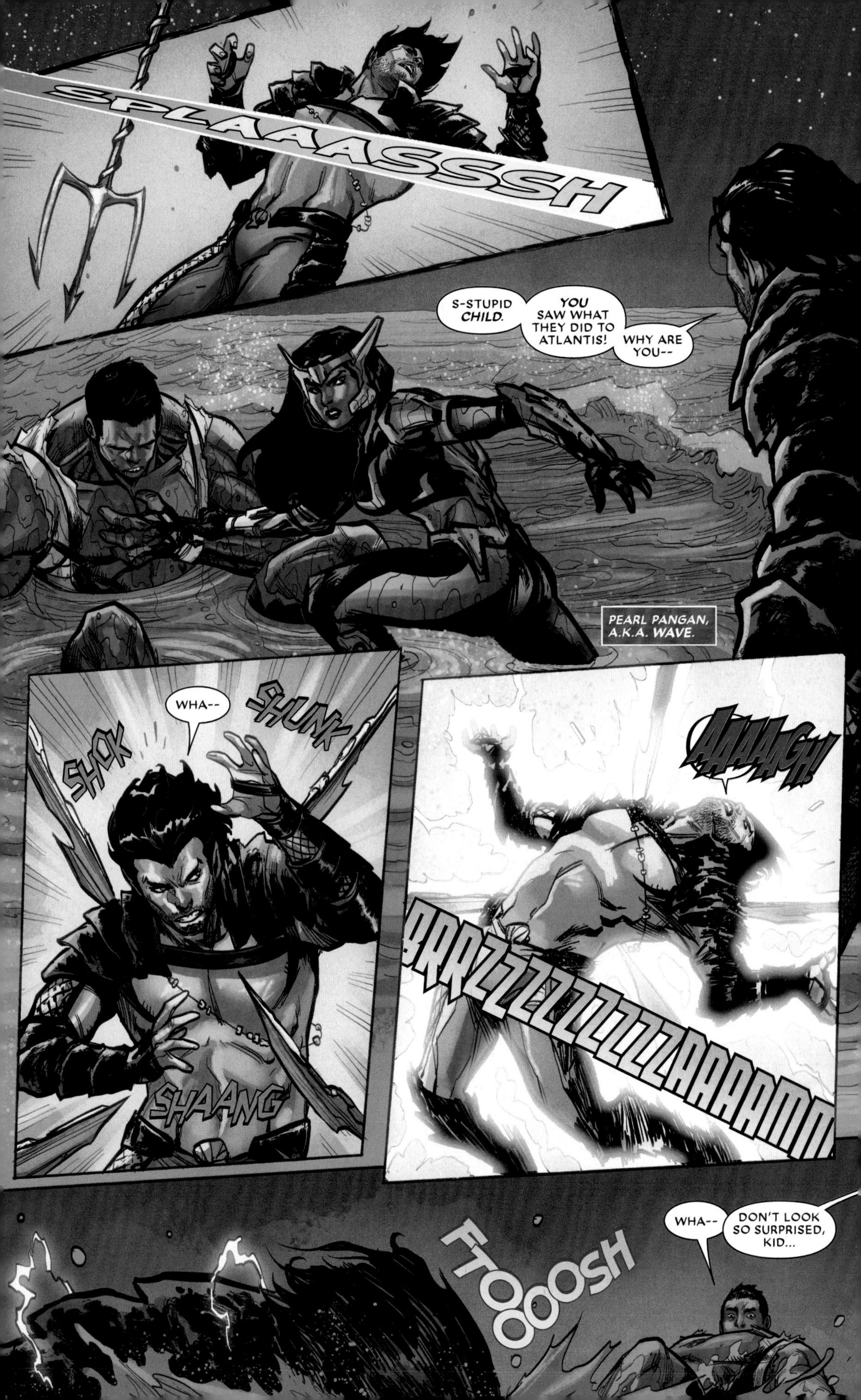
SPLAAASSSH
S-STUPID CHILD.
YOU SAW WHAT THEY DID TO ATLANTIS!
WHY ARE YOU--
PEARL PANGAN, A.K.A. WAVE.
WHA--
SHUNK
SHOK
SHAANG
AAAAAGH!
BRRZZZZZZZZZZAAAAMM
FTOOOOOSH
WHA--
DON'T LOOK SO SURPRISED, KID...

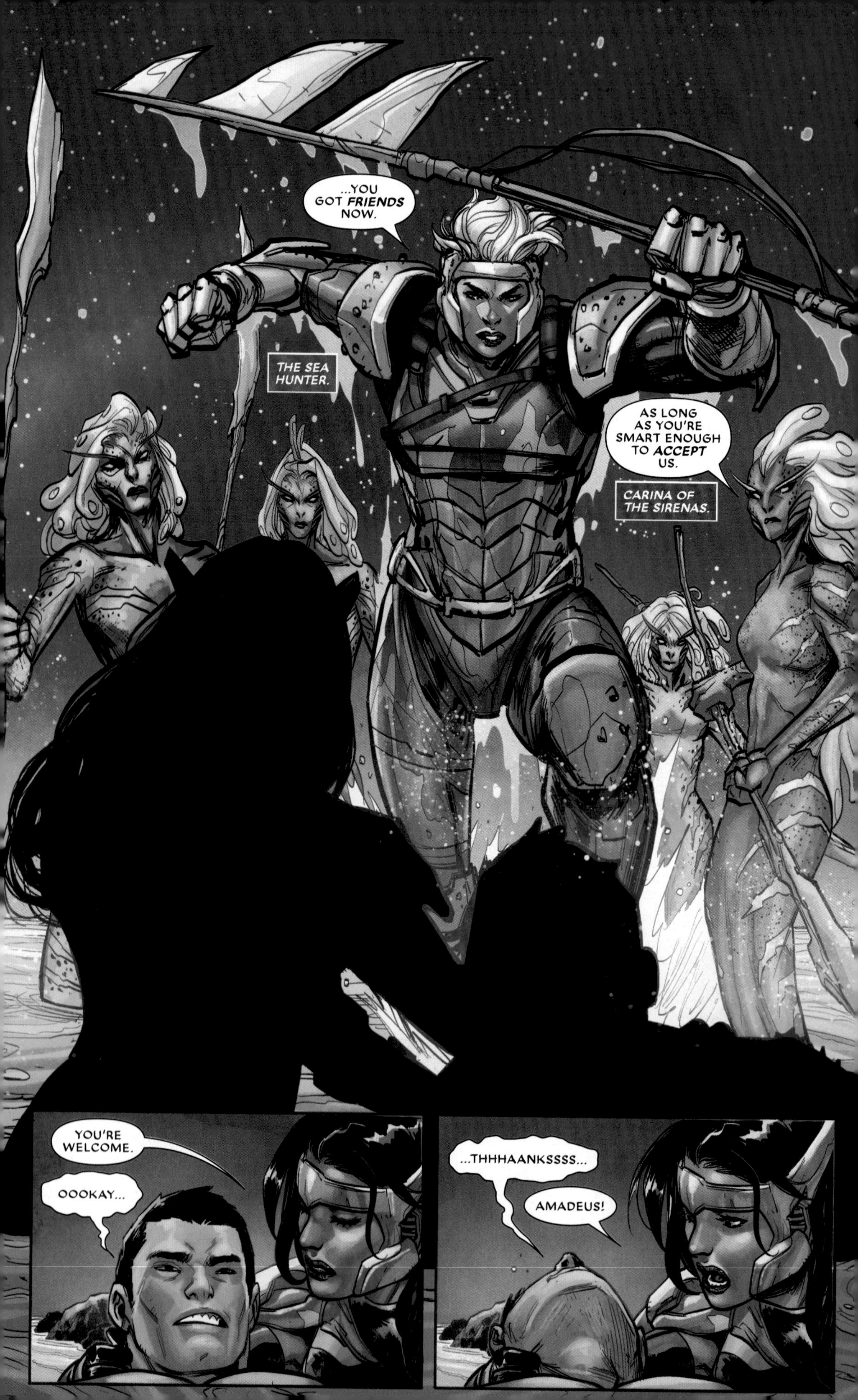
...YOU GOT FRIENDS NOW.
THE SEA HUNTER.
AS LONG AS YOU'RE SMART ENOUGH TO ACCEPT US.
CARINA OF THE SIRENAS.
YOU'RE WELCOME.
OOOKAY...
...THHHAANKSSSS...
AMADEUS!

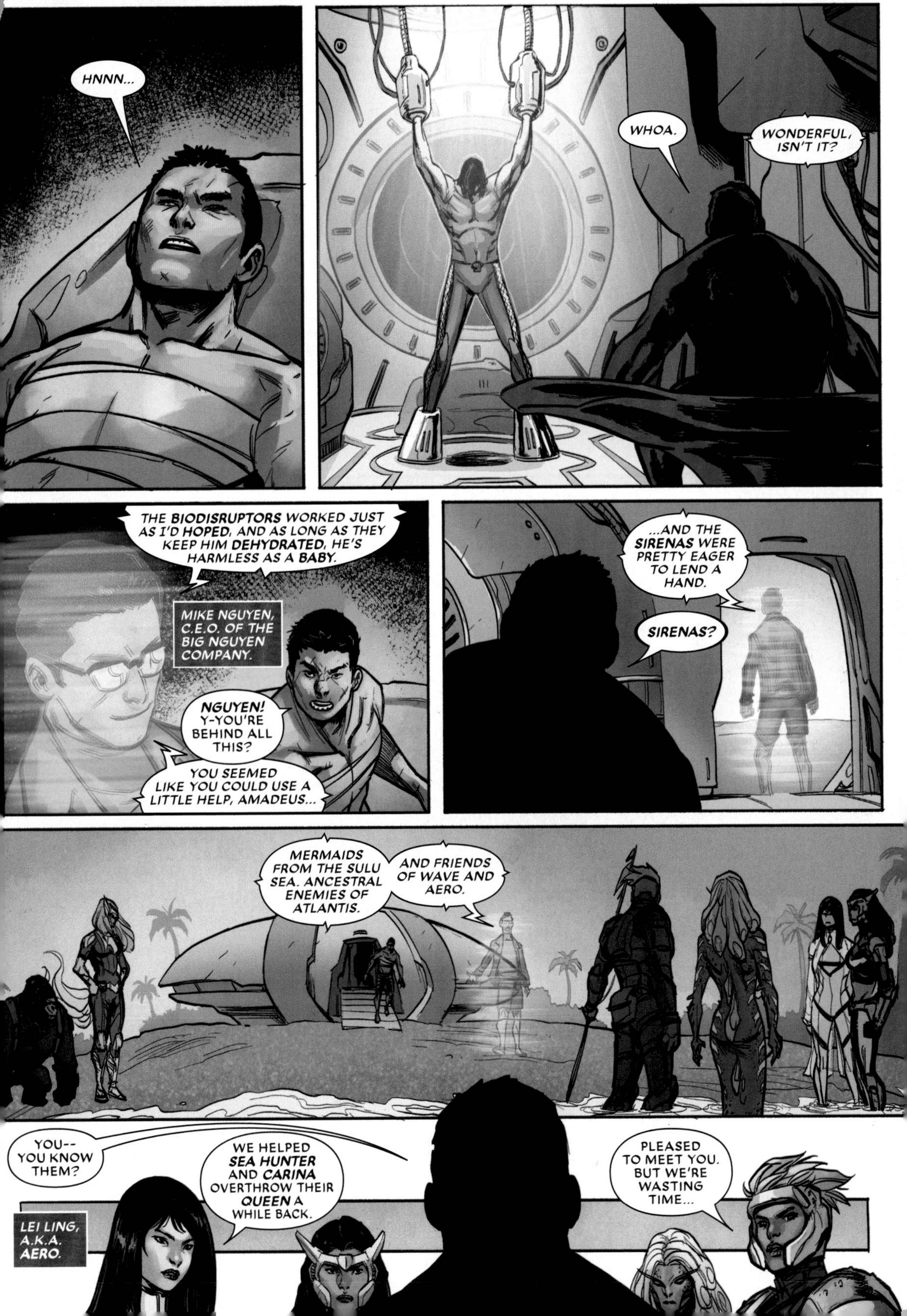
HNNN...
WHOA.
WONDERFUL, ISN'T IT?
THE BIODISRUPTORS WORKED JUST AS I'D HOPED, AND AS LONG AS THEY KEEP HIM DEHYDRATED, HE'S HARMLESS AS A BABY.
MIKE NGUYEN, C.E.O. OF THE BIG NGUYEN COMPANY.
NGUYEN! Y-YOU'RE BEHIND ALL THIS?
YOU SEEMED LIKE YOU COULD USE A LITTLE HELP, AMADEUS...
...AND THE SIRENAS WERE PRETTY EAGER TO LEND A HAND.
SIRENAS?
MERMAIDS FROM THE SULU SEA. ANCESTRAL ENEMIES OF ATLANTIS.
AND FRIENDS OF WAVE AND AERO.
YOU-- YOU KNOW THEM?
WE HELPED SEA HUNTER AND CARINA OVERTHROW THEIR QUEEN A WHILE BACK.
LEI LING, A.K.A. AERO.
PLEASED TO MEET YOU. BUT WE'RE WASTING TIME...

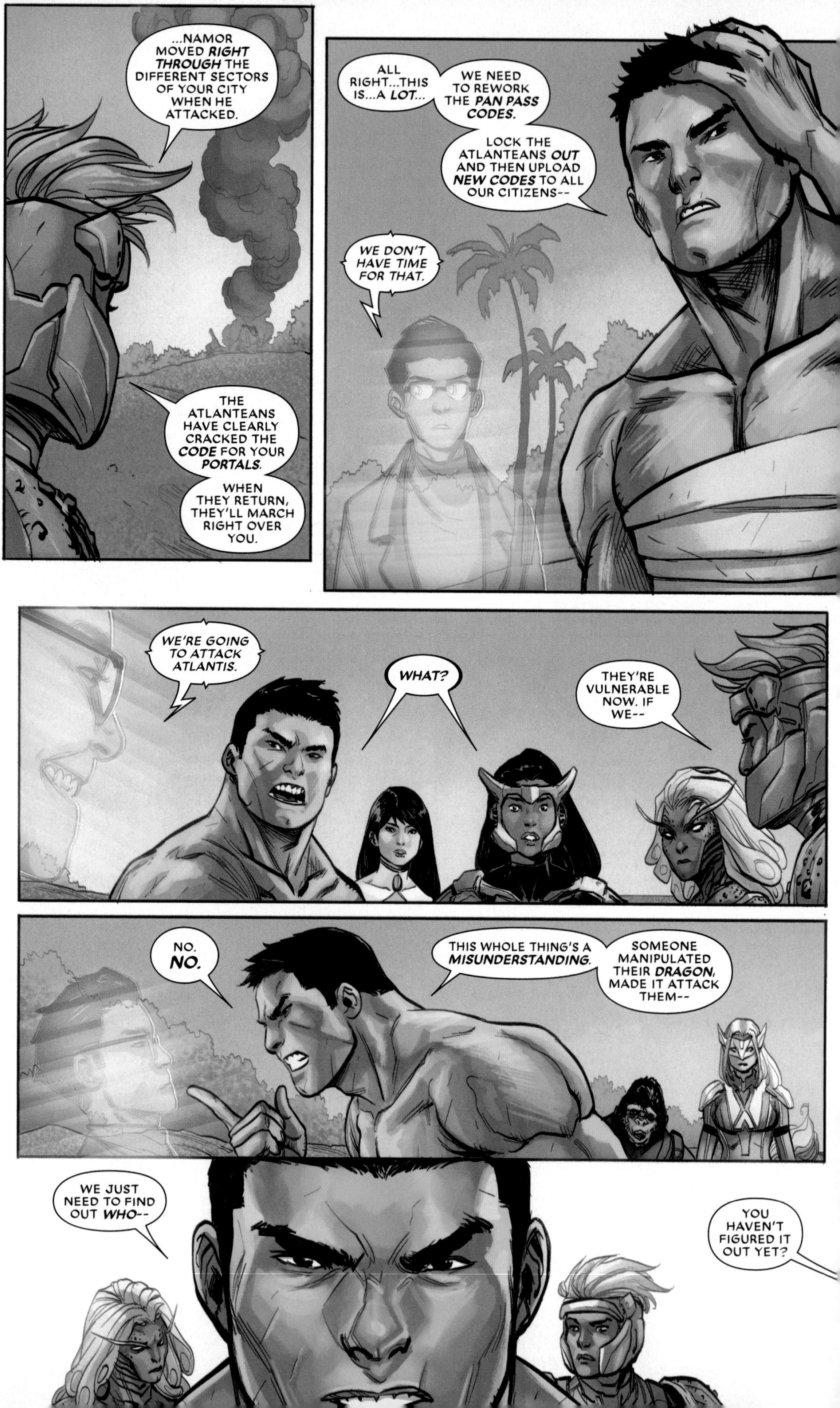
...NAMOR MOVED RIGHT THROUGH THE DIFFERENT SECTORS OF YOUR CITY WHEN HE ATTACKED.
THE ATLANTEANS HAVE CLEARLY CRACKED THE CODE FOR YOUR PORTALS.
WHEN THEY RETURN, THEY'LL MARCH RIGHT OVER YOU.
ALL RIGHT...THIS IS...A LOT...
WE NEED TO REWORK THE PAN PASS CODES.
LOCK THE ATLANTEANS OUT AND THEN UPLOAD NEW CODES TO ALL OUR CITIZENS--
WE DON'T HAVE TIME FOR THAT.
WE'RE GOING TO ATTACK ATLANTIS.
WHAT?
THEY'RE VULNERABLE NOW. IF WE--
NO. NO.
THIS WHOLE THING'S A MISUNDERSTANDING.
SOMEONE MANIPULATED THEIR DRAGON, MADE IT ATTACK THEM--
WE JUST NEED TO FIND OUT WHO--
YOU HAVEN'T FIGURED IT OUT YET?

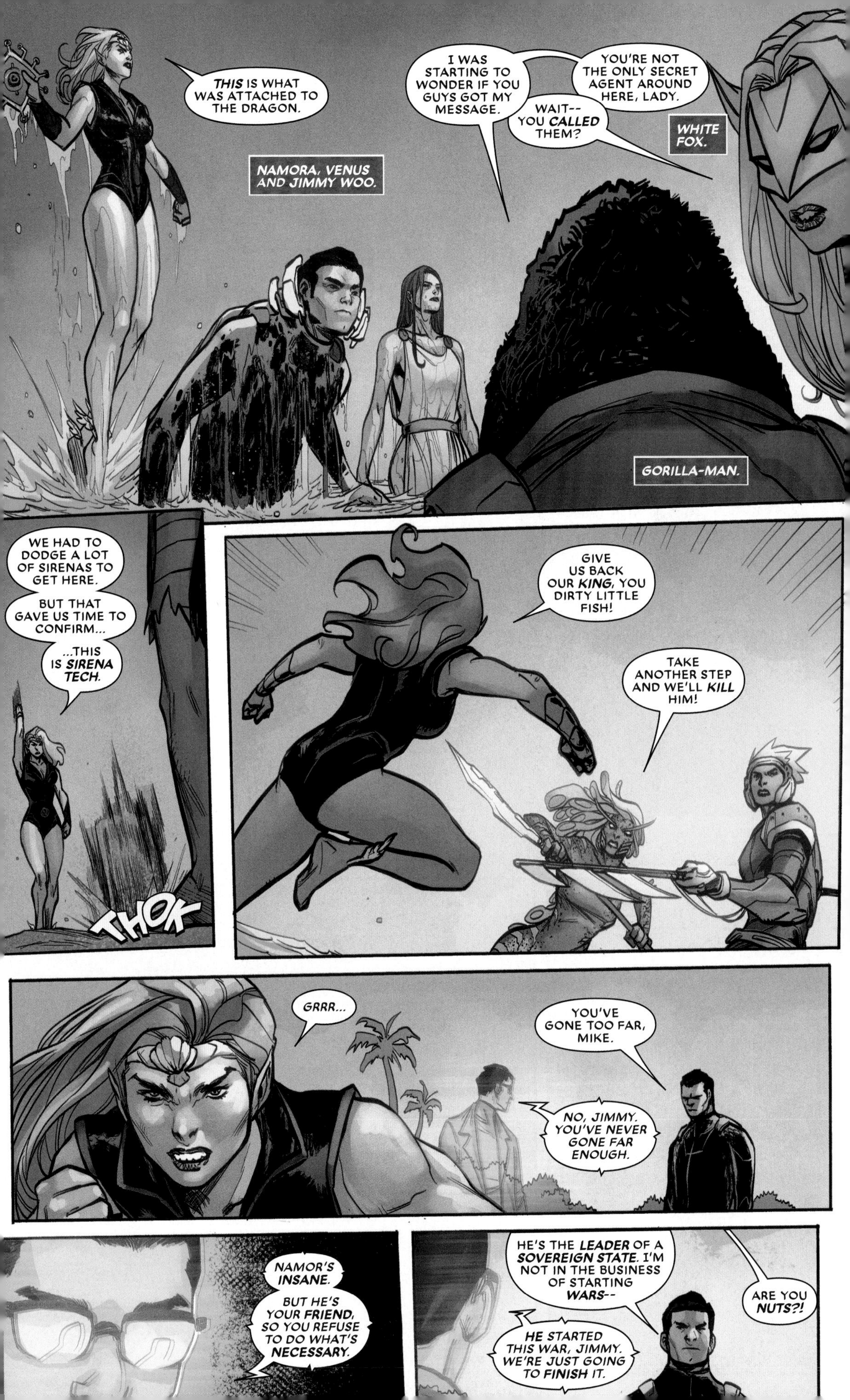
THIS IS WHAT WAS ATTACHED TO THE DRAGON.
NAMORA, VENUS AND JIMMY WOO.
I WAS STARTING TO WONDER IF YOU GUYS GOT MY MESSAGE.
YOU'RE NOT THE ONLY SECRET AGENT AROUND HERE, LADY.
WAIT-- YOU CALLED THEM?
WHITE FOX.
GORILLA-MAN.
WE HAD TO DODGE A LOT OF SIRENAS TO GET HERE.
BUT THAT GAVE US TIME TO CONFIRM...
...THIS IS SIRENA TECH.
THOK
GIVE US BACK OUR KING, YOU DIRTY LITTLE FISH!
TAKE ANOTHER STEP AND WE'LL KILL HIM!
GRRR...
YOU'VE GONE TOO FAR, MIKE.
NO, JIMMY. YOU'VE NEVER GONE FAR ENOUGH.
NAMOR'S INSANE.
BUT HE'S YOUR FRIEND, SO YOU REFUSE TO DO WHAT'S NECESSARY.
HE'S THE LEADER OF A SOVEREIGN STATE. I'M NOT IN THE BUSINESS OF STARTING WARS--
HE STARTED THIS WAR, JIMMY. WE'RE JUST GOING TO FINISH IT.
ARE YOU NUTS?!

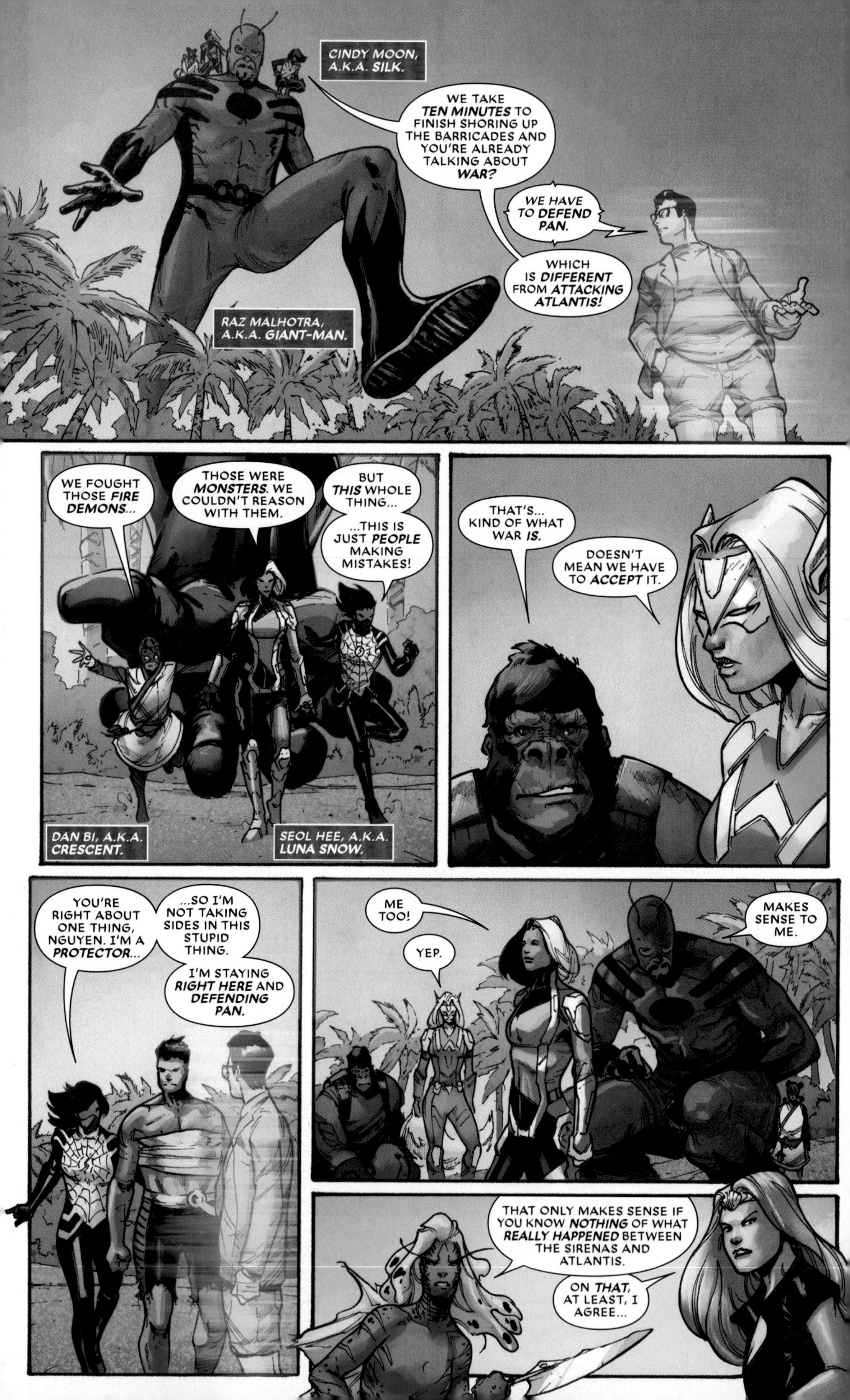
CINDY MOON, A.K.A. SILK.
WE TAKE TEN MINUTES TO FINISH SHORING UP THE BARRICADES AND YOU'RE ALREADY TALKING ABOUT WAR?
WE HAVE TO DEFEND PAN.
WHICH IS DIFFERENT FROM ATTACKING ATLANTIS!
RAZ MALHOTRA, A.K.A. GIANT-MAN.
WE FOUGHT THOSE FIRE DEMONS...
THOSE WERE MONSTERS. WE COULDN'T REASON WITH THEM.
BUT THIS WHOLE THING...
...THIS IS JUST PEOPLE MAKING MISTAKES!
DAN BI, A.K.A. CRESCENT.
SEOL HEE, A.K.A. LUNA SNOW.
THAT'S... KIND OF WHAT WAR IS.
DOESN'T MEAN WE HAVE TO ACCEPT IT.
YOU'RE RIGHT ABOUT ONE THING, NGUYEN. I'M A PROTECTOR...
...SO I'M NOT TAKING SIDES IN THIS STUPID THING.
I'M STAYING RIGHT HERE AND DEFENDING PAN.
ME TOO!
YEP.
MAKES SENSE TO ME.
THAT ONLY MAKES SENSE IF YOU KNOW NOTHING OF WHAT REALLY HAPPENED BETWEEN THE SIRENAS AND ATLANTIS.
ON THAT, AT LEAST, I AGREE...

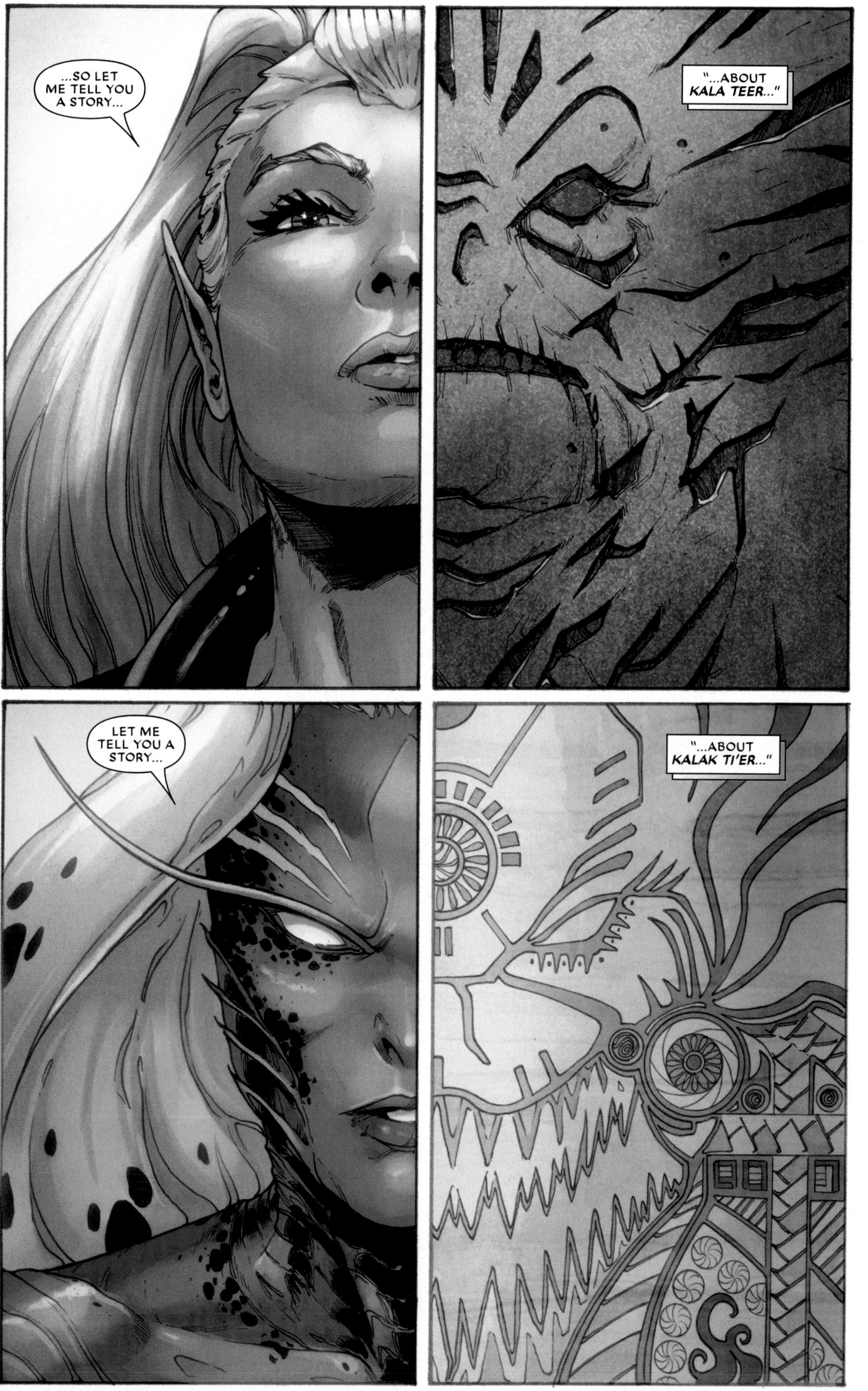
...SO LET ME TELL YOU A STORY...
"...ABOUT KALA TEER..."
LET ME TELL YOU A STORY...
"...ABOUT KALAK TI'ER..."

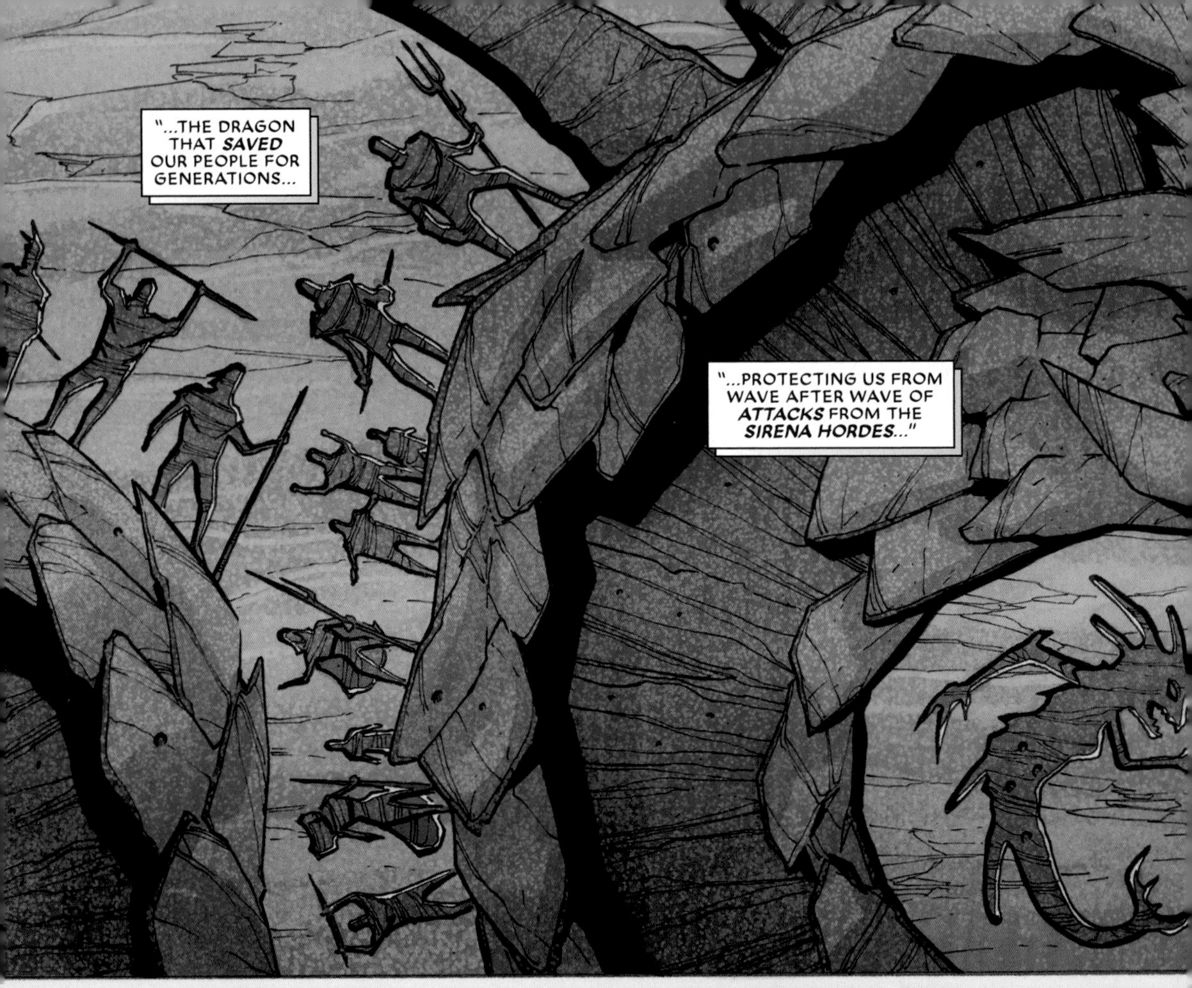
"...THE DRAGON THAT *SAVED* OUR PEOPLE FOR GENERATIONS...
"...PROTECTING US FROM WAVE AFTER WAVE OF *ATTACKS* FROM THE *SIRENA HORDES*..."

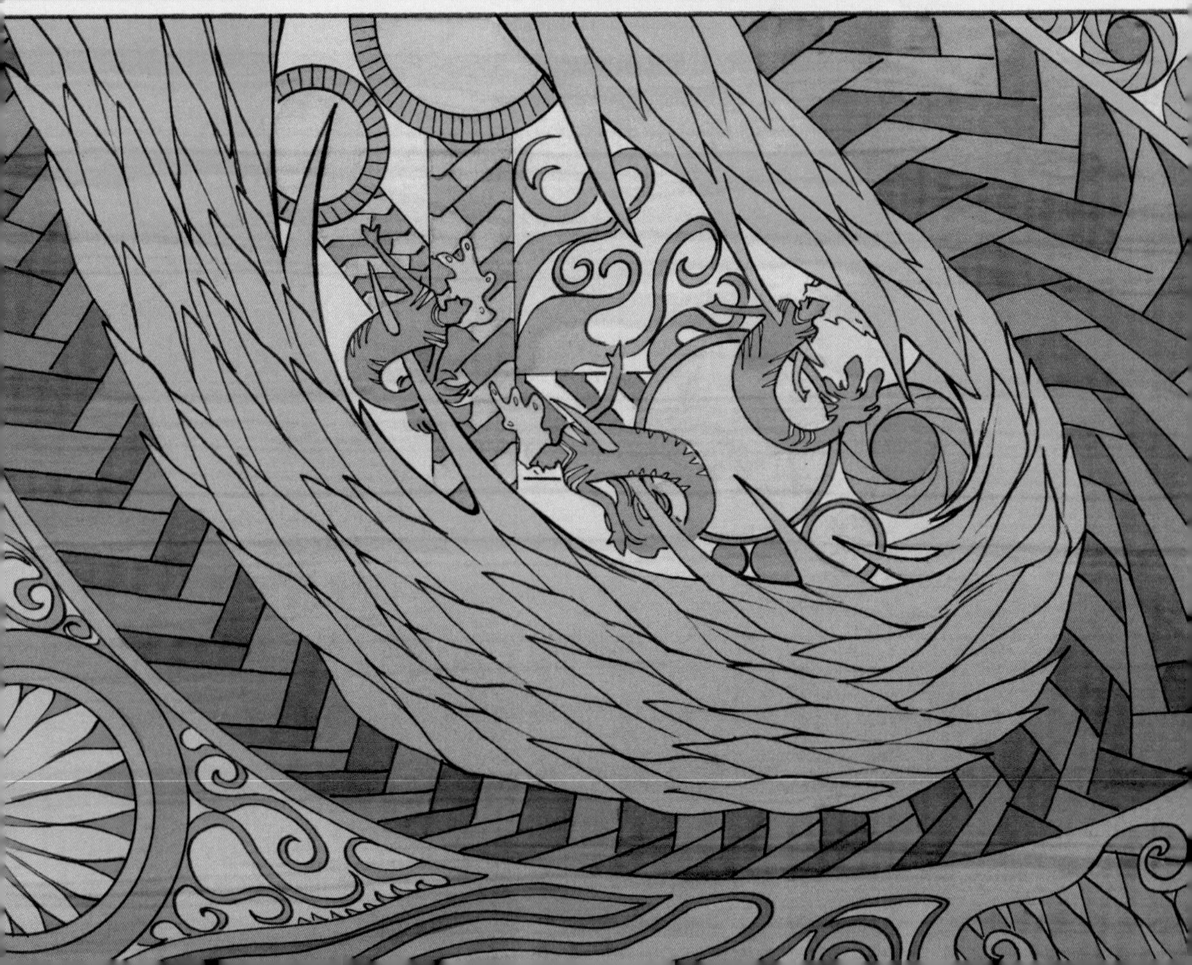

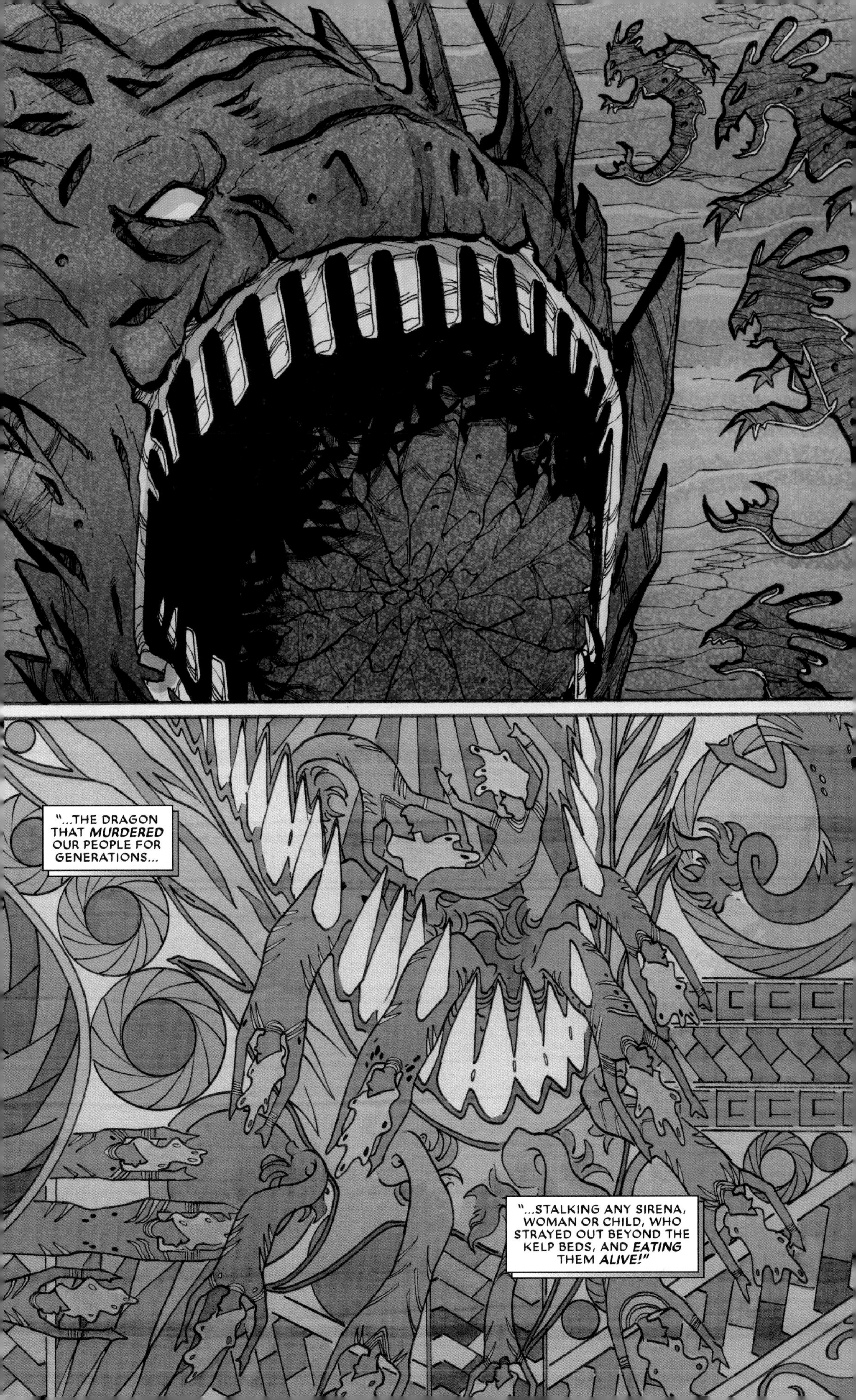
"...THE DRAGON THAT MURDERED OUR PEOPLE FOR GENERATIONS...
"...STALKING ANY SIRENA, WOMAN OR CHILD, WHO STRAYED OUT BEYOND THE KELP BEDS, AND EATING THEM ALIVE!"

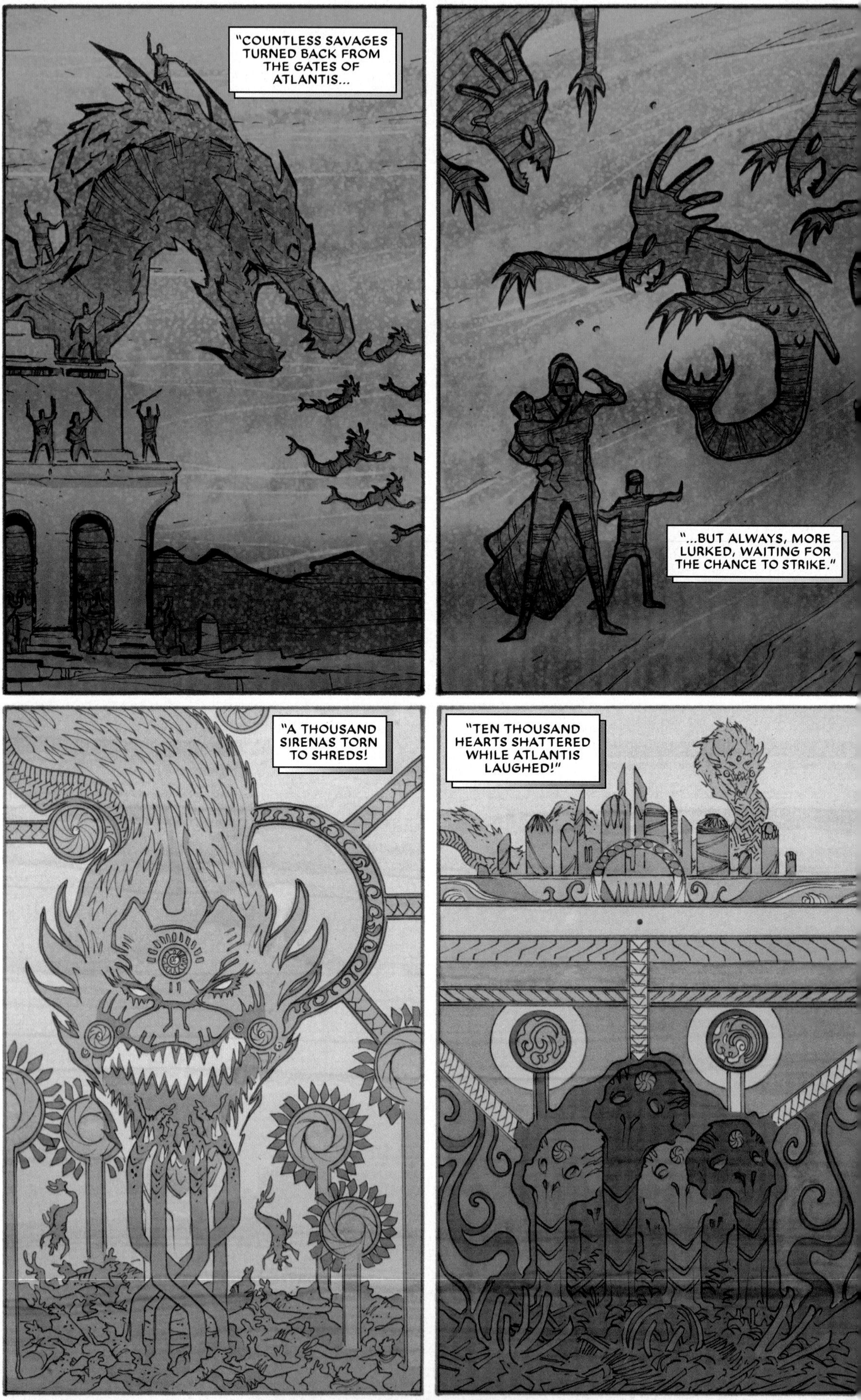
"COUNTLESS SAVAGES TURNED BACK FROM THE GATES OF ATLANTIS...
"...BUT ALWAYS, MORE LURKED, WAITING FOR THE CHANCE TO STRIKE."
"A THOUSAND SIRENAS TORN TO SHREDS!
"TEN THOUSAND HEARTS SHATTERED WHILE ATLANTIS LAUGHED!"

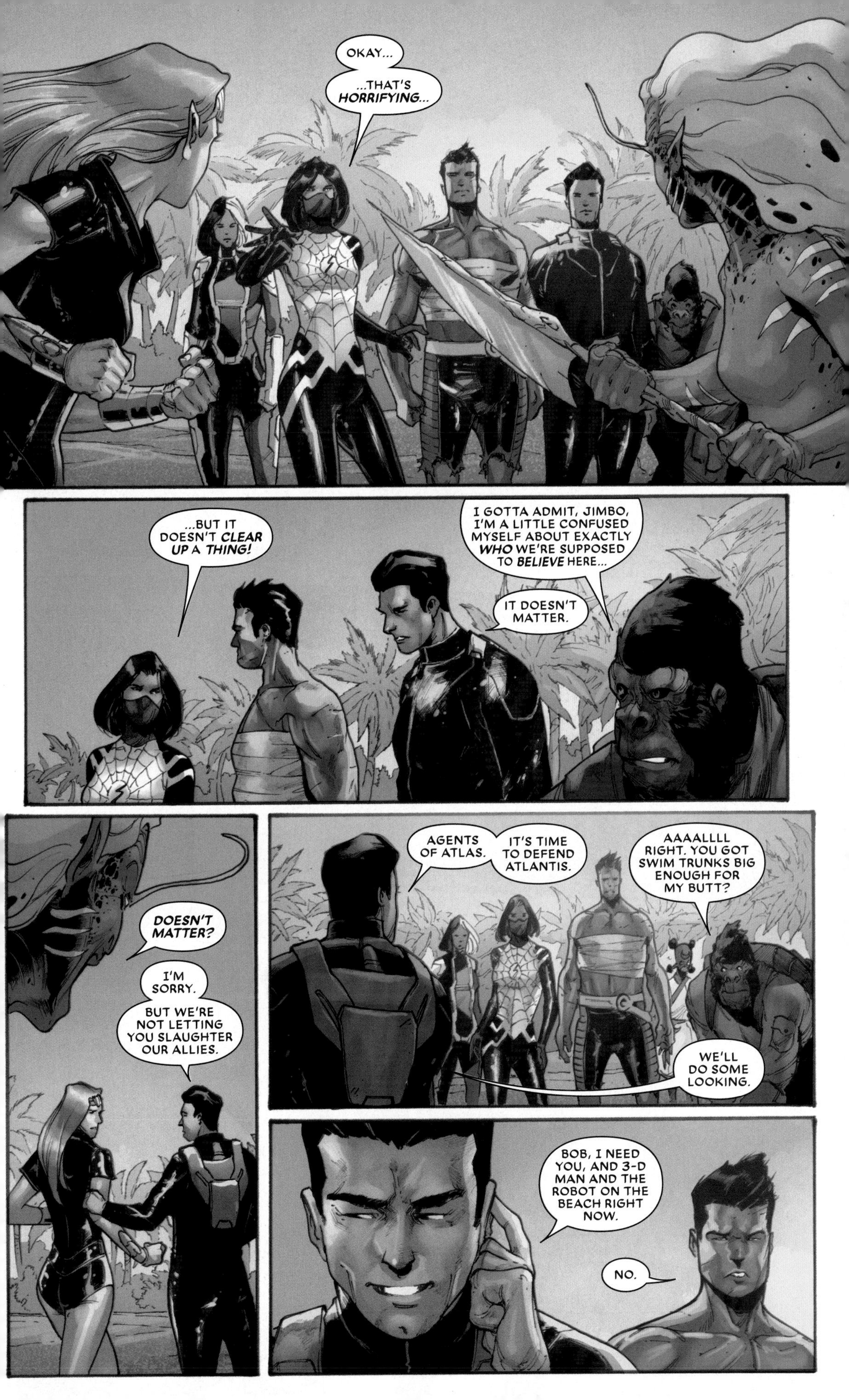

OKAY...
...THAT'S HORRIFYING...
...BUT IT DOESN'T CLEAR UP A THING!
I GOTTA ADMIT, JIMBO, I'M A LITTLE CONFUSED MYSELF ABOUT EXACTLY WHO WE'RE SUPPOSED TO BELIEVE HERE...
IT DOESN'T MATTER.
DOESN'T MATTER?
I'M SORRY.
BUT WE'RE NOT LETTING YOU SLAUGHTER OUR ALLIES.
AGENTS OF ATLAS.
IT'S TIME TO DEFEND ATLANTIS.
AAAALLLL RIGHT. YOU GOT SWIM TRUNKS BIG ENOUGH FOR MY BUTT?
WE'LL DO SOME LOOKING.
BOB, I NEED YOU, AND 3-D MAN AND THE ROBOT ON THE BEACH RIGHT NOW.
NO.

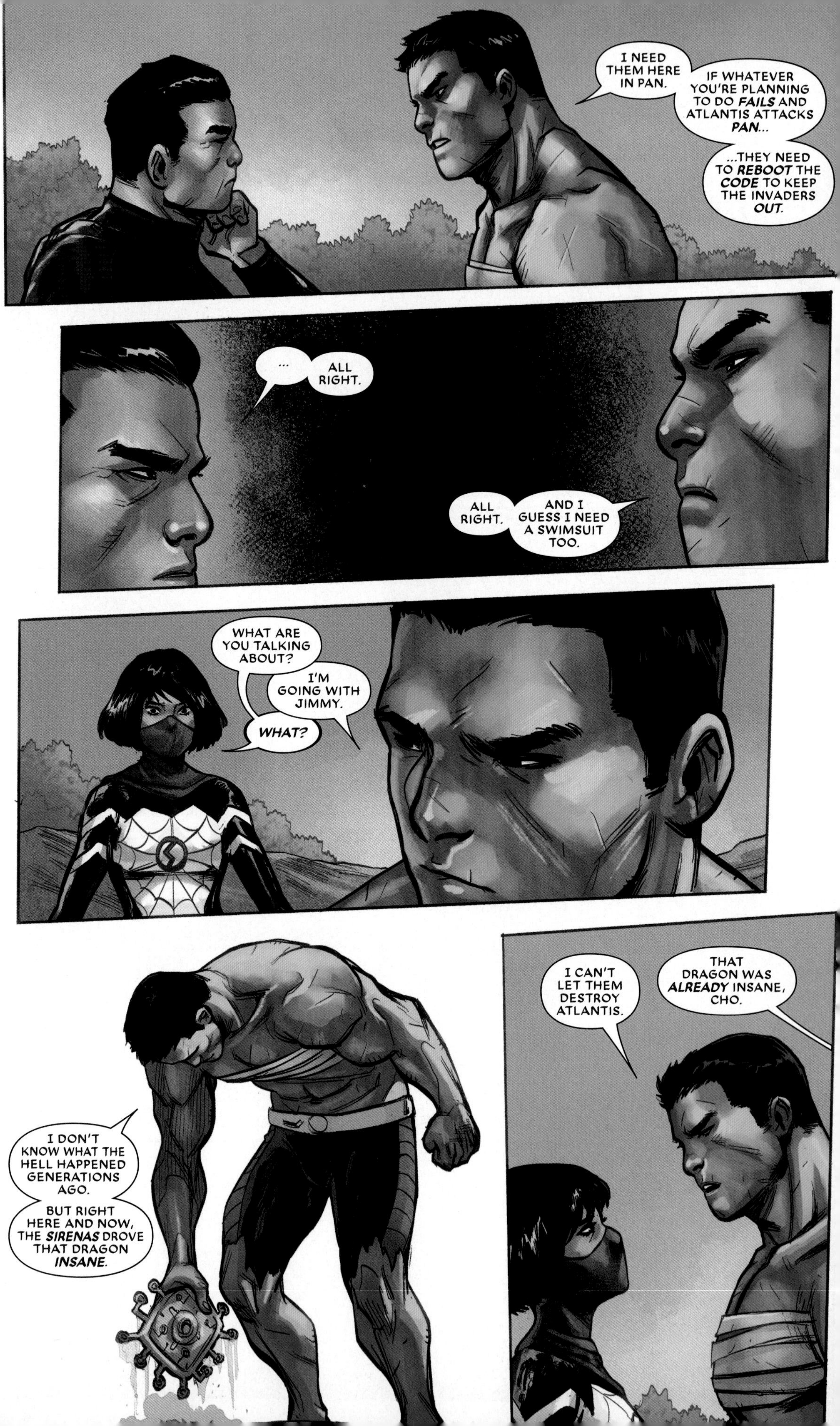
I NEED THEM HERE IN PAN.
IF WHATEVER YOU'RE PLANNING TO DO FAILS AND ATLANTIS ATTACKS PAN...
...THEY NEED TO REBOOT THE CODE TO KEEP THE INVADERS OUT.
... ALL RIGHT.
ALL RIGHT.
AND I GUESS I NEED A SWIMSUIT TOO.
WHAT ARE YOU TALKING ABOUT?
I'M GOING WITH JIMMY.
WHAT?
I DON'T KNOW WHAT THE HELL HAPPENED GENERATIONS AGO.
BUT RIGHT HERE AND NOW, THE SIRENAS DROVE THAT DRAGON INSANE.
I CAN'T LET THEM DESTROY ATLANTIS.
THAT DRAGON WAS ALREADY INSANE, CHO.

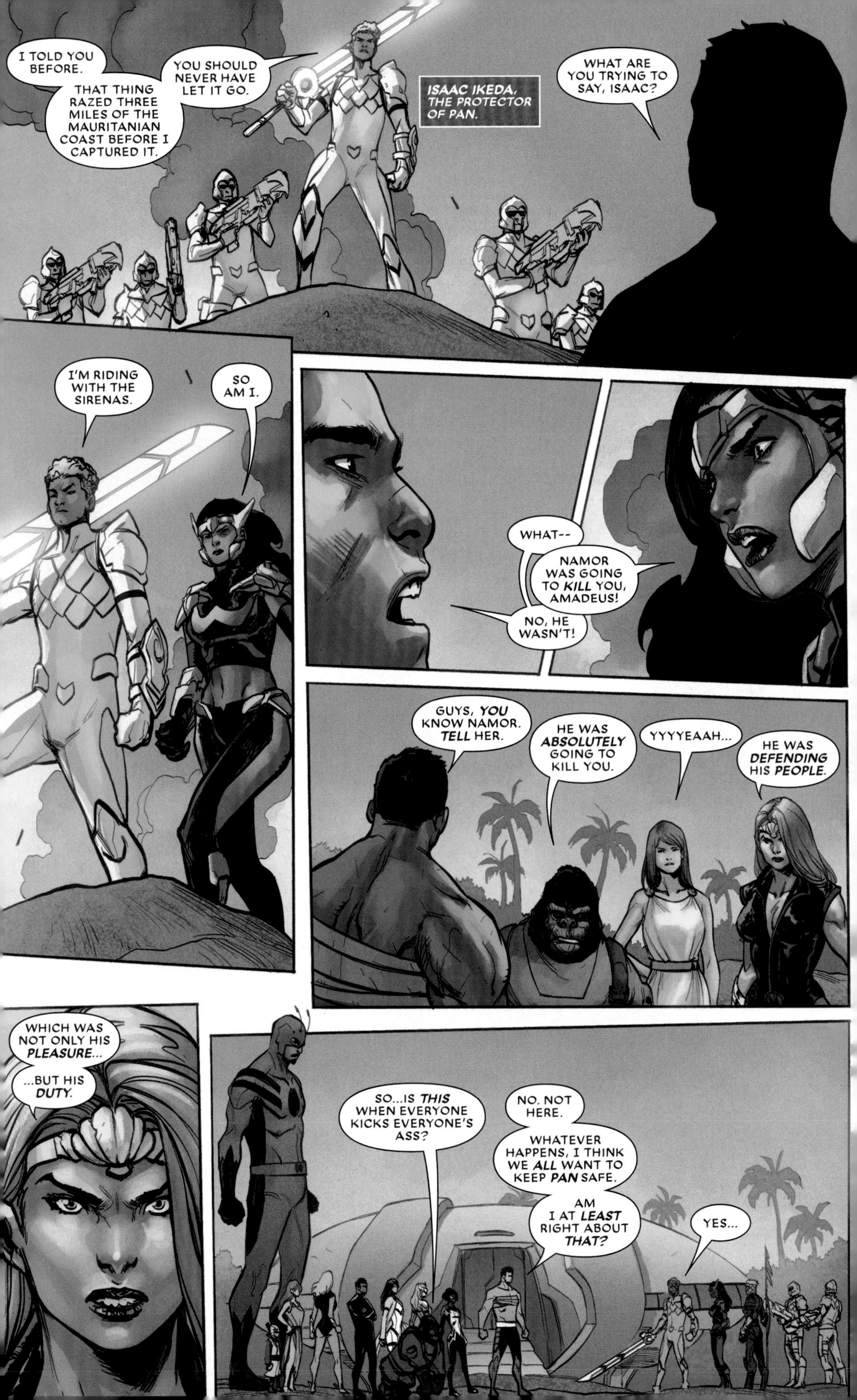
I TOLD YOU BEFORE.
THAT THING RAZED THREE MILES OF THE MAURITANIAN COAST BEFORE I CAPTURED IT.
YOU SHOULD NEVER HAVE LET IT GO.
ISAAC IKEDA, THE PROTECTOR OF PAN.
WHAT ARE YOU TRYING TO SAY, ISAAC?
I'M RIDING WITH THE SIRENAS.
SO AM I.
WHAT--
NAMOR WAS GOING TO KILL YOU, AMADEUS!
NO, HE WASN'T!
GUYS, YOU KNOW NAMOR. TELL HER.
HE WAS ABSOLUTELY GOING TO KILL YOU.
YYYYEAAH...
HE WAS DEFENDING HIS PEOPLE.
WHICH WAS NOT ONLY HIS PLEASURE...
...BUT HIS DUTY.
SO...IS THIS WHEN EVERYONE KICKS EVERYONE'S ASS?
NO. NOT HERE.
WHATEVER HAPPENS, I THINK WE ALL WANT TO KEEP PAN SAFE.
AM I AT LEAST RIGHT ABOUT THAT?
YES...

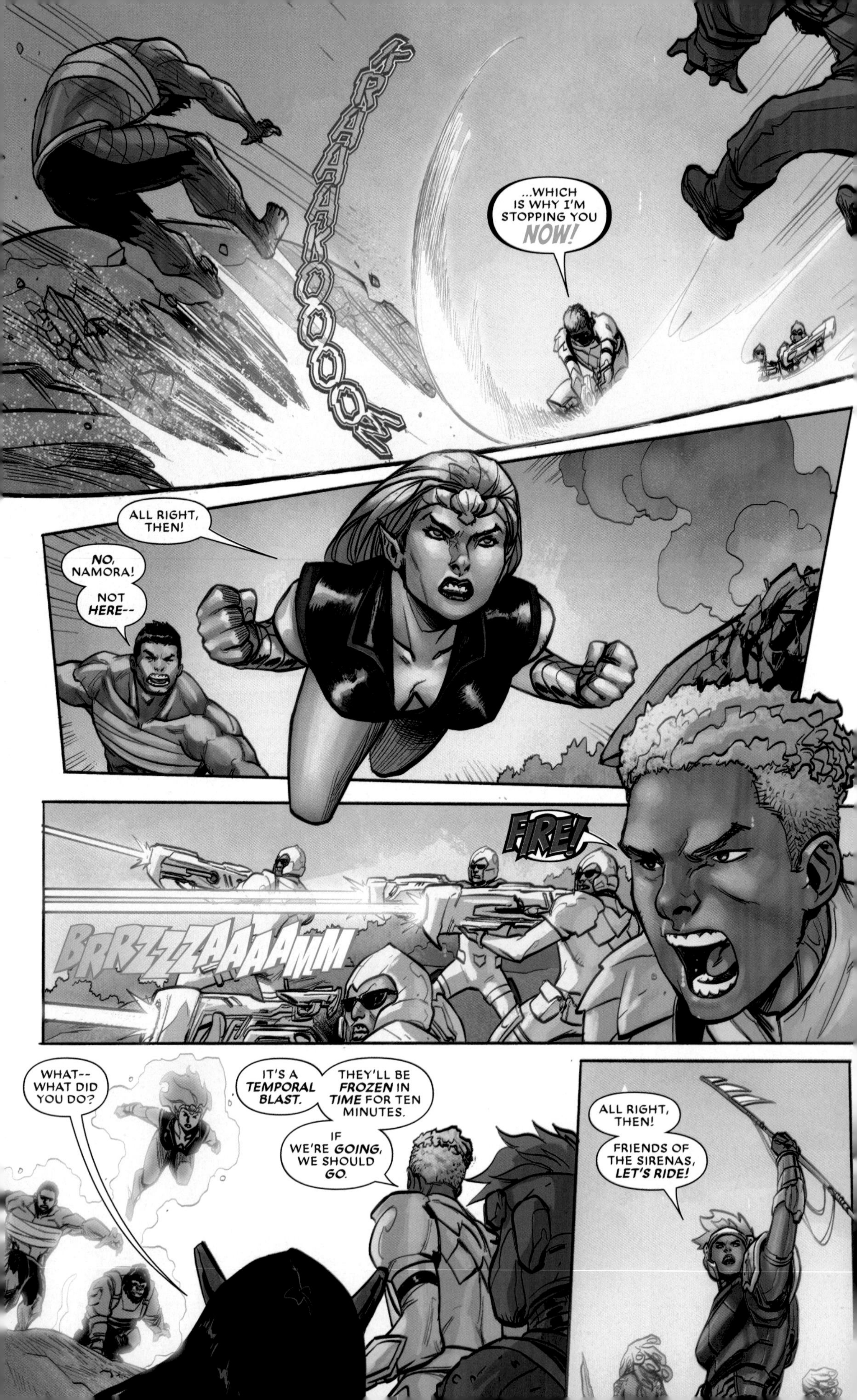
KRAAAKOOOOOM
...WHICH IS WHY I'M STOPPING YOU NOW!
ALL RIGHT, THEN!
NO, NAMORA!
NOT HERE--
FIRE!
BRRZZZAAAAMM
WHAT-- WHAT DID YOU DO?
IT'S A TEMPORAL BLAST.
THEY'LL BE FROZEN IN TIME FOR TEN MINUTES.
IF WE'RE GOING, WE SHOULD GO.
ALL RIGHT, THEN!
FRIENDS OF THE SIRENAS, LET'S RIDE!

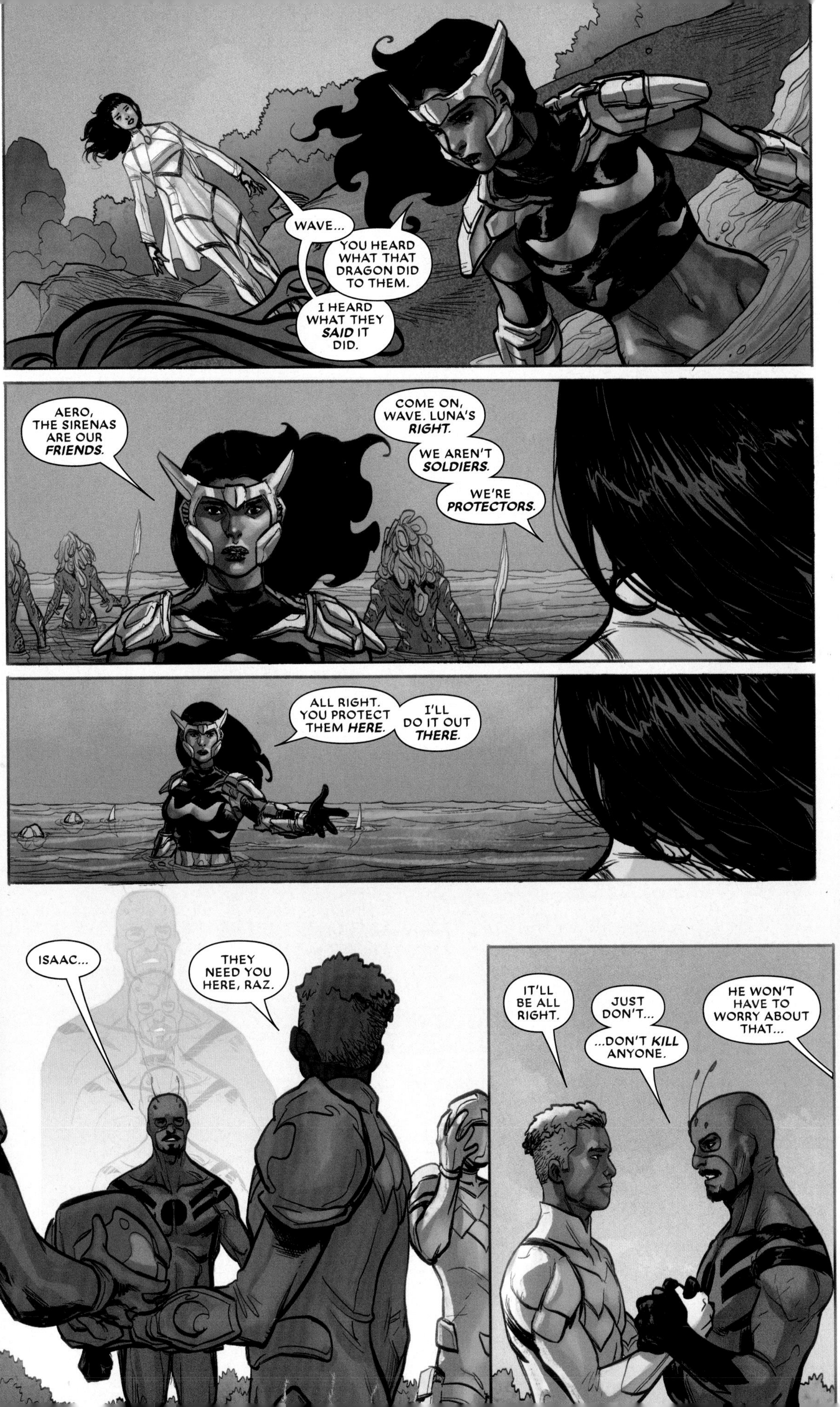

WAVE...
YOU HEARD WHAT THAT DRAGON DID TO THEM.
I HEARD WHAT THEY *SAID* IT DID.
AERO, THE SIRENAS ARE OUR *FRIENDS*.
COME ON, WAVE. LUNA'S *RIGHT*.
WE AREN'T *SOLDIERS*.
WE'RE *PROTECTORS*.
ALL RIGHT. YOU PROTECT THEM *HERE*.
I'LL DO IT OUT *THERE*.
ISAAC...
THEY NEED YOU HERE, RAZ.
IT'LL BE ALL RIGHT.
JUST DON'T...
...DON'T *KILL* ANYONE.
HE WON'T HAVE TO WORRY ABOUT THAT...

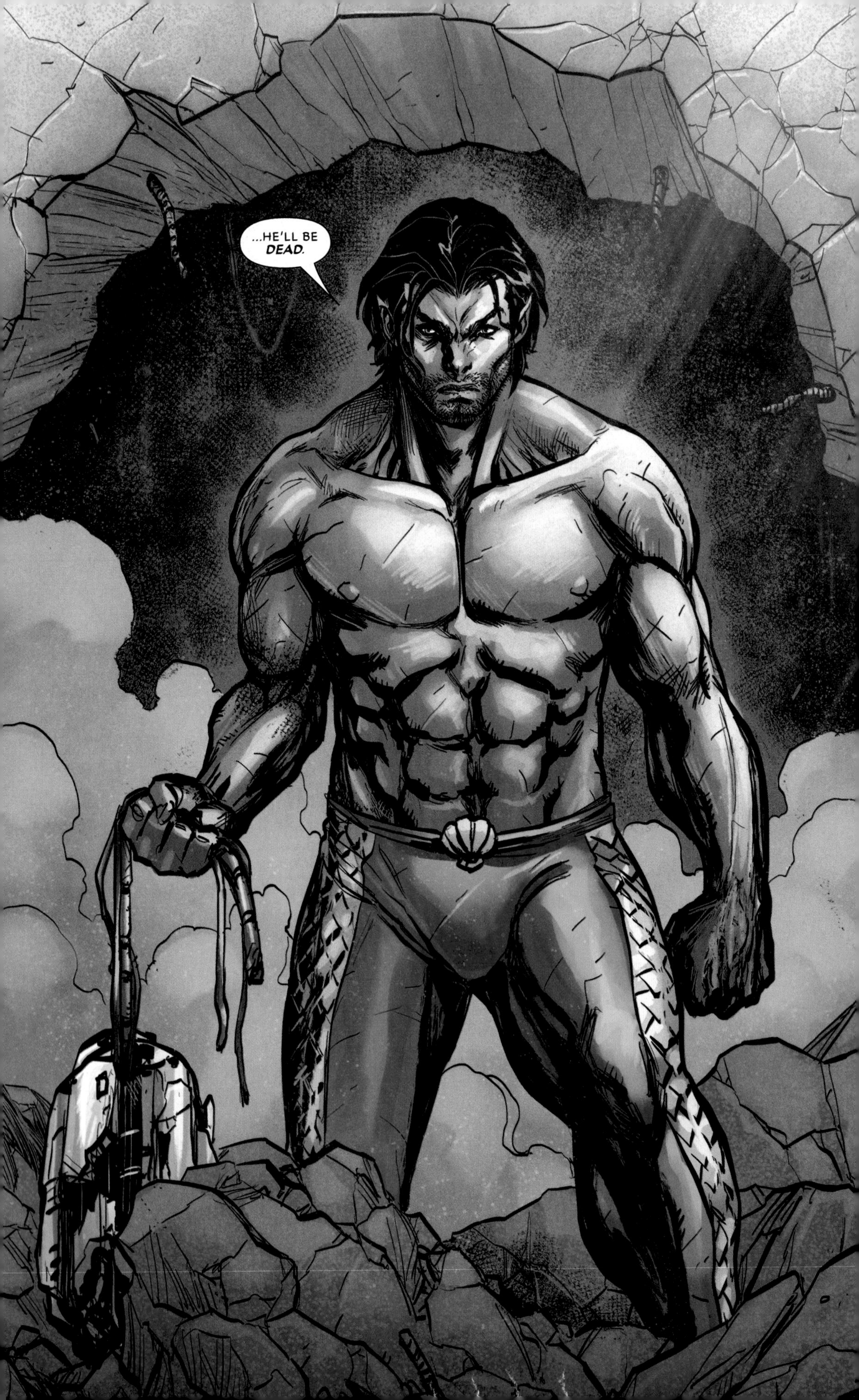
...HE'LL BE DEAD.

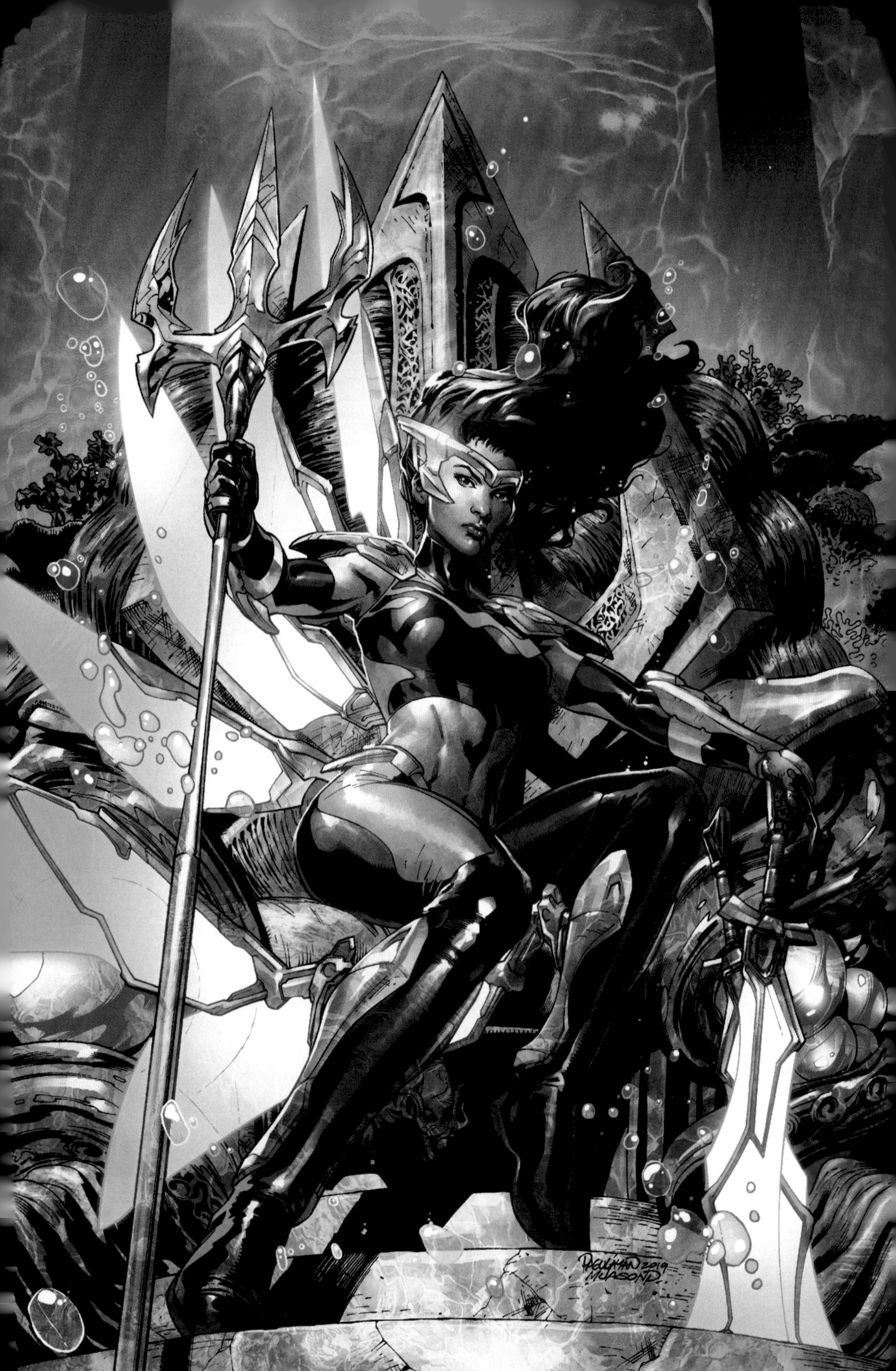

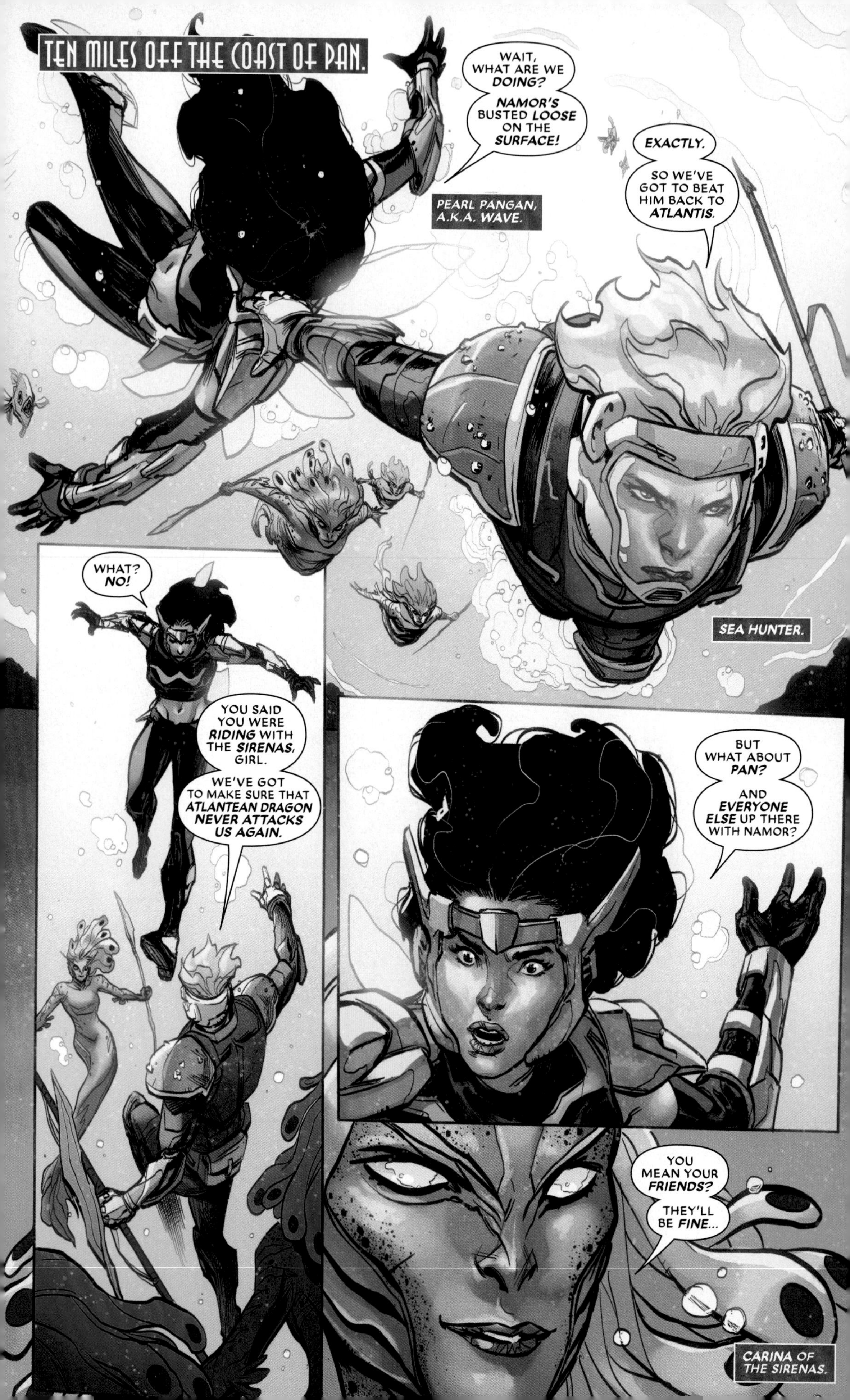
TEN MILES OFF THE COAST OF PAN.
WAIT, WHAT ARE WE DOING? NAMOR'S BUSTED LOOSE ON THE SURFACE!
PEARL PANGAN, A.K.A. WAVE.
EXACTLY. SO WE'VE GOT TO BEAT HIM BACK TO ATLANTIS.
SEA HUNTER.
WHAT? NO!
YOU SAID YOU WERE RIDING WITH THE SIRENAS, GIRL. WE'VE GOT TO MAKE SURE THAT ATLANTEAN DRAGON NEVER ATTACKS US AGAIN.
BUT WHAT ABOUT PAN? AND EVERYONE ELSE UP THERE WITH NAMOR?
YOU MEAN YOUR FRIENDS? THEY'LL BE FINE...
CARINA OF THE SIRENAS.

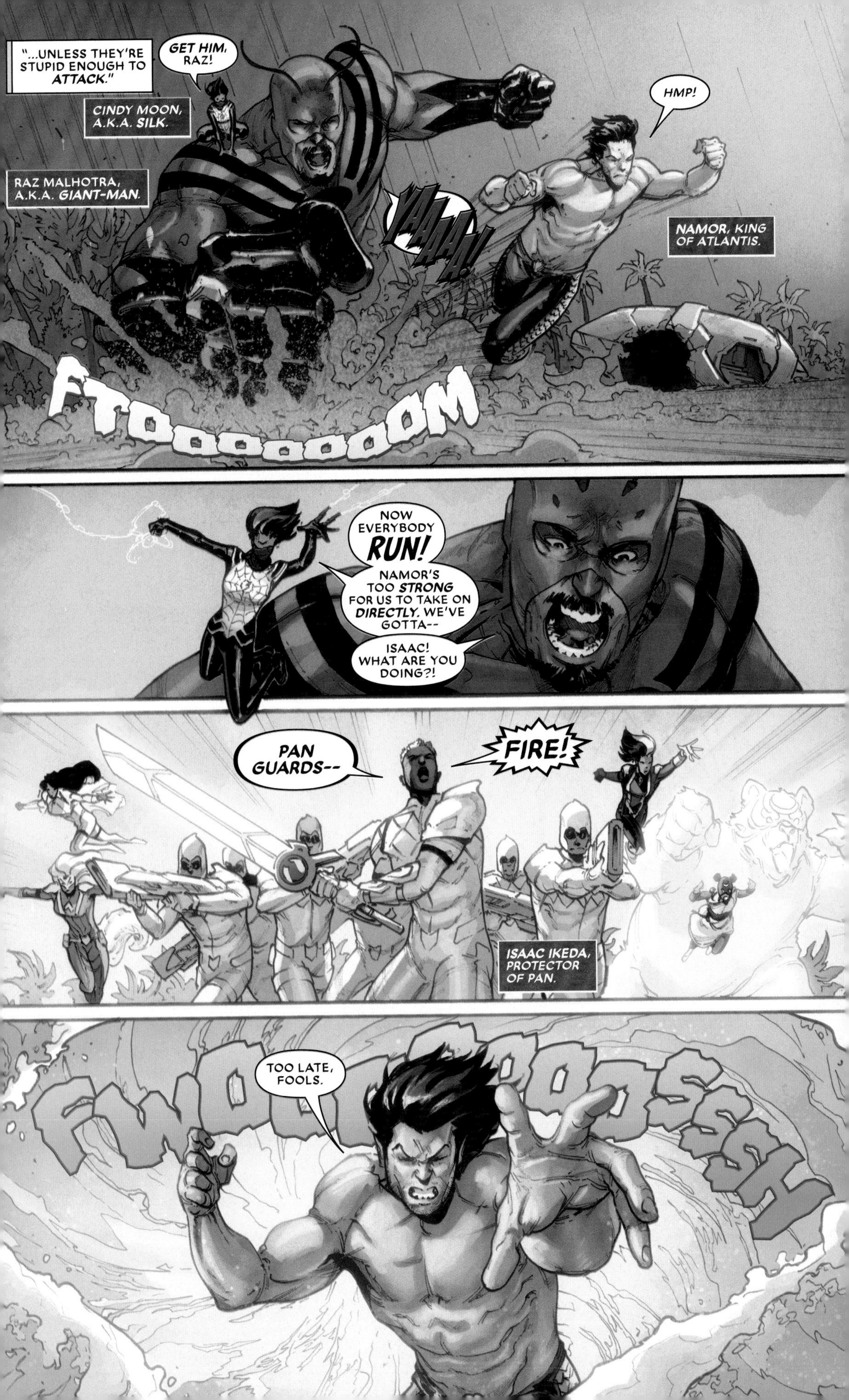
"...UNLESS THEY'RE STUPID ENOUGH TO *ATTACK*."
GET HIM, RAZ!
CINDY MOON, A.K.A. *SILK*.
RAZ MALHOTRA, A.K.A. *GIANT-MAN*.
HMP!
YAAAAAH!
NAMOR, KING OF ATLANTIS.
FTOOOOOOOOM
NOW EVERYBODY *RUN!*
NAMOR'S TOO *STRONG* FOR US TO TAKE ON *DIRECTLY*. WE'VE GOTTA--
ISAAC! WHAT ARE YOU DOING?!
PAN GUARDS--
FIRE!
ISAAC IKEDA, PROTECTOR OF PAN.
TOO LATE, FOOLS.

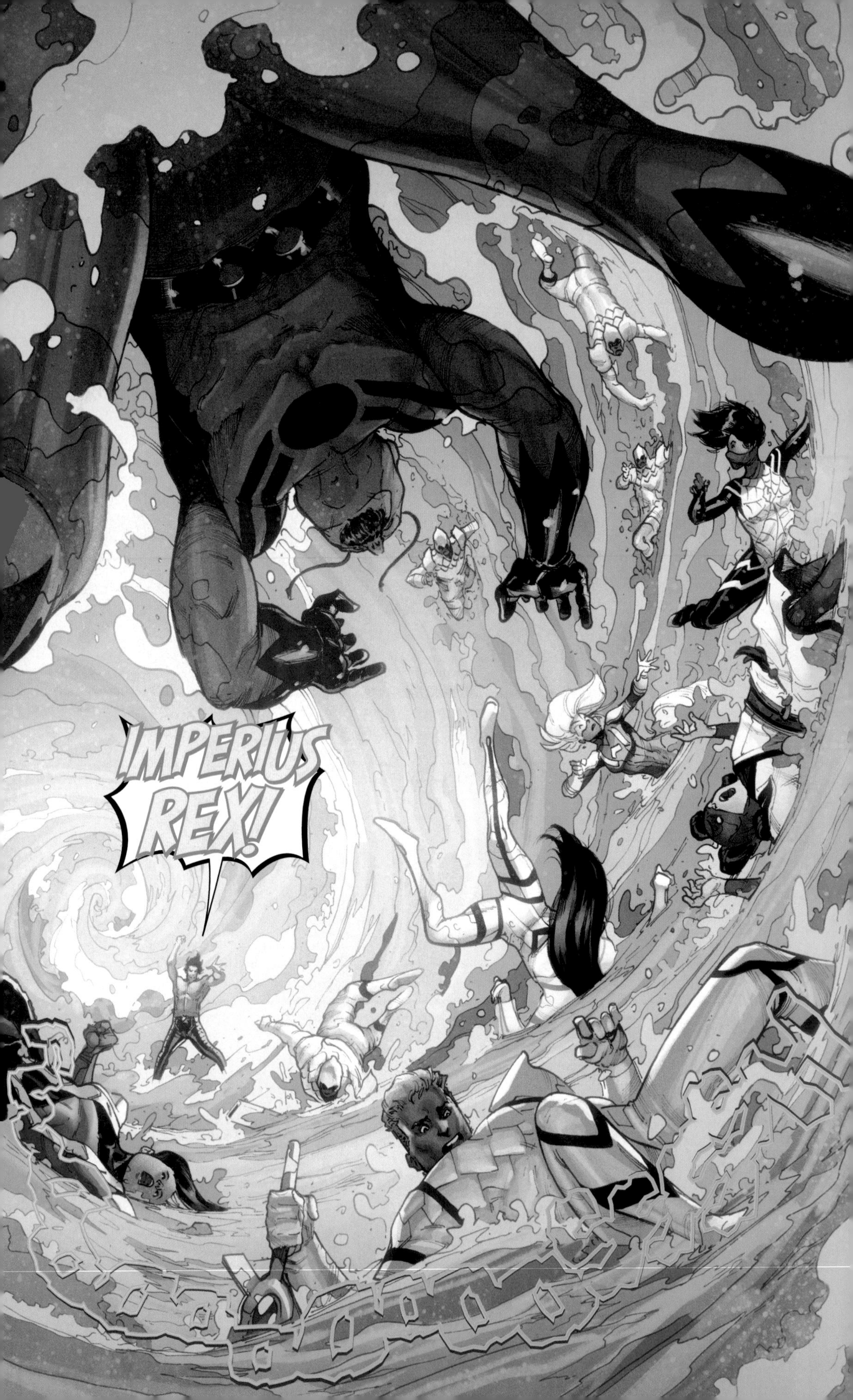
IMPERIUS REX!

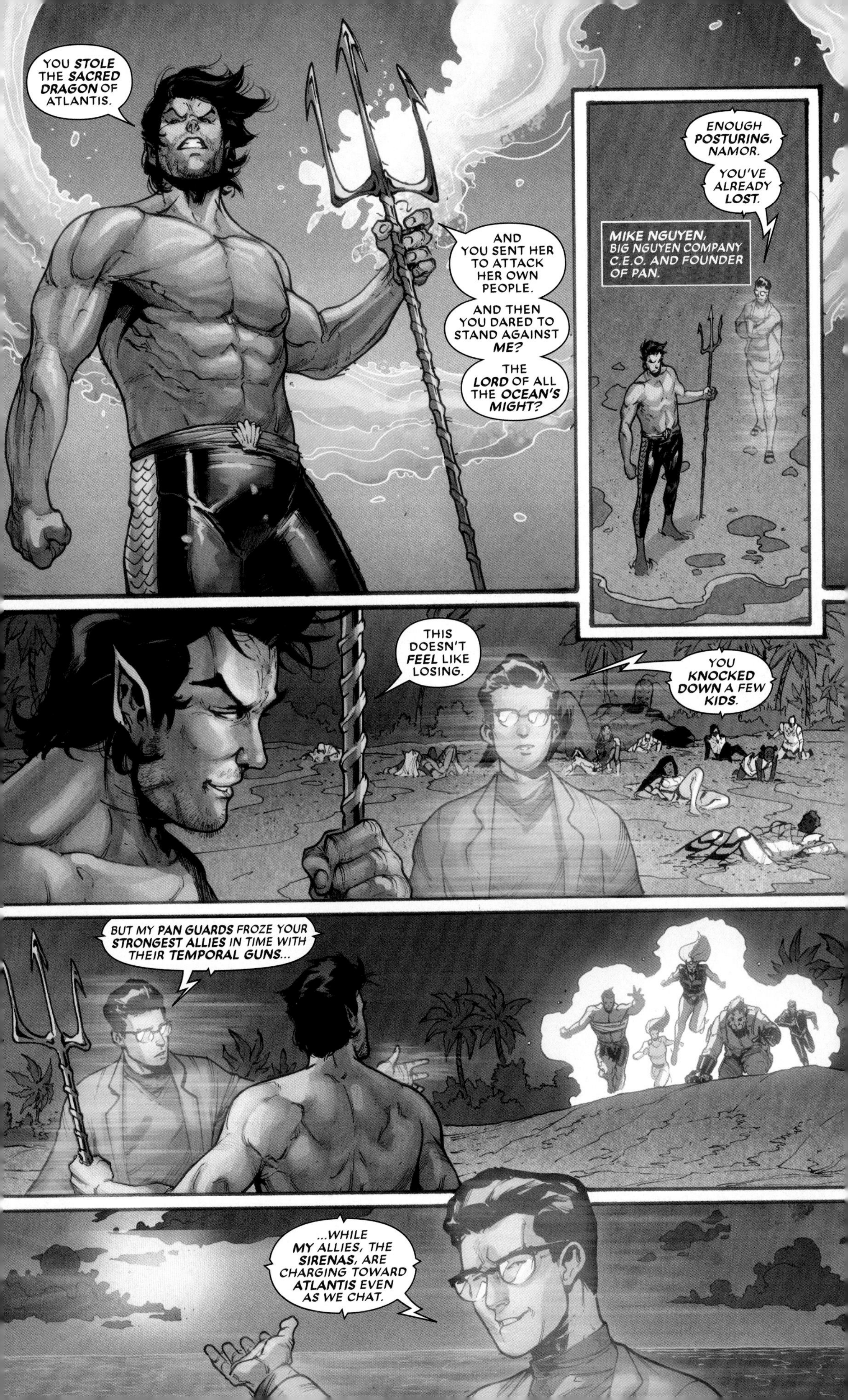

YOU STOLE THE SACRED DRAGON OF ATLANTIS.
AND YOU SENT HER TO ATTACK HER OWN PEOPLE.
AND THEN YOU DARED TO STAND AGAINST ME?
THE LORD OF ALL THE OCEAN'S MIGHT?
ENOUGH POSTURING, NAMOR.
YOU'VE ALREADY LOST.
MIKE NGUYEN, BIG NGUYEN COMPANY C.E.O. AND FOUNDER OF PAN.
THIS DOESN'T FEEL LIKE LOSING.
YOU KNOCKED DOWN A FEW KIDS.
BUT MY PAN GUARDS FROZE YOUR STRONGEST ALLIES IN TIME WITH THEIR TEMPORAL GUNS...
...WHILE MY ALLIES, THE SIRENAS, ARE CHARGING TOWARD ATLANTIS EVEN AS WE CHAT.

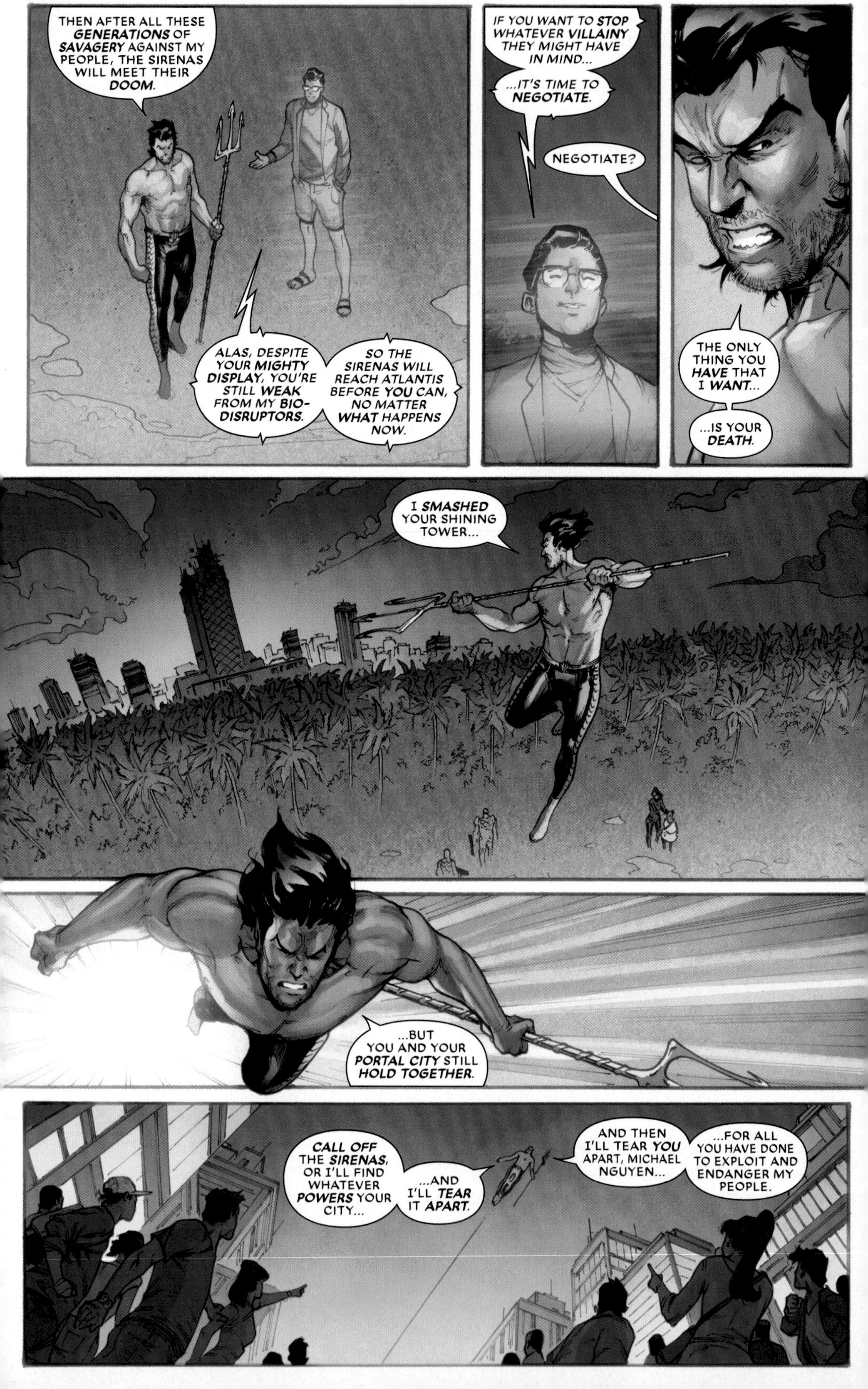
THEN AFTER ALL THESE GENERATIONS OF SAVAGERY AGAINST MY PEOPLE, THE SIRENAS WILL MEET THEIR DOOM.
ALAS, DESPITE YOUR MIGHTY DISPLAY, YOU'RE STILL WEAK FROM MY BIO-DISRUPTORS.
SO THE SIRENAS WILL REACH ATLANTIS BEFORE YOU CAN, NO MATTER WHAT HAPPENS NOW.
IF YOU WANT TO STOP WHATEVER VILLAINY THEY MIGHT HAVE IN MIND...
...IT'S TIME TO NEGOTIATE.
NEGOTIATE?
THE ONLY THING YOU HAVE THAT I WANT...
...IS YOUR DEATH.
I SMASHED YOUR SHINING TOWER...
...BUT YOU AND YOUR PORTAL CITY STILL HOLD TOGETHER.
CALL OFF THE SIRENAS, OR I'LL FIND WHATEVER POWERS YOUR CITY...
...AND I'LL TEAR IT APART.
AND THEN I'LL TEAR YOU APART, MICHAEL NGUYEN...
...FOR ALL YOU HAVE DONE TO EXPLOIT AND ENDANGER MY PEOPLE.

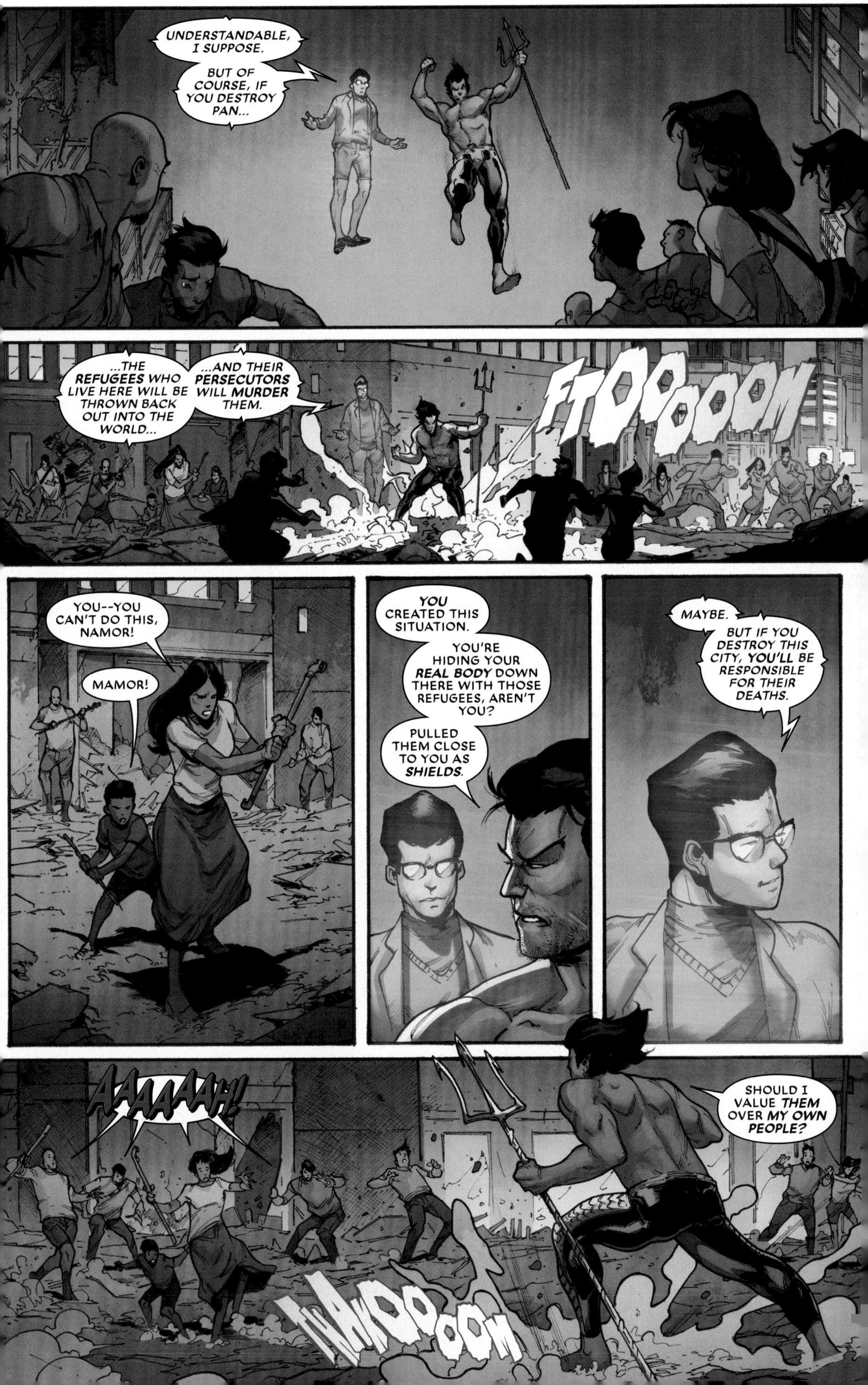
UNDERSTANDABLE, I SUPPOSE.
BUT OF COURSE, IF YOU DESTROY PAN...
...THE REFUGEES WHO LIVE HERE WILL BE THROWN BACK OUT INTO THE WORLD...
...AND THEIR PERSECUTORS WILL MURDER THEM.
FTOOOOOOM
YOU--YOU CAN'T DO THIS, NAMOR!
MAMOR!
YOU CREATED THIS SITUATION.
YOU'RE HIDING YOUR REAL BODY DOWN THERE WITH THOSE REFUGEES, AREN'T YOU?
PULLED THEM CLOSE TO YOU AS SHIELDS.
MAYBE.
BUT IF YOU DESTROY THIS CITY, YOU'LL BE RESPONSIBLE FOR THEIR DEATHS.
AAAAAAH!
SHOULD I VALUE THEM OVER MY OWN PEOPLE?
THAKOOOOM

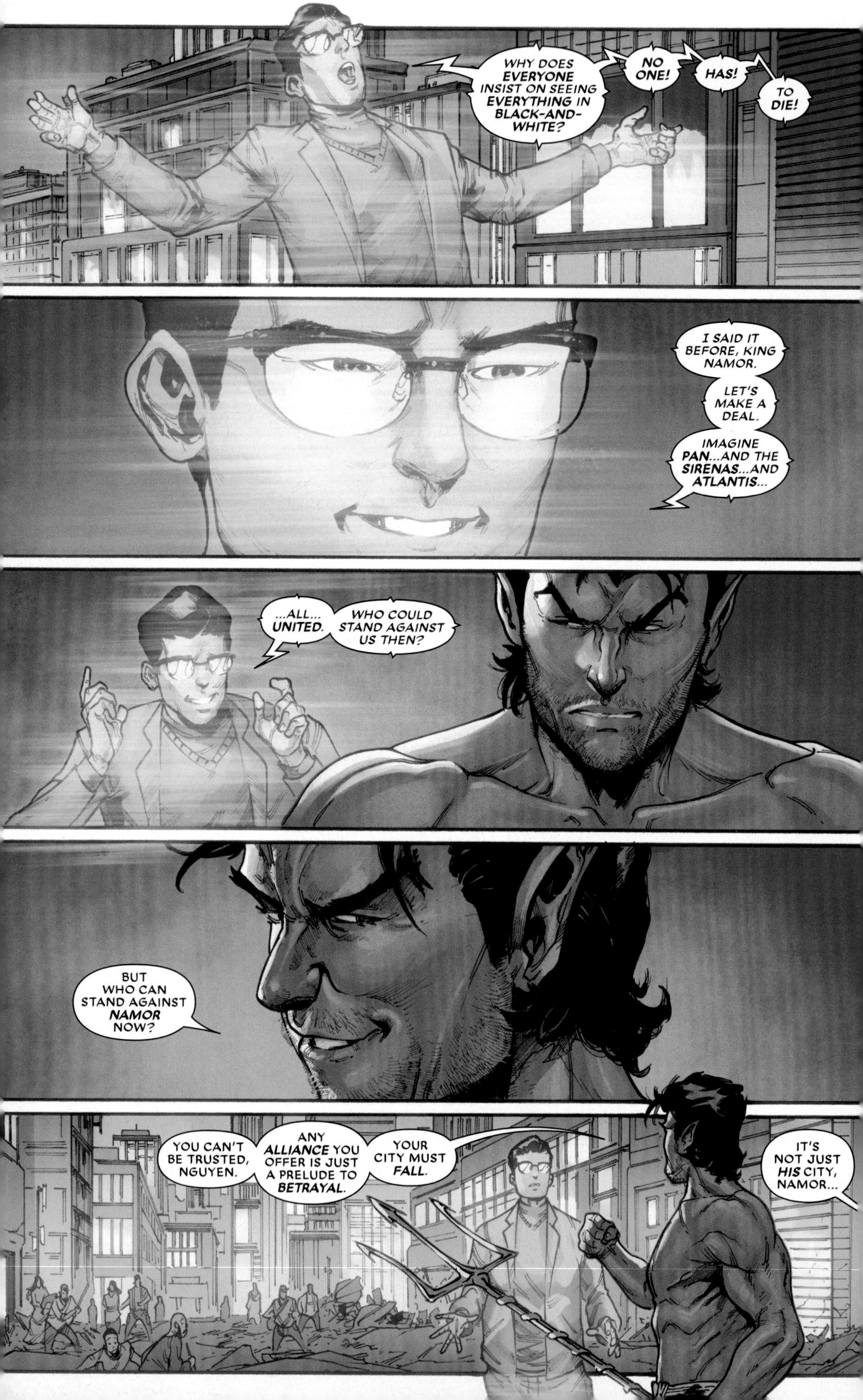
WHY DOES EVERYONE INSIST ON SEEING EVERYTHING IN BLACK-AND-WHITE?
NO ONE!
HAS!
TO DIE!
I SAID IT BEFORE, KING NAMOR.
LET'S MAKE A DEAL.
IMAGINE PAN...AND THE SIRENAS...AND ATLANTIS...
...ALL... UNITED.
WHO COULD STAND AGAINST US THEN?
BUT WHO CAN STAND AGAINST NAMOR NOW?
YOU CAN'T BE TRUSTED, NGUYEN.
ANY ALLIANCE YOU OFFER IS JUST A PRELUDE TO BETRAYAL.
YOUR CITY MUST FALL.
IT'S NOT JUST HIS CITY, NAMOR...

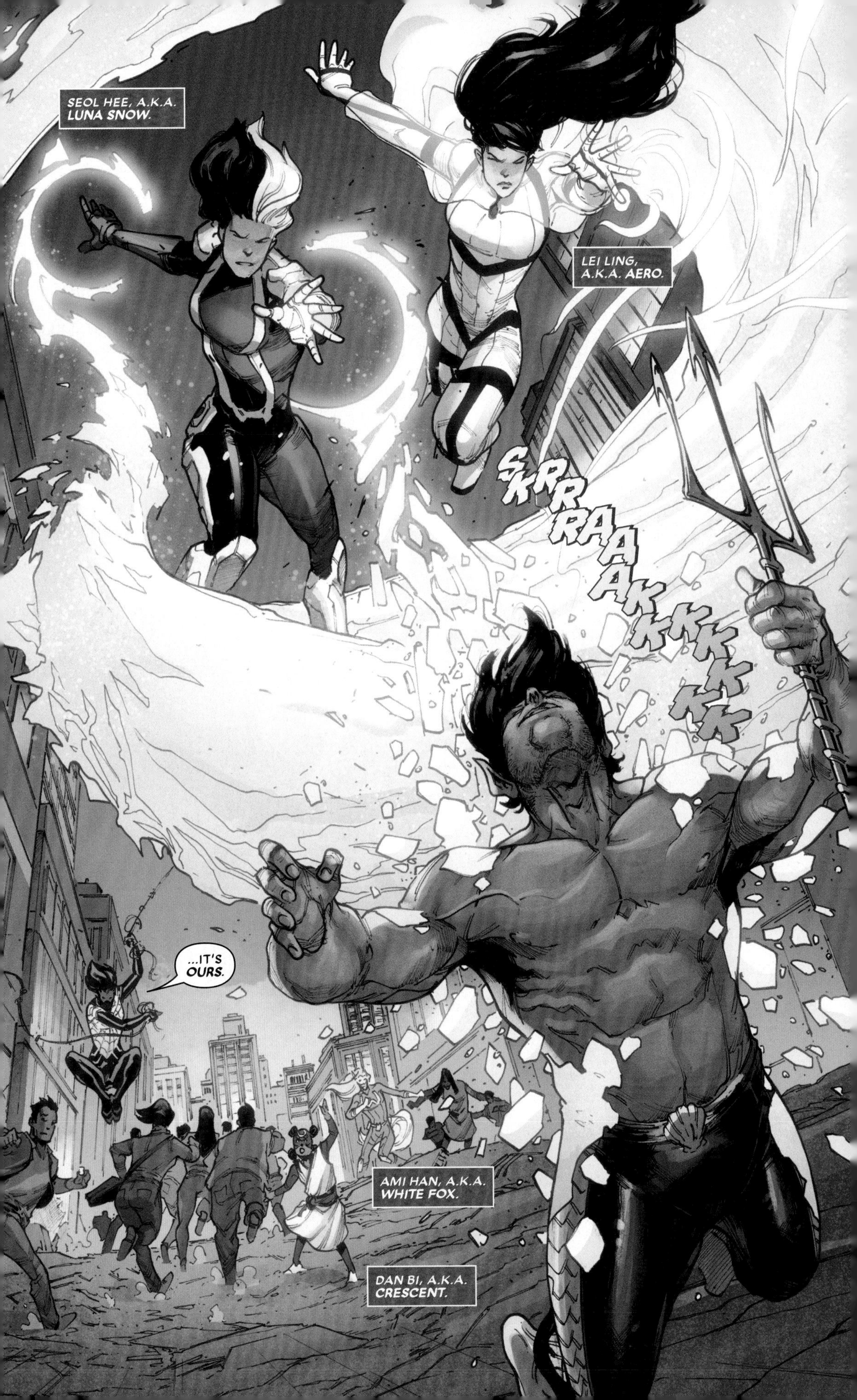
SEOL HEE, A.K.A. LUNA SNOW.
LEI LING, A.K.A. AERO.
SKRRRAAAAKKKKKKKKK
...IT'S OURS.
AMI HAN, A.K.A. WHITE FOX.
DAN BI, A.K.A. CRESCENT.

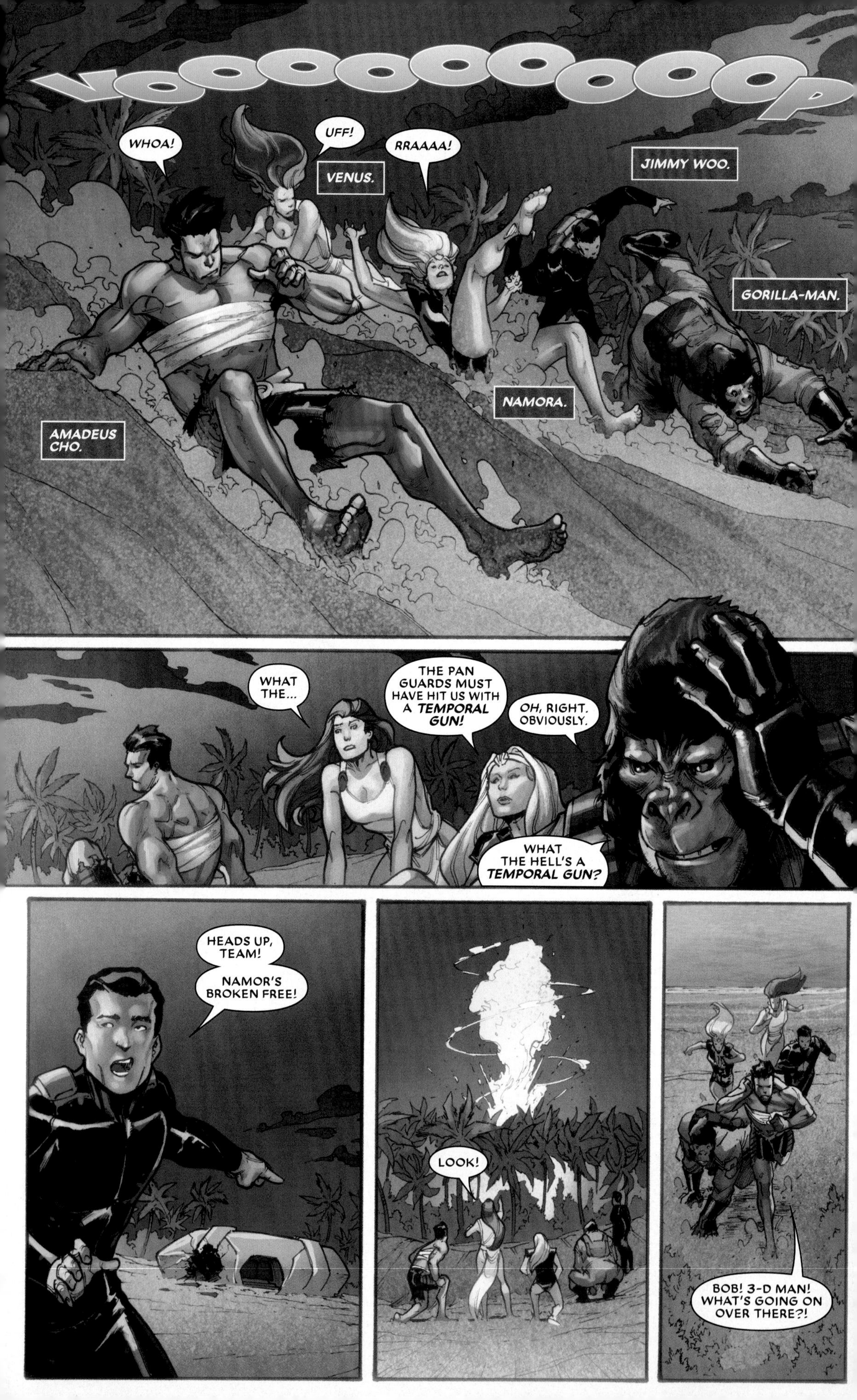
VOOOOOOOOOP
WHOA!
UFF!
VENUS.
RRAAAA!
JIMMY WOO.
GORILLA-MAN.
NAMORA.
AMADEUS CHO.
WHAT THE...
THE PAN GUARDS MUST HAVE HIT US WITH A TEMPORAL GUN!
OH, RIGHT. OBVIOUSLY.
WHAT THE HELL'S A TEMPORAL GUN?
HEADS UP, TEAM!
NAMOR'S BROKEN FREE!
LOOK!
BOB! 3-D MAN! WHAT'S GOING ON OVER THERE?!

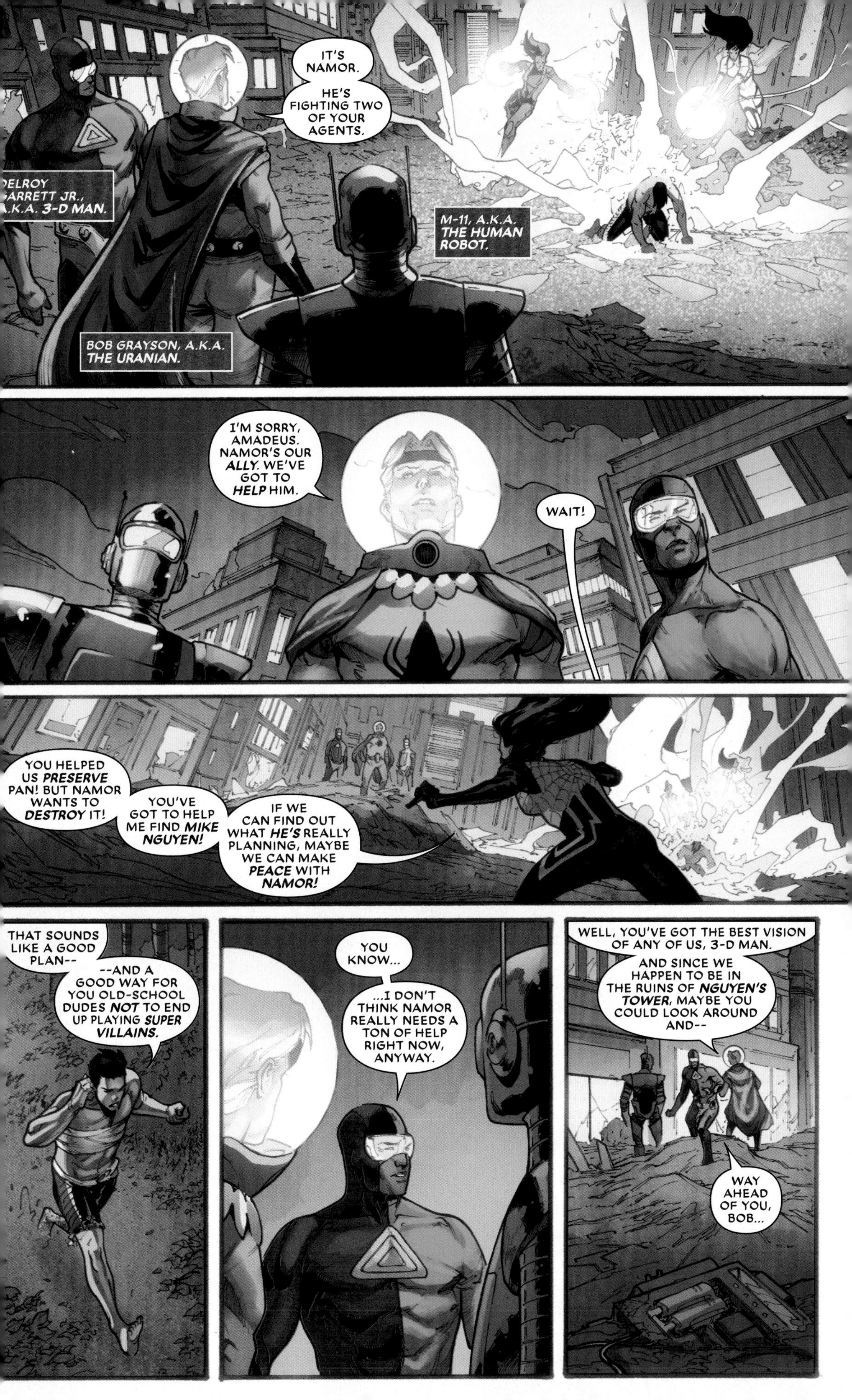

IT'S NAMOR.
HE'S FIGHTING TWO OF YOUR AGENTS.
DELROY GARRETT JR., A.K.A. 3-D MAN.
M-11, A.K.A. THE HUMAN ROBOT.
BOB GRAYSON, A.K.A. THE URANIAN.
I'M SORRY, AMADEUS. NAMOR'S OUR ALLY. WE'VE GOT TO HELP HIM.
WAIT!
YOU HELPED US PRESERVE PAN! BUT NAMOR WANTS TO DESTROY IT!
YOU'VE GOT TO HELP ME FIND MIKE NGUYEN!
IF WE CAN FIND OUT WHAT HE'S REALLY PLANNING, MAYBE WE CAN MAKE PEACE WITH NAMOR!
THAT SOUNDS LIKE A GOOD PLAN--
--AND A GOOD WAY FOR YOU OLD-SCHOOL DUDES NOT TO END UP PLAYING SUPER VILLAINS.
YOU KNOW...
...I DON'T THINK NAMOR REALLY NEEDS A TON OF HELP RIGHT NOW, ANYWAY.
WELL, YOU'VE GOT THE BEST VISION OF ANY OF US, 3-D MAN.
AND SINCE WE HAPPEN TO BE IN THE RUINS OF NGUYEN'S TOWER, MAYBE YOU COULD LOOK AROUND AND--
WAY AHEAD OF YOU, BOB...

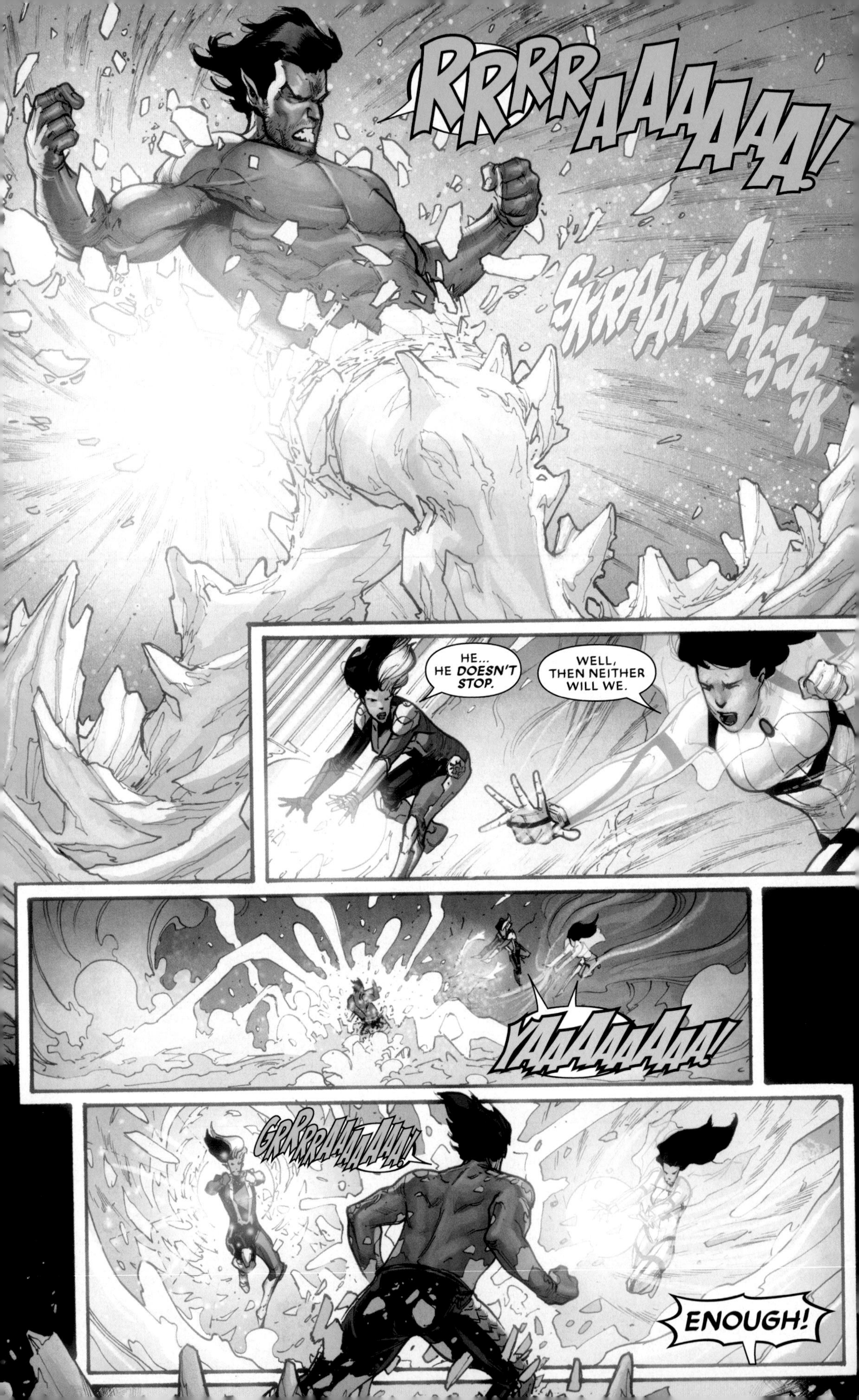
RRRRAAAAAAA!
SKRAAKAASSSK
HE... HE DOESN'T STOP.
WELL, THEN NEITHER WILL WE.
YAAAAAAAA!
GRRRRAAAAAAA!
ENOUGH!

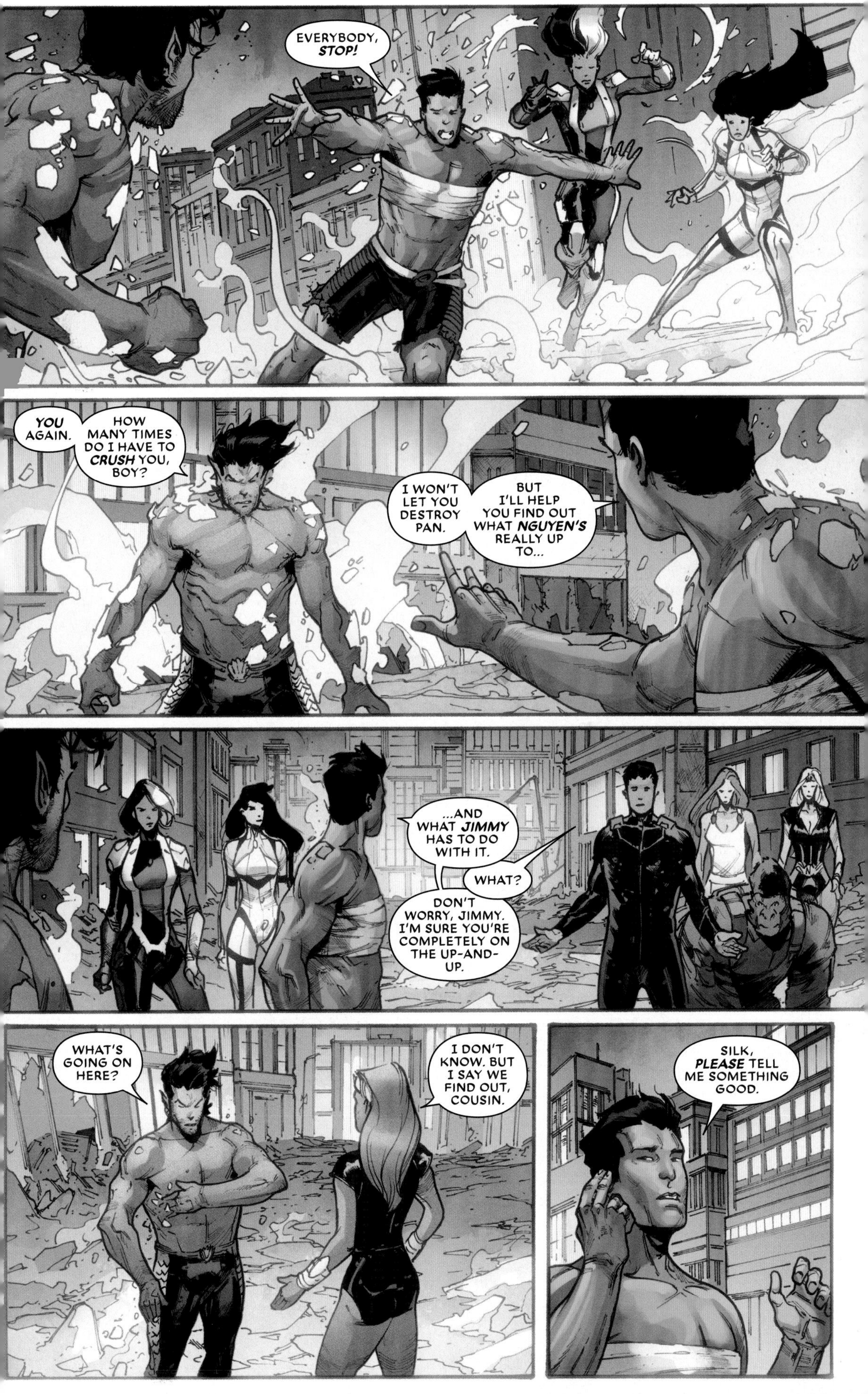
EVERYBODY, STOP!
YOU AGAIN.
HOW MANY TIMES DO I HAVE TO CRUSH YOU, BOY?
I WON'T LET YOU DESTROY PAN.
BUT I'LL HELP YOU FIND OUT WHAT NGUYEN'S REALLY UP TO...
...AND WHAT JIMMY HAS TO DO WITH IT.
WHAT?
DON'T WORRY, JIMMY. I'M SURE YOU'RE COMPLETELY ON THE UP-AND-UP.
WHAT'S GOING ON HERE?
I DON'T KNOW. BUT I SAY WE FIND OUT, COUSIN.
SILK, PLEASE TELL ME SOMETHING GOOD.

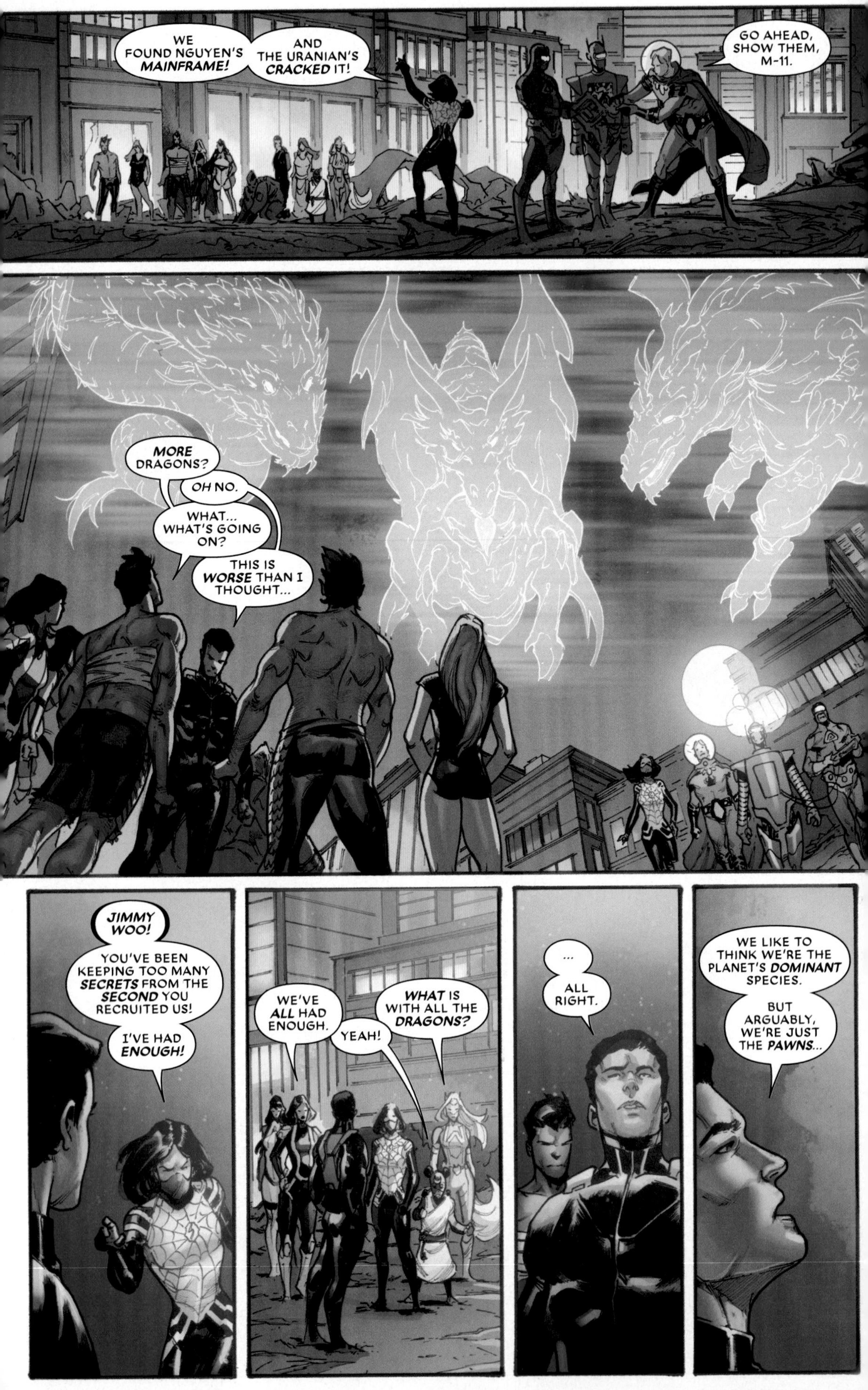
WE FOUND NGUYEN'S MAINFRAME!
AND THE URANIAN'S CRACKED IT!
GO AHEAD, SHOW THEM, M-11.
MORE DRAGONS?
OH NO.
WHAT... WHAT'S GOING ON?
THIS IS WORSE THAN I THOUGHT...
JIMMY WOO!
YOU'VE BEEN KEEPING TOO MANY SECRETS FROM THE SECOND YOU RECRUITED US!
I'VE HAD ENOUGH!
WE'VE ALL HAD ENOUGH.
YEAH!
WHAT IS WITH ALL THE DRAGONS?
...
ALL RIGHT.
WE LIKE TO THINK WE'RE THE PLANET'S DOMINANT SPECIES.
BUT ARGUABLY, WE'RE JUST THE PAWNS...

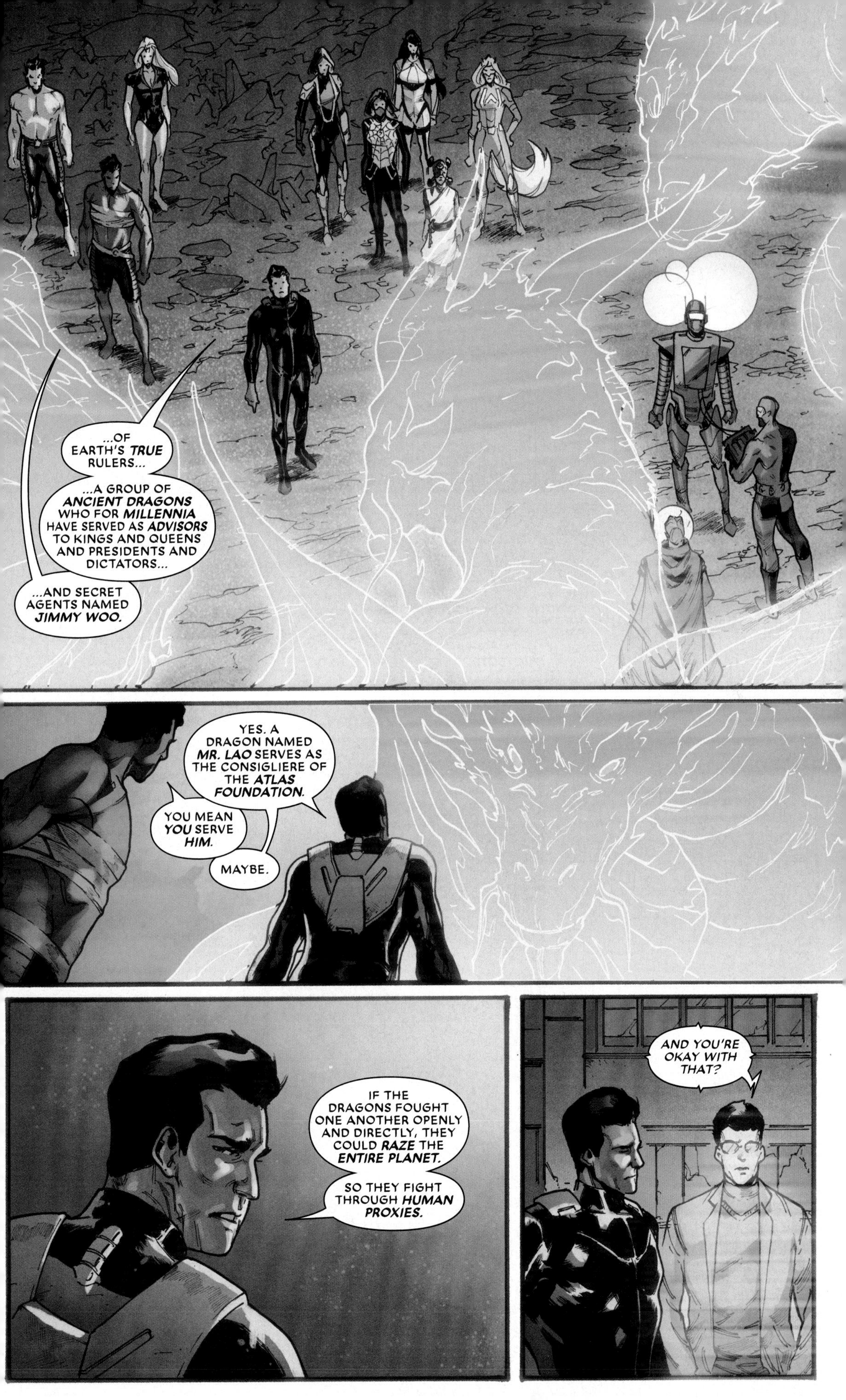

...OF EARTH'S TRUE RULERS...
...A GROUP OF ANCIENT DRAGONS WHO FOR MILLENNIA HAVE SERVED AS ADVISORS TO KINGS AND QUEENS AND PRESIDENTS AND DICTATORS...
...AND SECRET AGENTS NAMED JIMMY WOO.
YES. A DRAGON NAMED MR. LAO SERVES AS THE CONSIGLIERE OF THE ATLAS FOUNDATION.
YOU MEAN YOU SERVE HIM.
MAYBE.
IF THE DRAGONS FOUGHT ONE ANOTHER OPENLY AND DIRECTLY, THEY COULD RAZE THE ENTIRE PLANET.
SO THEY FIGHT THROUGH HUMAN PROXIES.
AND YOU'RE OKAY WITH THAT?

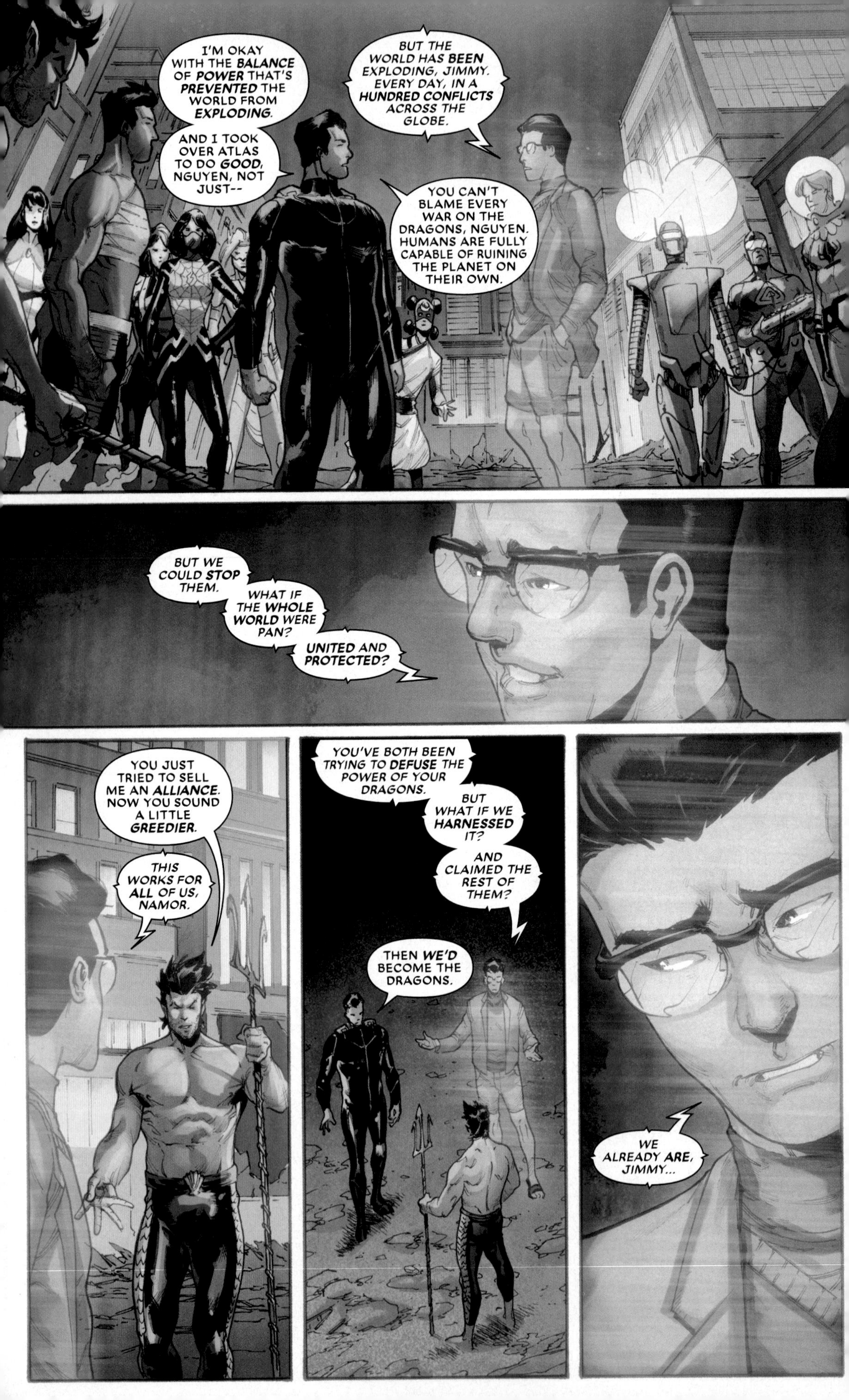
I'M OKAY WITH THE BALANCE OF POWER THAT'S PREVENTED THE WORLD FROM EXPLODING.
AND I TOOK OVER ATLAS TO DO GOOD, NGUYEN, NOT JUST--
BUT THE WORLD HAS BEEN EXPLODING, JIMMY. EVERY DAY, IN A HUNDRED CONFLICTS ACROSS THE GLOBE.
YOU CAN'T BLAME EVERY WAR ON THE DRAGONS, NGUYEN. HUMANS ARE FULLY CAPABLE OF RUINING THE PLANET ON THEIR OWN.
BUT WE COULD STOP THEM.
WHAT IF THE WHOLE WORLD WERE PAN?
UNITED AND PROTECTED?
YOU JUST TRIED TO SELL ME AN ALLIANCE. NOW YOU SOUND A LITTLE GREEDIER.
THIS WORKS FOR ALL OF US, NAMOR.
YOU'VE BOTH BEEN TRYING TO DEFUSE THE POWER OF YOUR DRAGONS.
BUT WHAT IF WE HARNESSED IT?
AND CLAIMED THE REST OF THEM?
THEN WE'D BECOME THE DRAGONS.
WE ALREADY ARE, JIMMY...

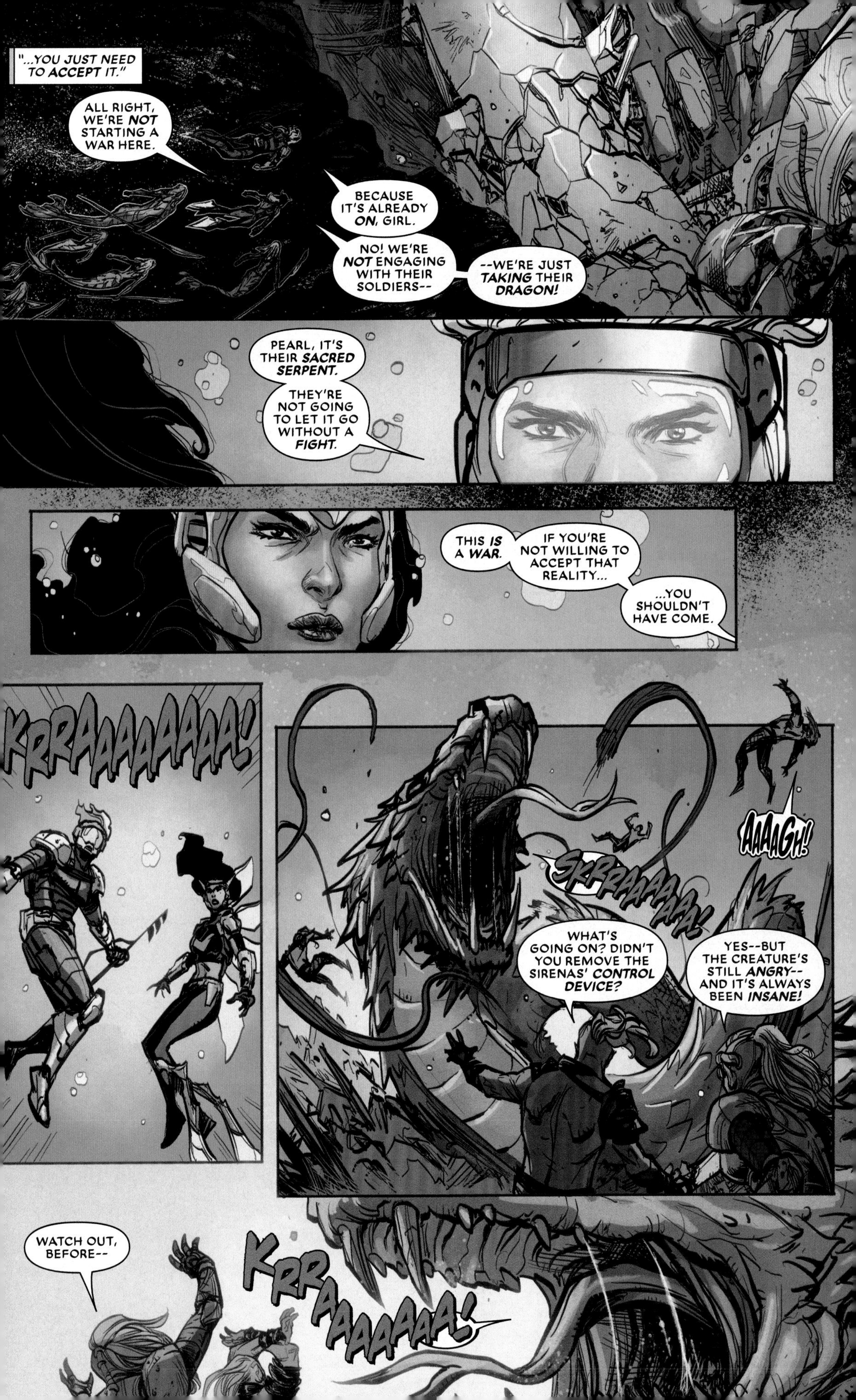
"...YOU JUST NEED TO ACCEPT IT."
ALL RIGHT, WE'RE NOT STARTING A WAR HERE.
BECAUSE IT'S ALREADY ON, GIRL.
NO! WE'RE NOT ENGAGING WITH THEIR SOLDIERS--
--WE'RE JUST TAKING THEIR DRAGON!
PEARL, IT'S THEIR SACRED SERPENT.
THEY'RE NOT GOING TO LET IT GO WITHOUT A FIGHT.
THIS IS A WAR.
IF YOU'RE NOT WILLING TO ACCEPT THAT REALITY...
...YOU SHOULDN'T HAVE COME.
KRRAAAAAAAA!
AAAAGH!
SKRRAAAAAAAA!
WHAT'S GOING ON? DIDN'T YOU REMOVE THE SIRENAS' CONTROL DEVICE?
YES--BUT THE CREATURE'S STILL ANGRY-- AND IT'S ALWAYS BEEN INSANE!
WATCH OUT, BEFORE--
KRRAAAAAAA!

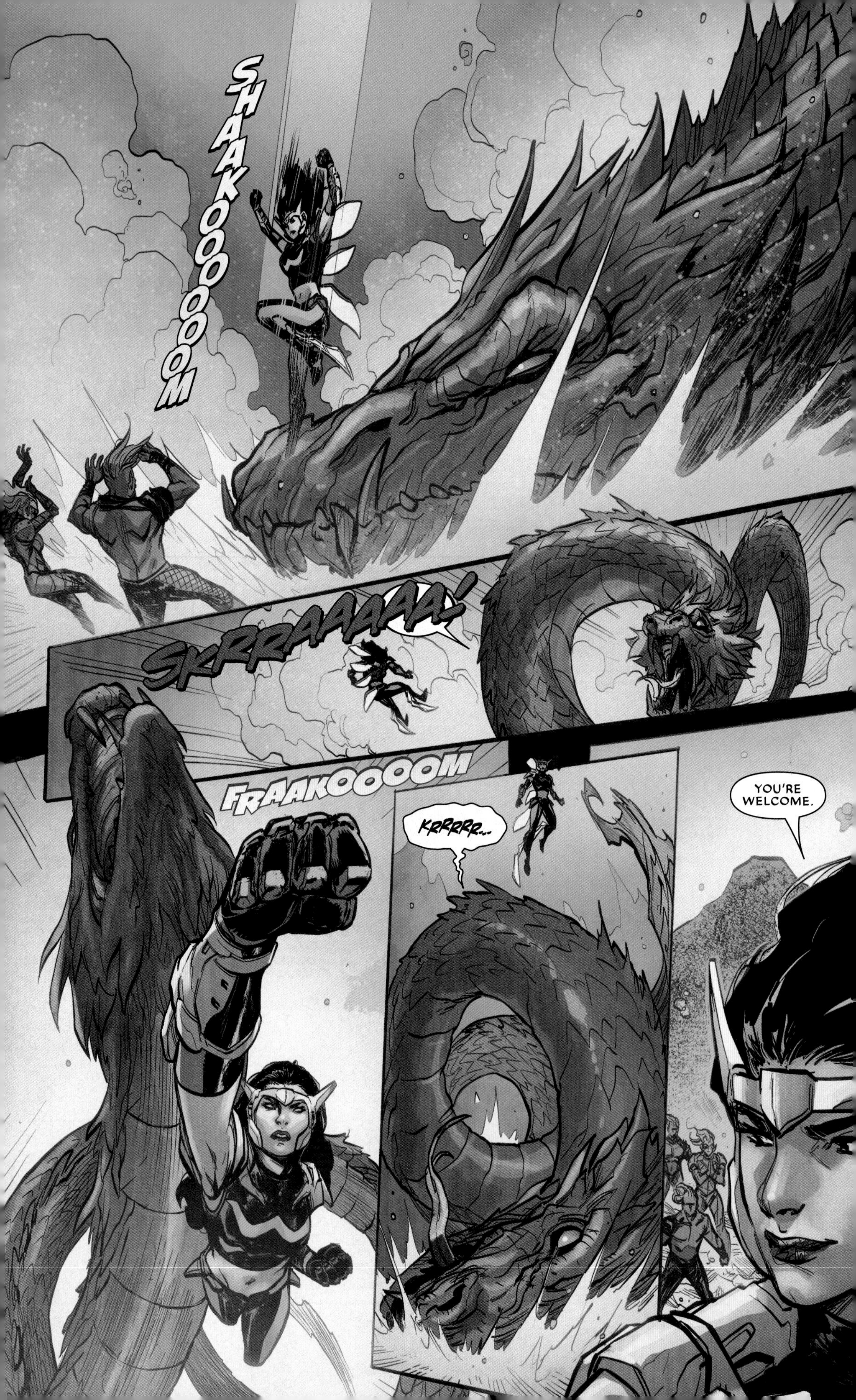
SHAAKOOOOOOOM
SKRRAAAAAA!
FRAAKOOOOOM
KRRRRR...
YOU'RE WELCOME.

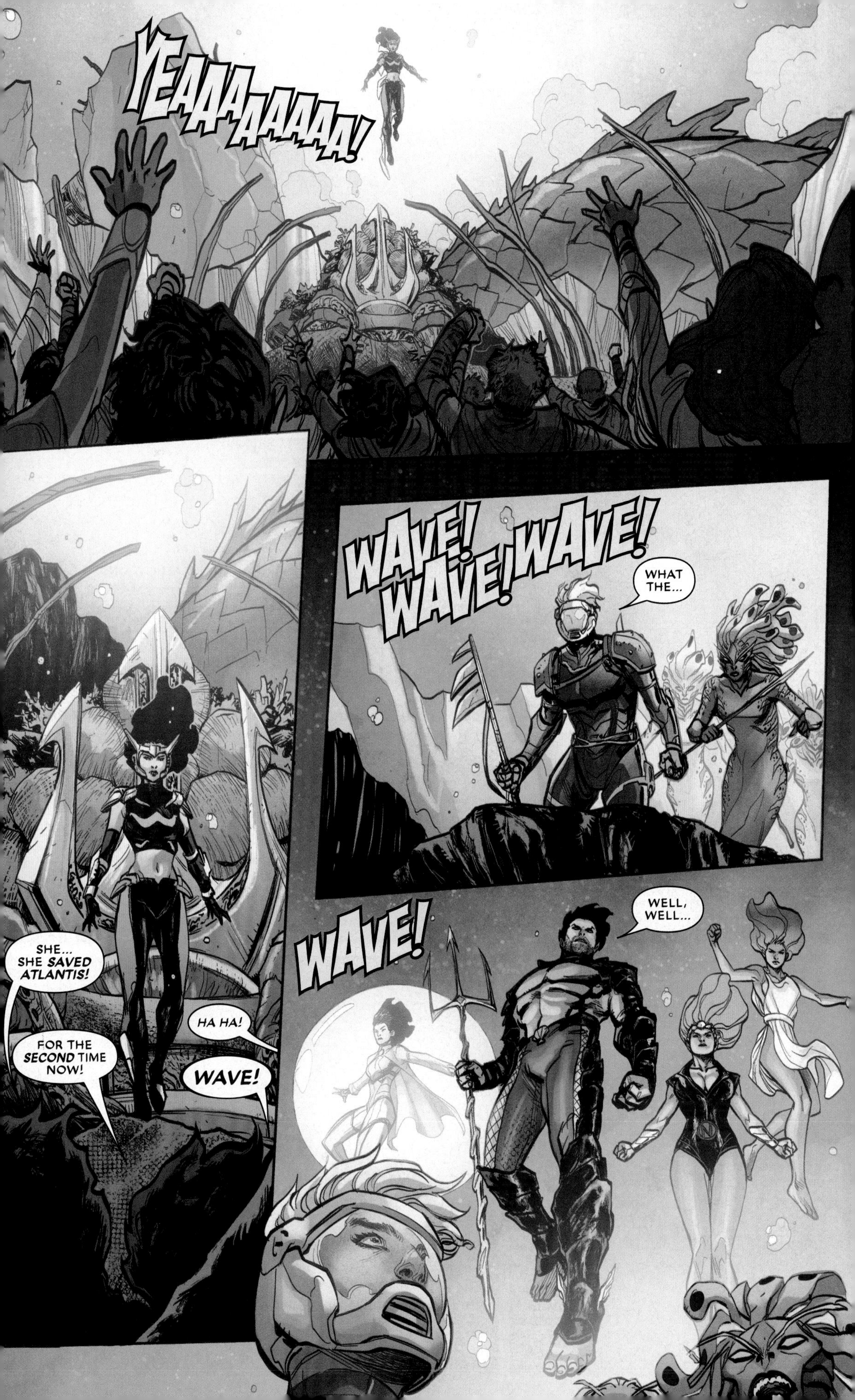
YEAAAAAAAA!
SHE... SHE SAVED ATLANTIS!
FOR THE SECOND TIME NOW!
HA HA!
WAVE!
WAVE! WAVE! WAVE!
WHAT THE...
WAVE!
WELL, WELL...

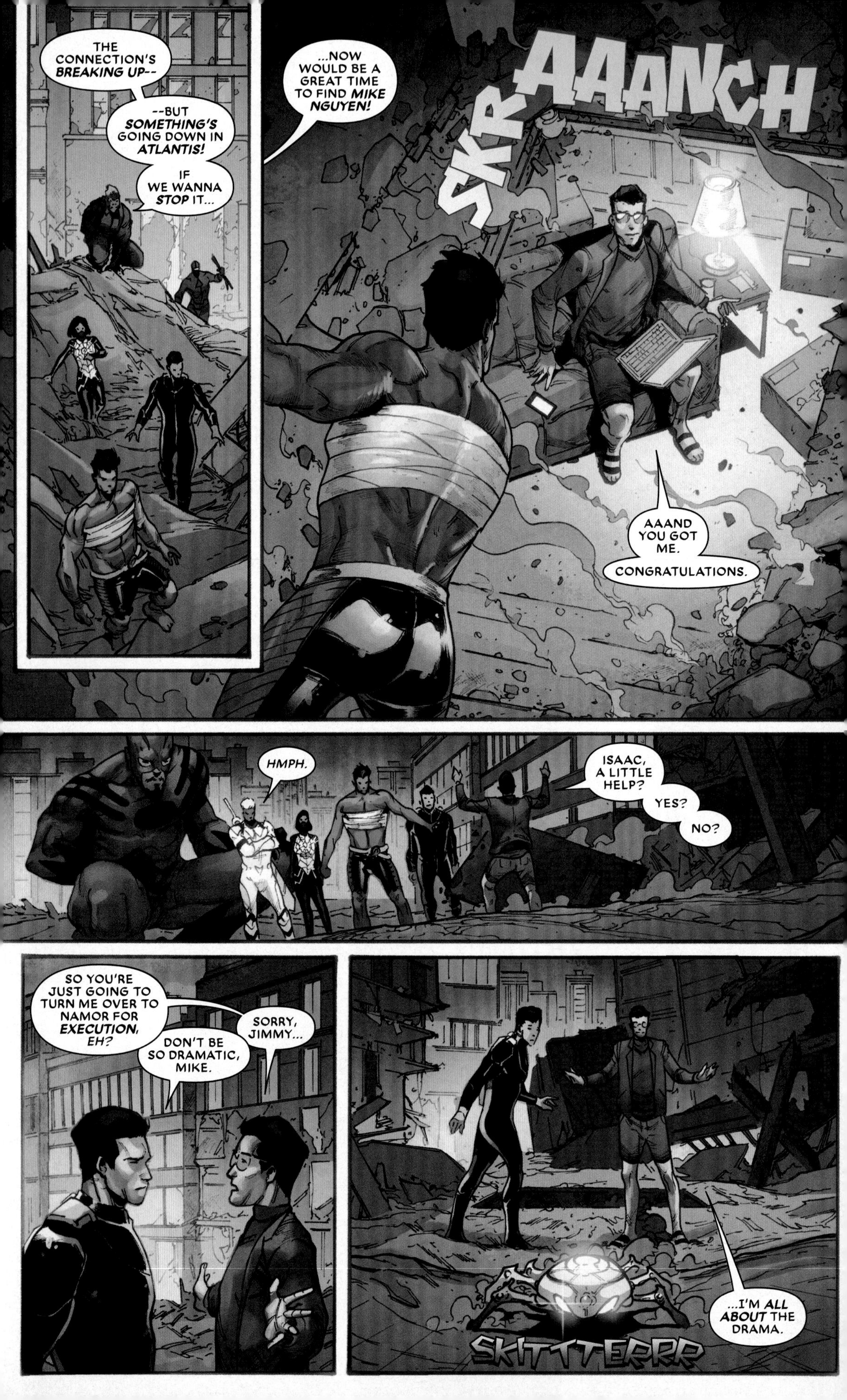
THE CONNECTION'S BREAKING UP--
--BUT SOMETHING'S GOING DOWN IN ATLANTIS!
IF WE WANNA STOP IT...
...NOW WOULD BE A GREAT TIME TO FIND MIKE NGUYEN!
SKRAAANCH
AAAND YOU GOT ME.
CONGRATULATIONS.
HMPH.
ISAAC, A LITTLE HELP?
YES?
NO?
SO YOU'RE JUST GOING TO TURN ME OVER TO NAMOR FOR EXECUTION, EH?
SORRY, JIMMY...
DON'T BE SO DRAMATIC, MIKE.
...I'M ALL ABOUT THE DRAMA.
SKITTTERRR

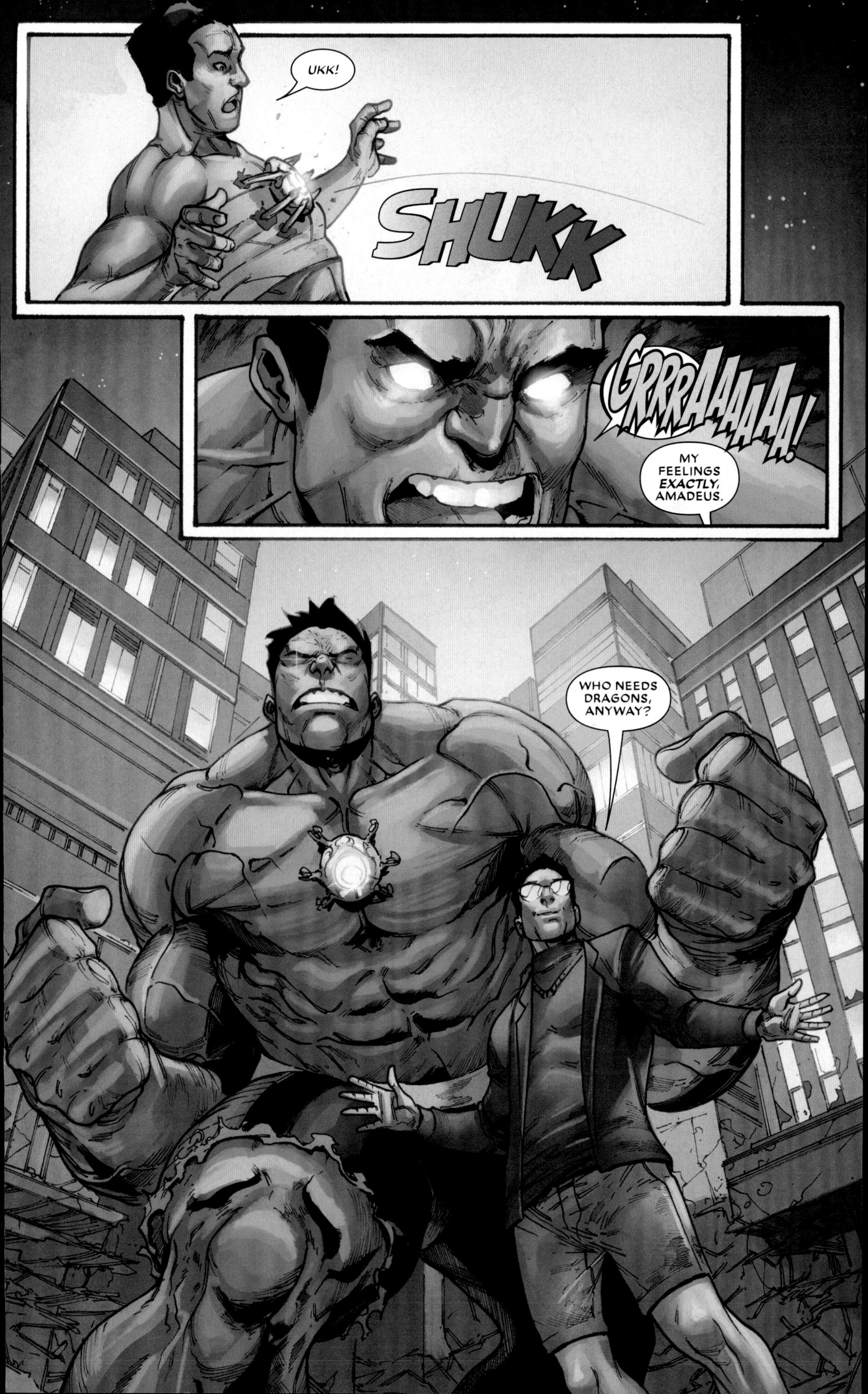
UKK!
SHUKK
GRRRAAAAAA!
MY FEELINGS EXACTLY, AMADEUS.
WHO NEEDS DRAGONS, ANYWAY?

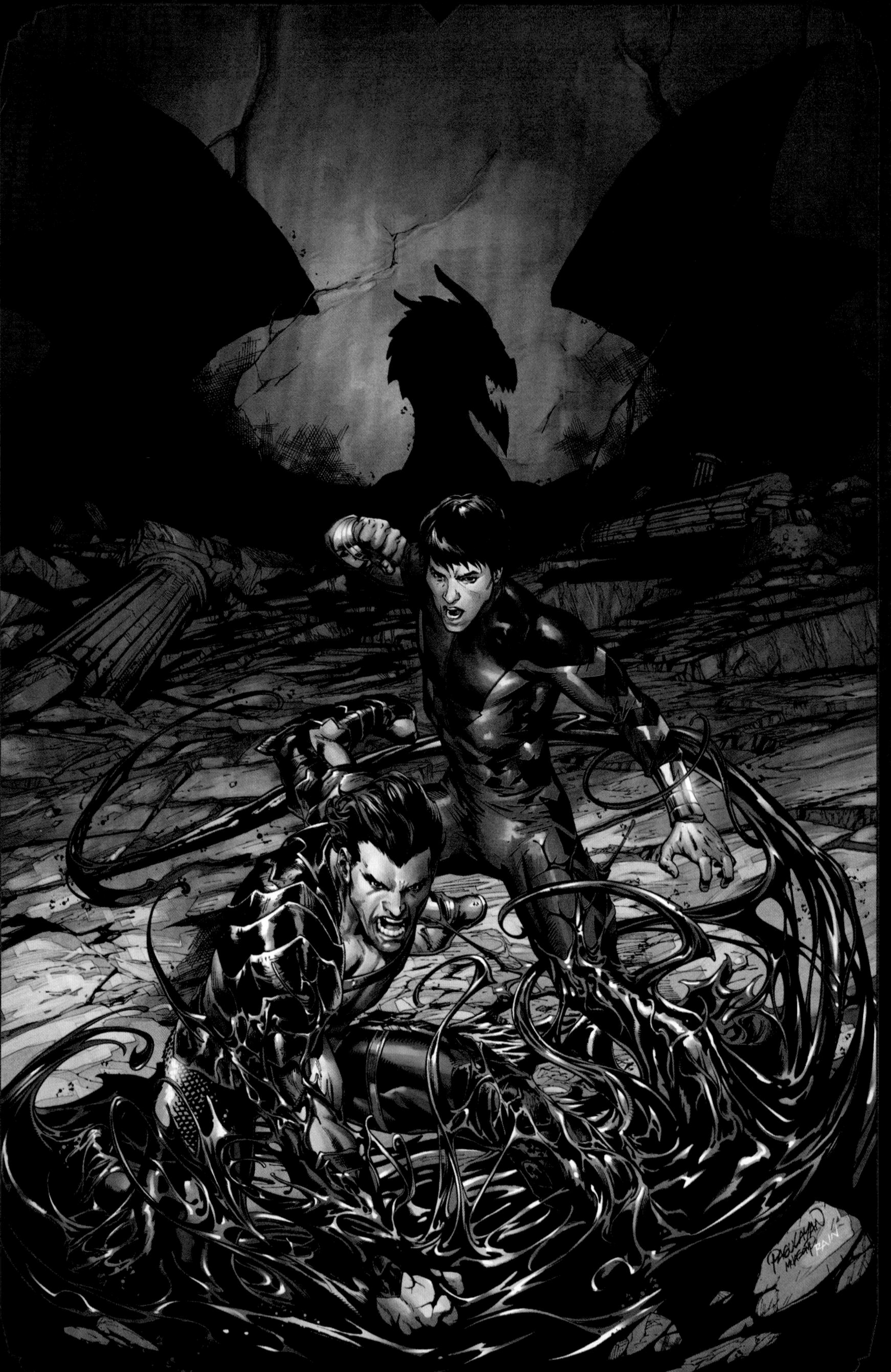

5

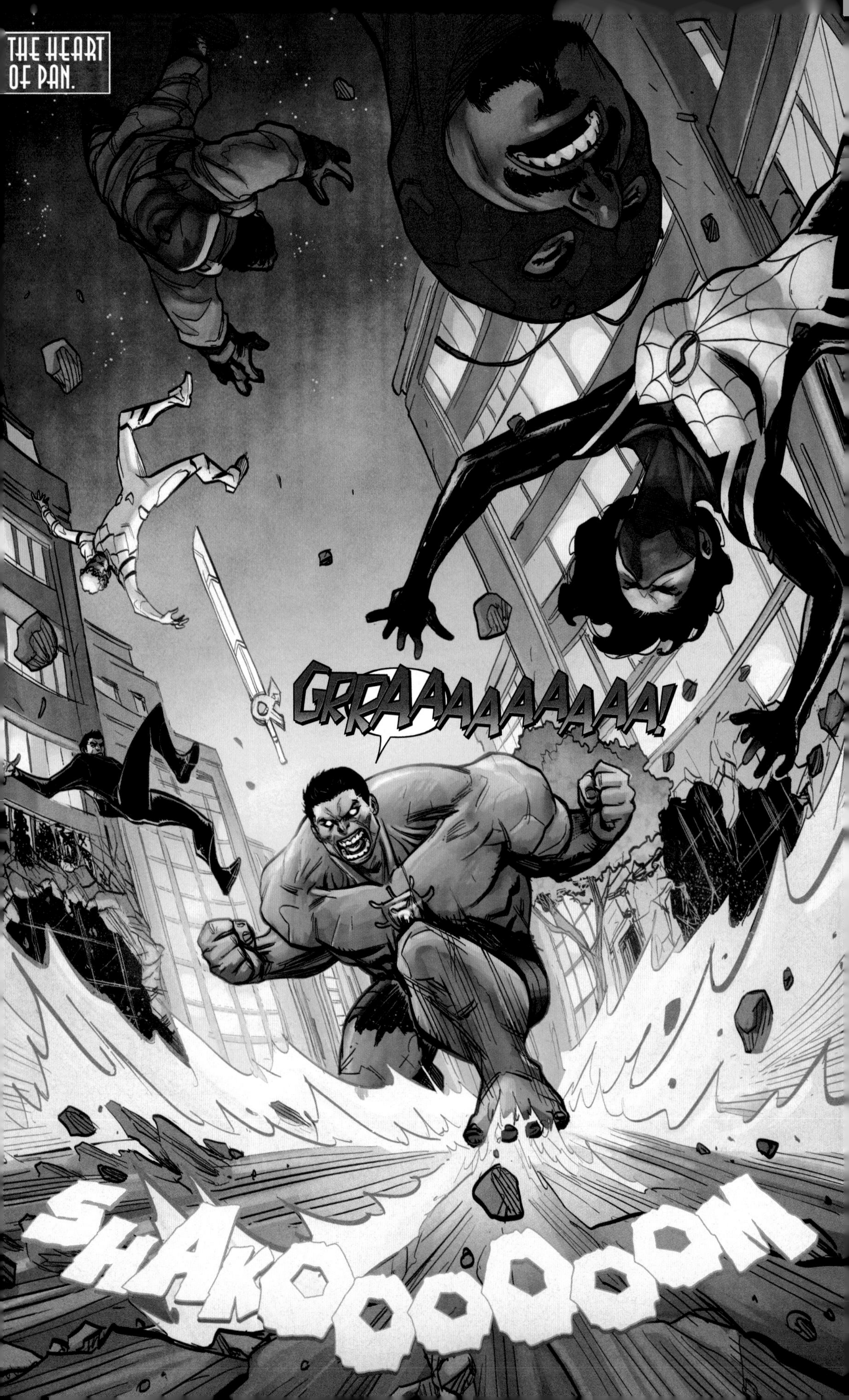
THE HEART OF PAN.
GRRAAAAAAAAA!
SHAKOOOOOOM

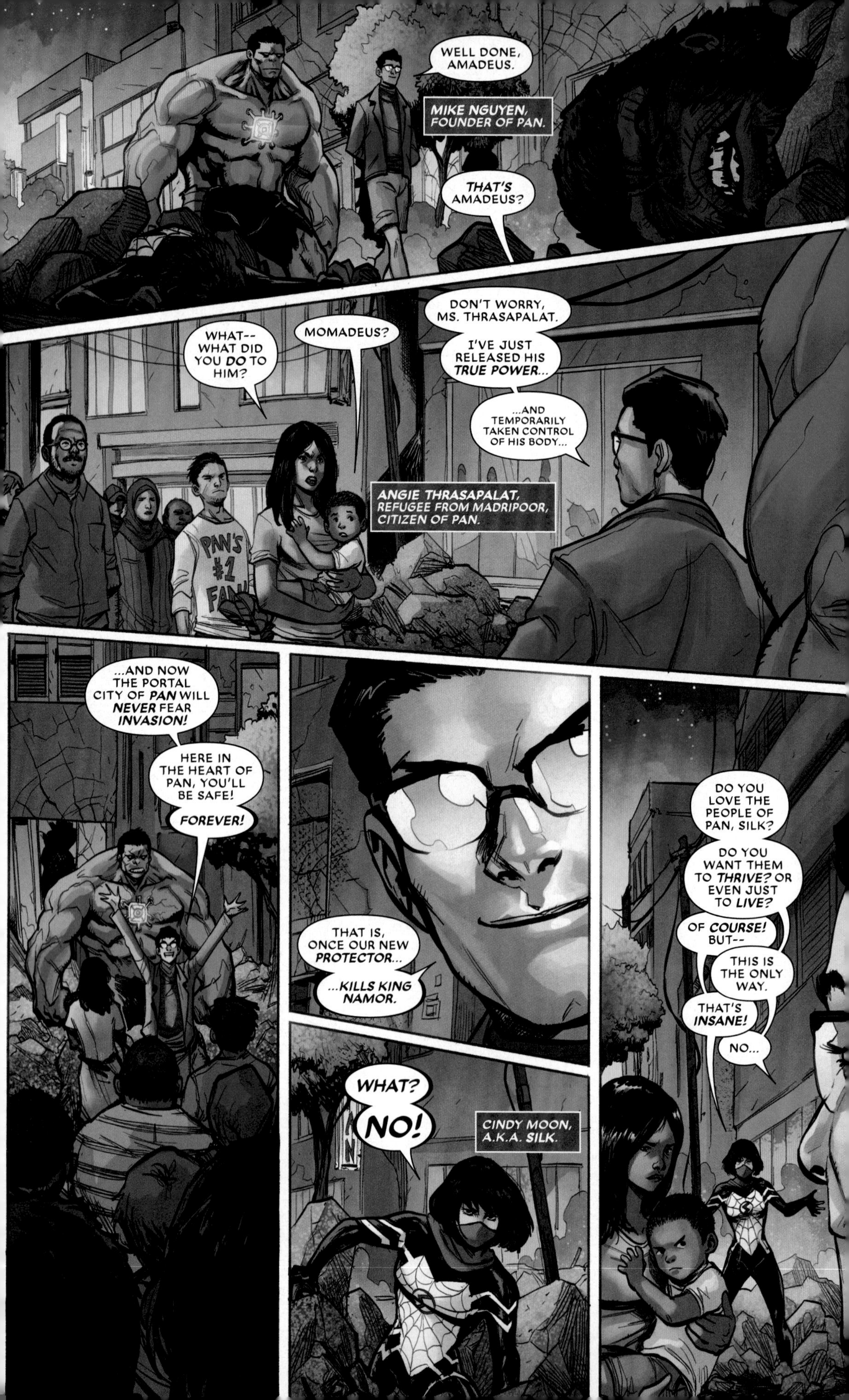
WELL DONE, AMADEUS.
MIKE NGUYEN, FOUNDER OF PAN.
THAT'S AMADEUS?
WHAT-- WHAT DID YOU DO TO HIM?
MOMADEUS?
DON'T WORRY, MS. THRASAPALAT.
I'VE JUST RELEASED HIS TRUE POWER...
...AND TEMPORARILY TAKEN CONTROL OF HIS BODY...
ANGIE THRASAPALAT, REFUGEE FROM MADRIPOOR, CITIZEN OF PAN.
PAN'S #1 FAN
...AND NOW THE PORTAL CITY OF PAN WILL NEVER FEAR INVASION!
HERE IN THE HEART OF PAN, YOU'LL BE SAFE!
FOREVER!
THAT IS, ONCE OUR NEW PROTECTOR...
...KILLS KING NAMOR.
WHAT?
NO!
CINDY MOON, A.K.A. SILK.
DO YOU LOVE THE PEOPLE OF PAN, SILK?
DO YOU WANT THEM TO THRIVE? OR EVEN JUST TO LIVE?
OF COURSE! BUT--
THIS IS THE ONLY WAY.
THAT'S INSANE!
NO...

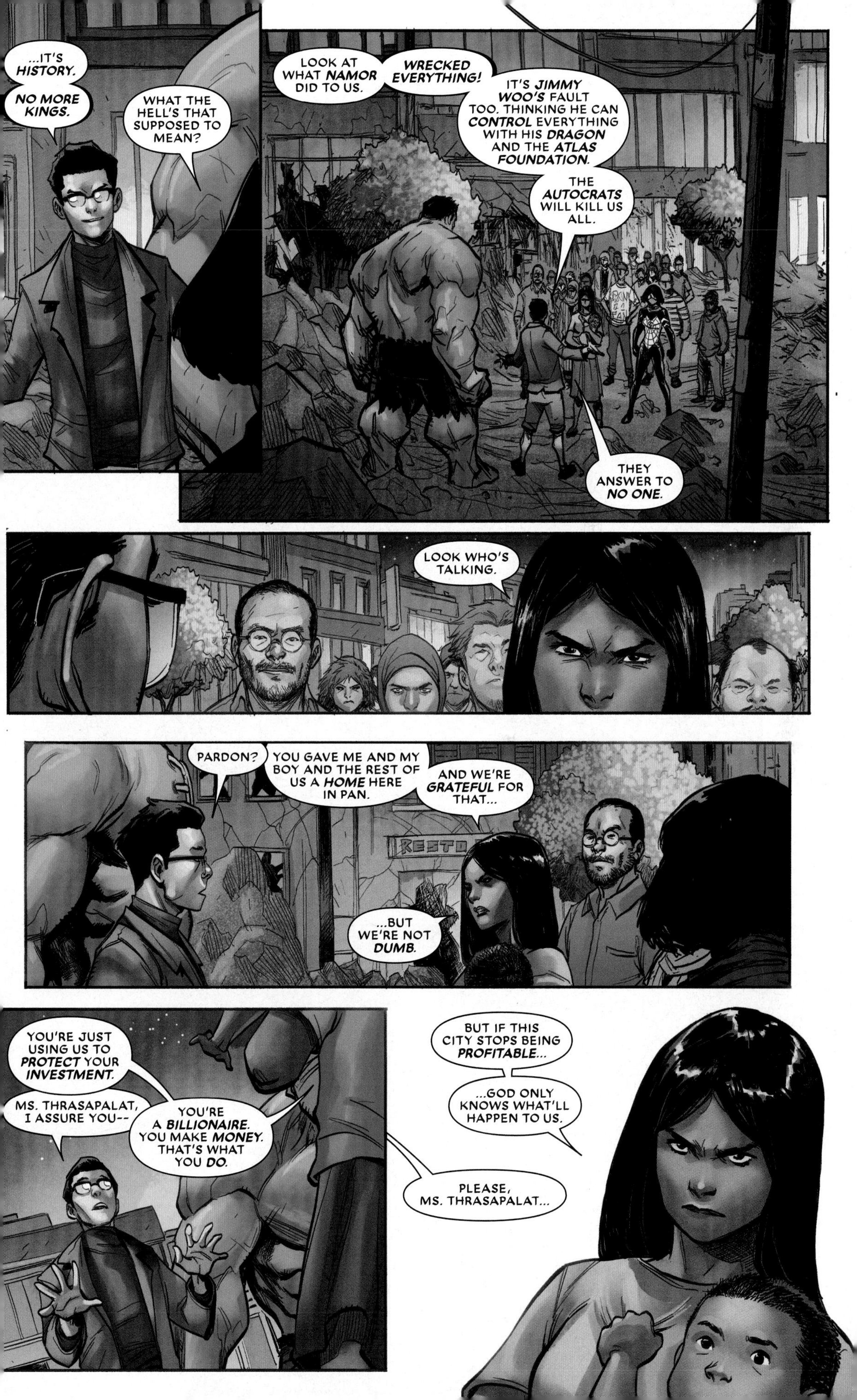
...IT'S HISTORY.
NO MORE KINGS.
WHAT THE HELL'S THAT SUPPOSED TO MEAN?
LOOK AT WHAT NAMOR DID TO US.
WRECKED EVERYTHING!
IT'S JIMMY WOO'S FAULT TOO. THINKING HE CAN CONTROL EVERYTHING WITH HIS DRAGON AND THE ATLAS FOUNDATION.
THE AUTOCRATS WILL KILL US ALL.
THEY ANSWER TO NO ONE.
LOOK WHO'S TALKING.
PARDON?
YOU GAVE ME AND MY BOY AND THE REST OF US A HOME HERE IN PAN.
AND WE'RE GRATEFUL FOR THAT...
...BUT WE'RE NOT DUMB.
YOU'RE JUST USING US TO PROTECT YOUR INVESTMENT.
MS. THRASAPALAT, I ASSURE YOU--
YOU'RE A BILLIONAIRE. YOU MAKE MONEY. THAT'S WHAT YOU DO.
BUT IF THIS CITY STOPS BEING PROFITABLE...
...GOD ONLY KNOWS WHAT'LL HAPPEN TO US.
PLEASE, MS. THRASAPALAT...

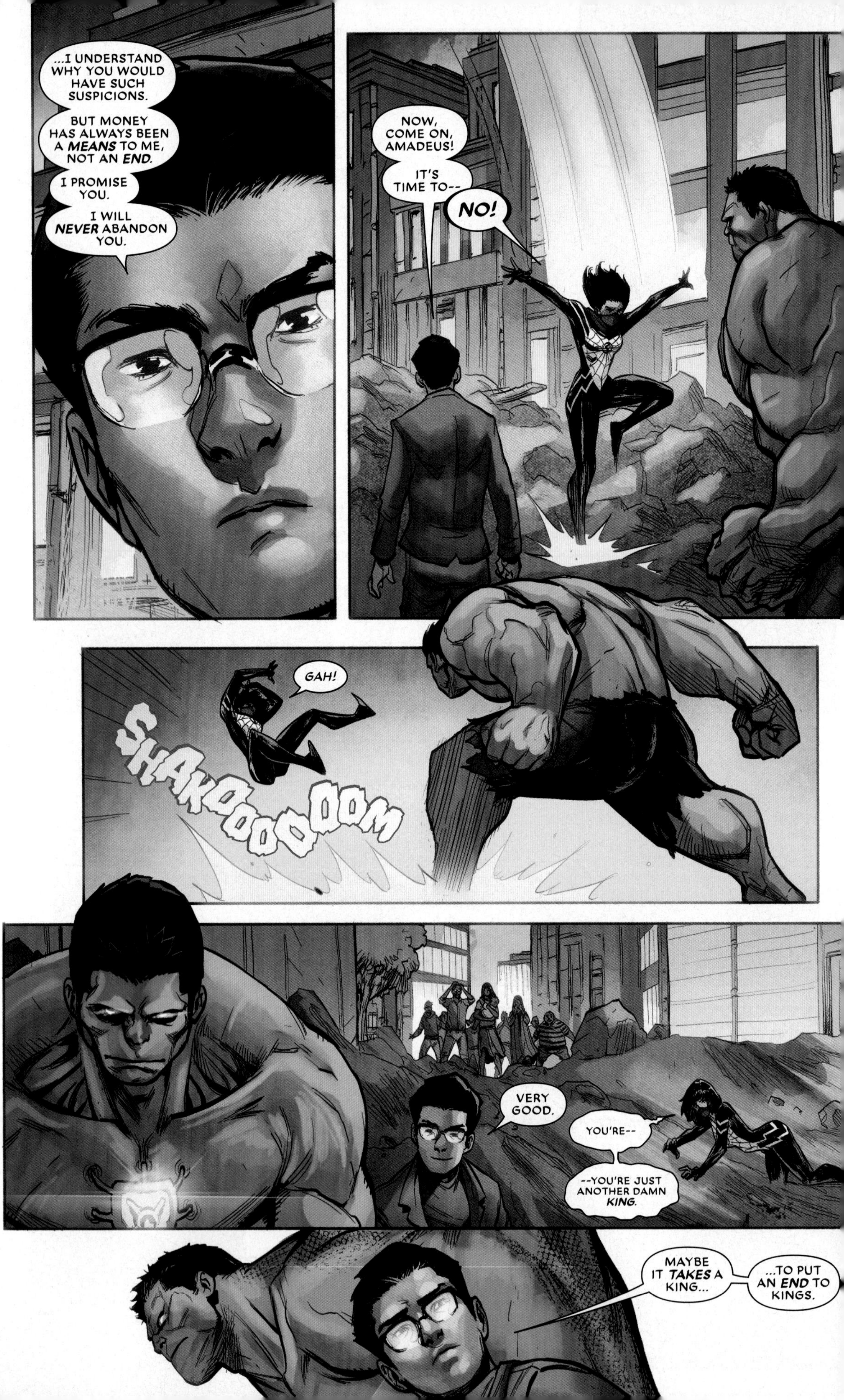
...I UNDERSTAND WHY YOU WOULD HAVE SUCH SUSPICIONS.
BUT MONEY HAS ALWAYS BEEN A MEANS TO ME, NOT AN END.
I PROMISE YOU.
I WILL NEVER ABANDON YOU.
NOW, COME ON, AMADEUS!
IT'S TIME TO--
NO!
GAH!
SHAKOOOOOOM
VERY GOOD.
YOU'RE--
--YOU'RE JUST ANOTHER DAMN KING.
MAYBE IT TAKES A KING...
...TO PUT AN END TO KINGS.

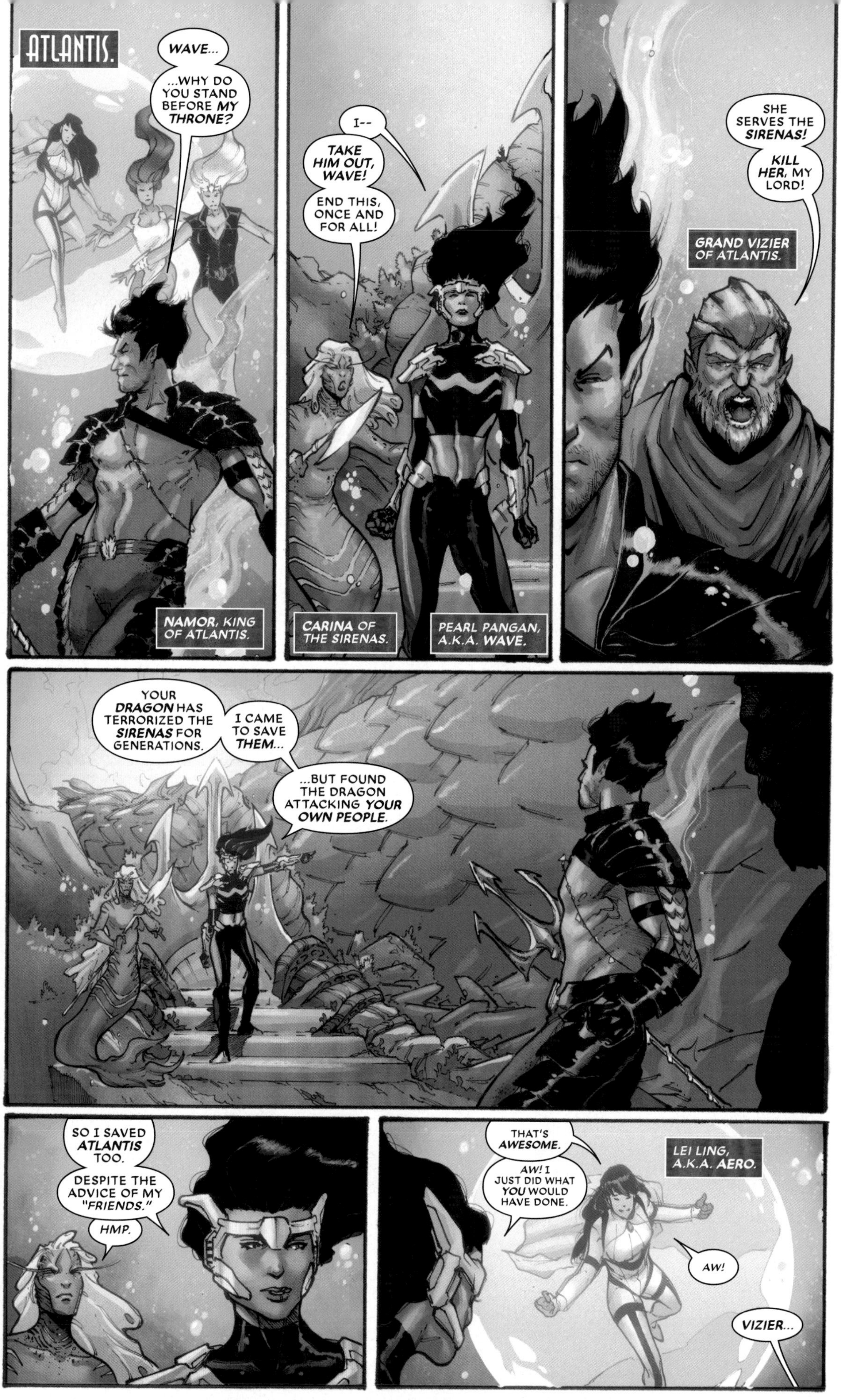
ATLANTIS.
WAVE...
...WHY DO YOU STAND BEFORE MY THRONE?
NAMOR, KING OF ATLANTIS.
I--
TAKE HIM OUT, WAVE!
END THIS, ONCE AND FOR ALL!
CARINA OF THE SIRENAS.
PEARL PANGAN, A.K.A. WAVE.
SHE SERVES THE SIRENAS!
KILL HER, MY LORD!
GRAND VIZIER OF ATLANTIS.
YOUR DRAGON HAS TERRORIZED THE SIRENAS FOR GENERATIONS.
I CAME TO SAVE THEM...
...BUT FOUND THE DRAGON ATTACKING YOUR OWN PEOPLE.
SO I SAVED ATLANTIS TOO.
DESPITE THE ADVICE OF MY "FRIENDS."
HMP.
THAT'S AWESOME.
AW! I JUST DID WHAT YOU WOULD HAVE DONE.
LEI LING, A.K.A. AERO.
AW!
VIZIER...

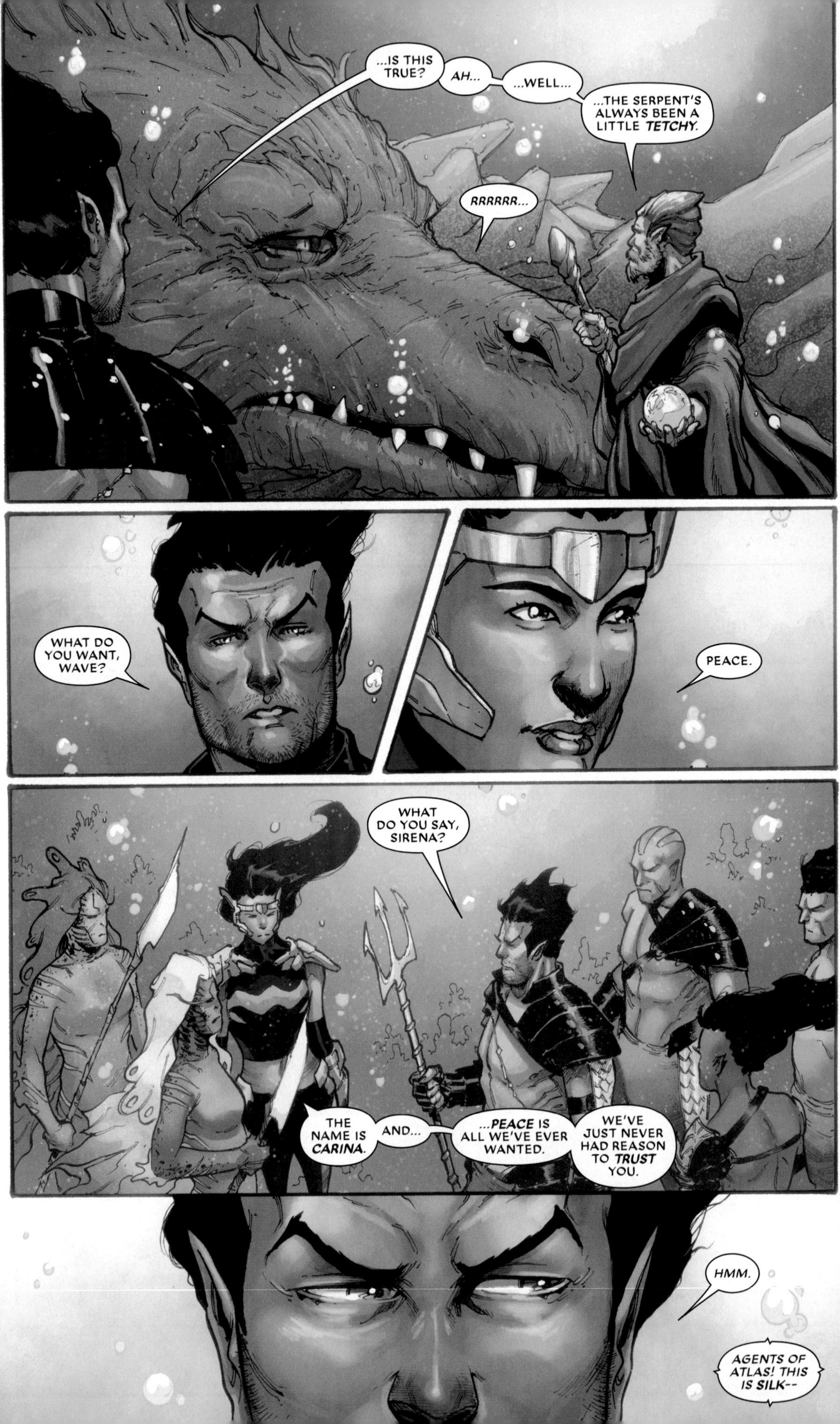
...IS THIS TRUE?
AH...
...WELL...
...THE SERPENT'S ALWAYS BEEN A LITTLE *TETCHY*.
RRRRRR...
WHAT DO YOU WANT, WAVE?
PEACE.
WHAT DO YOU SAY, SIRENA?
THE NAME IS *CARINA*.
AND...
...*PEACE* IS ALL WE'VE EVER WANTED.
WE'VE JUST NEVER HAD REASON TO *TRUST* YOU.
HMM.
AGENTS OF ATLAS! THIS IS *SILK*--

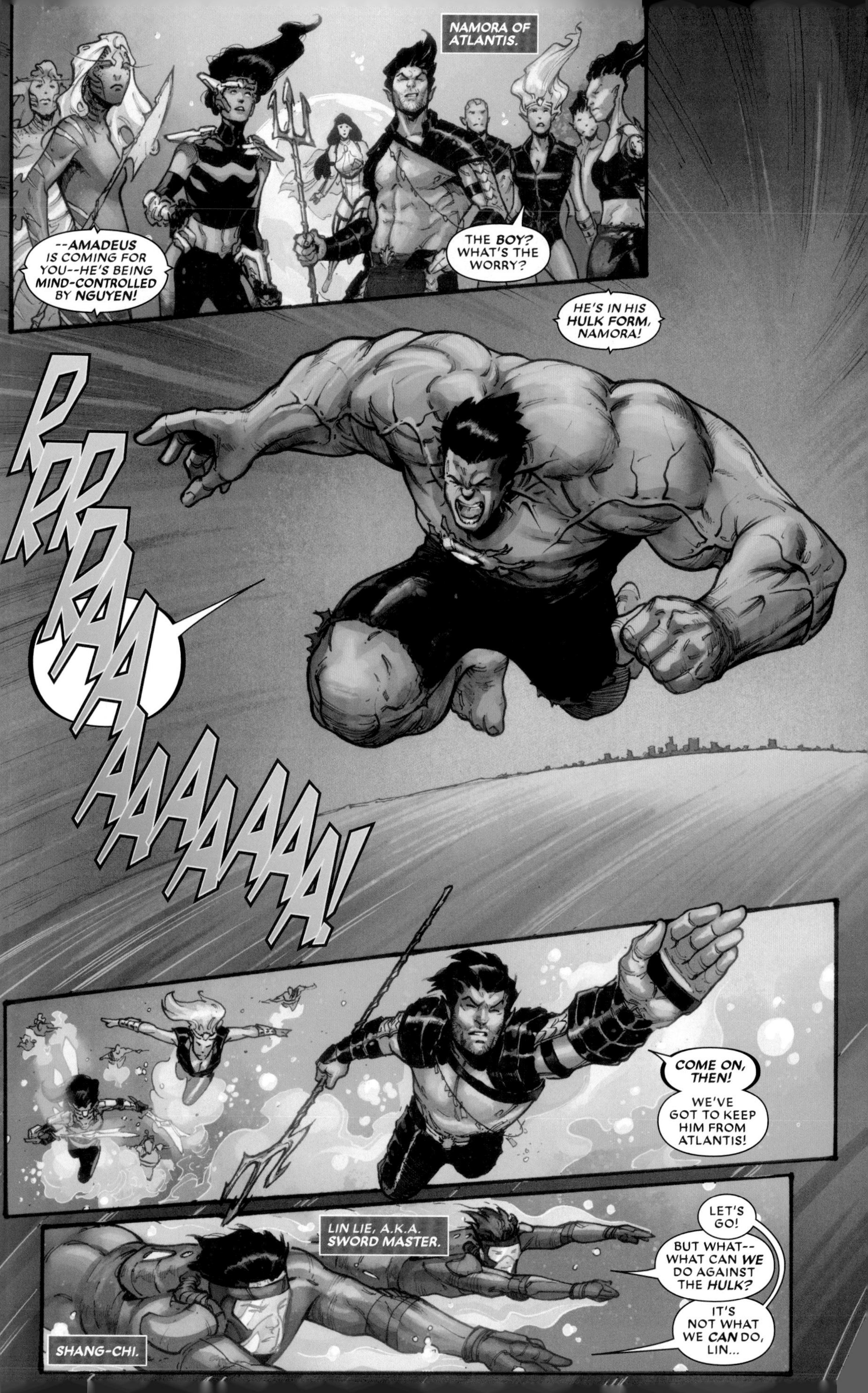
NAMORA OF ATLANTIS.
--AMADEUS IS COMING FOR YOU--HE'S BEING MIND-CONTROLLED BY NGUYEN!
THE BOY? WHAT'S THE WORRY?
HE'S IN HIS HULK FORM, NAMORA!
RRRRAAAAAAAAAAA!
COME ON, THEN!
WE'VE GOT TO KEEP HIM FROM ATLANTIS!
LIN LIE, A.K.A. SWORD MASTER.
SHANG-CHI.
LET'S GO!
BUT WHAT--WHAT CAN WE DO AGAINST THE HULK?
IT'S NOT WHAT WE CAN DO, LIN...

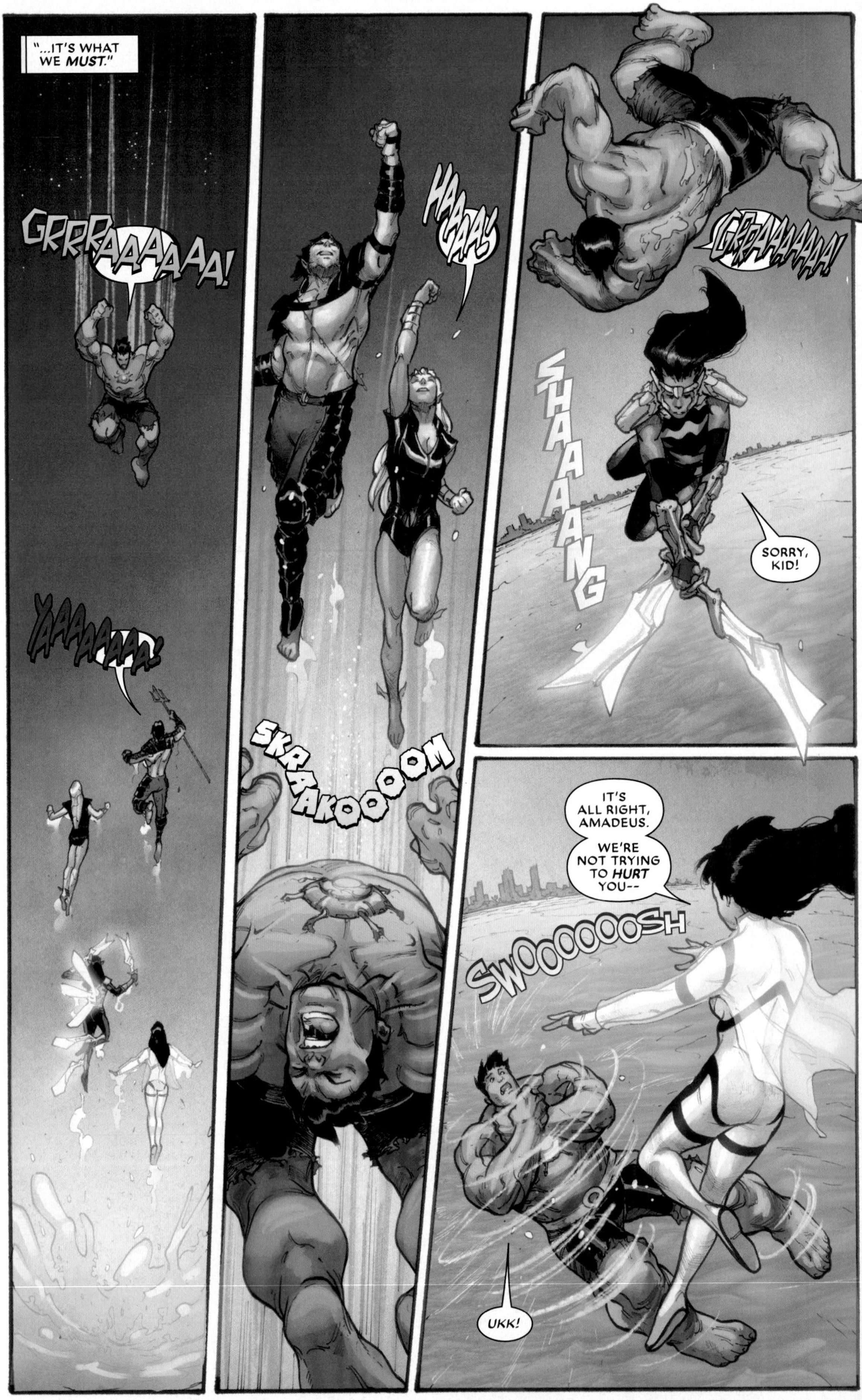
"...IT'S WHAT WE MUST."
GRRRAAAAAAAA!
YAAAAAAAA!
HAAAAA!
SKRAAKOOOOOM
GRRAAAAAAAA!
SHAAAAANG
SORRY, KID!
IT'S ALL RIGHT, AMADEUS.
WE'RE NOT TRYING TO HURT YOU--
SWOOOOOOOSH
UKK!

GRRRAAAAAA!

SPEAK FOR YOURSELF.

KTHOOOOOOM

RRRAARR!

I KNOW YOU CAN HEAR ME, NGUYEN!

CALL OFF YOUR MONSTER OR SUFFER THE CONSEQUENCES!

I'M DONE WITH *NEGOTIATING*, NAMOR.

I THINK YOU SAID IT BEST THE LAST TIME WE SPOKE.

"THE ONLY THING YOU HAVE THAT I WANT..."

FTOOOOOOSSH

"...IS YOUR DEATH."

DO YOU THINK EVERYONE ELSE IS A *FOOL?*

YOU READY FOR THIS?

ALWAYS.

MY *SCIENTISTS* FOUND THE TRUE LOCATION OF YOUR *HEART OF PAN...*

...AND *THAT'S* WHERE I'M TAKING THIS BATTLE.

WHA-- HE--HE'S *TELEPORTING* US!

BEFORE *I* DIE...

WOOOO-

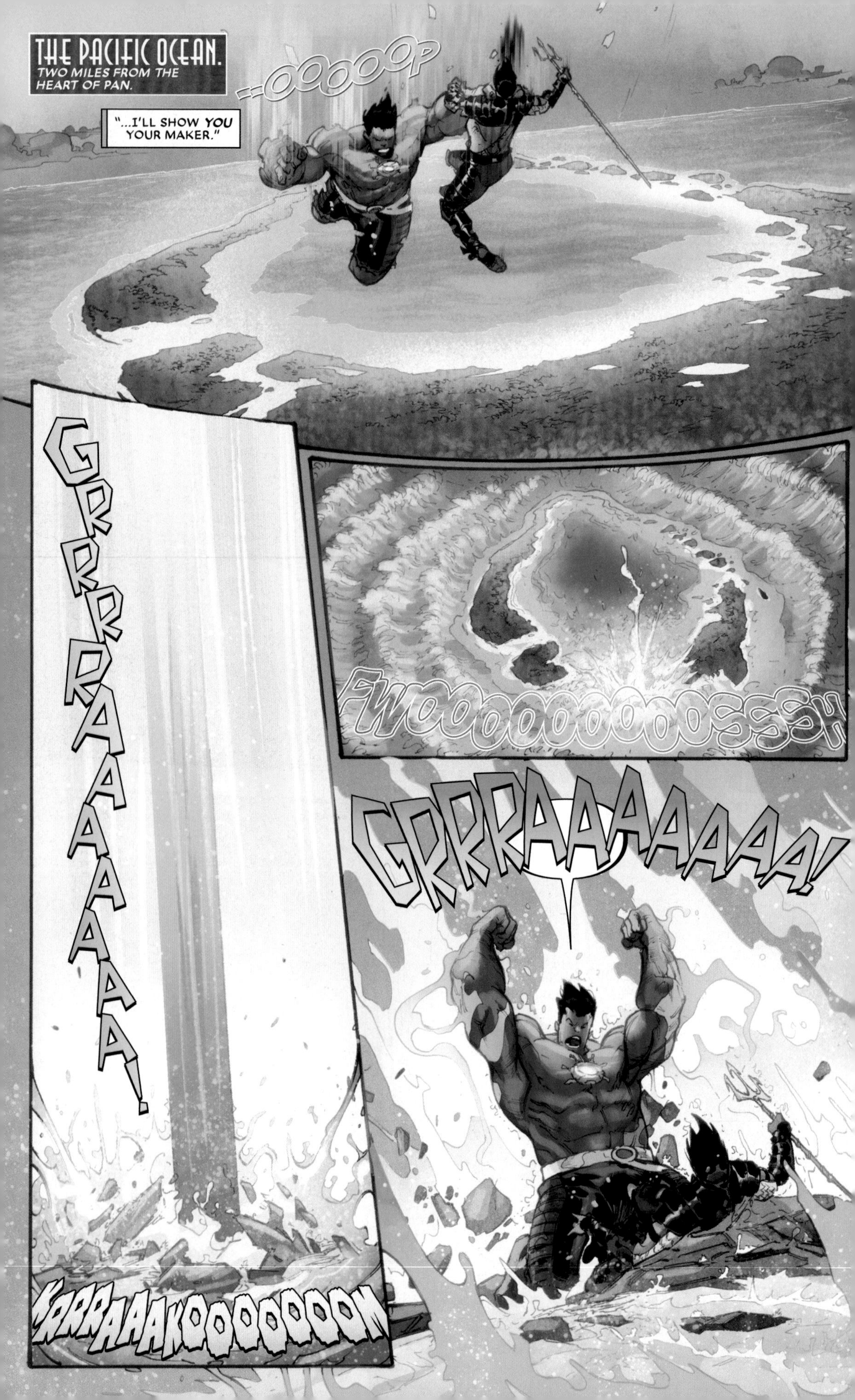
THE PACIFIC OCEAN.
TWO MILES FROM THE HEART OF PAN.
"...I'LL SHOW YOU YOUR MAKER."
--OOOOOOP
GRRRRAAAAAAA!
FWOOOOOOOOOOOSSSH
GRRRAAAAAAAA!
KRRRAAAKOOOOOOOM

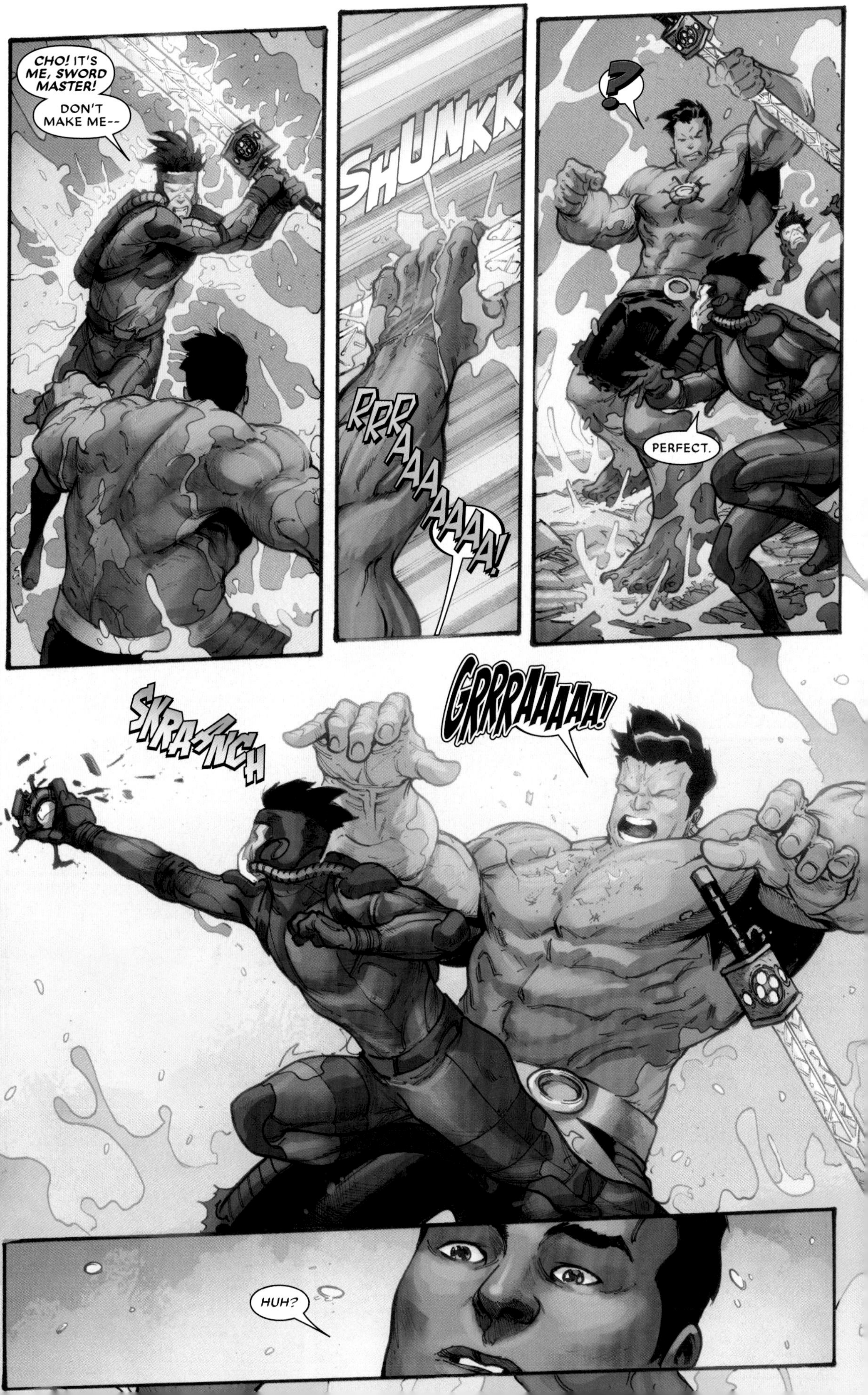
CHO! IT'S ME, SWORD MASTER!
DON'T MAKE ME--
SHUNKK
RRRAAAAAAA!
?
PERFECT.
SKRAANCH
GRRRAAAAAA!
HUH?

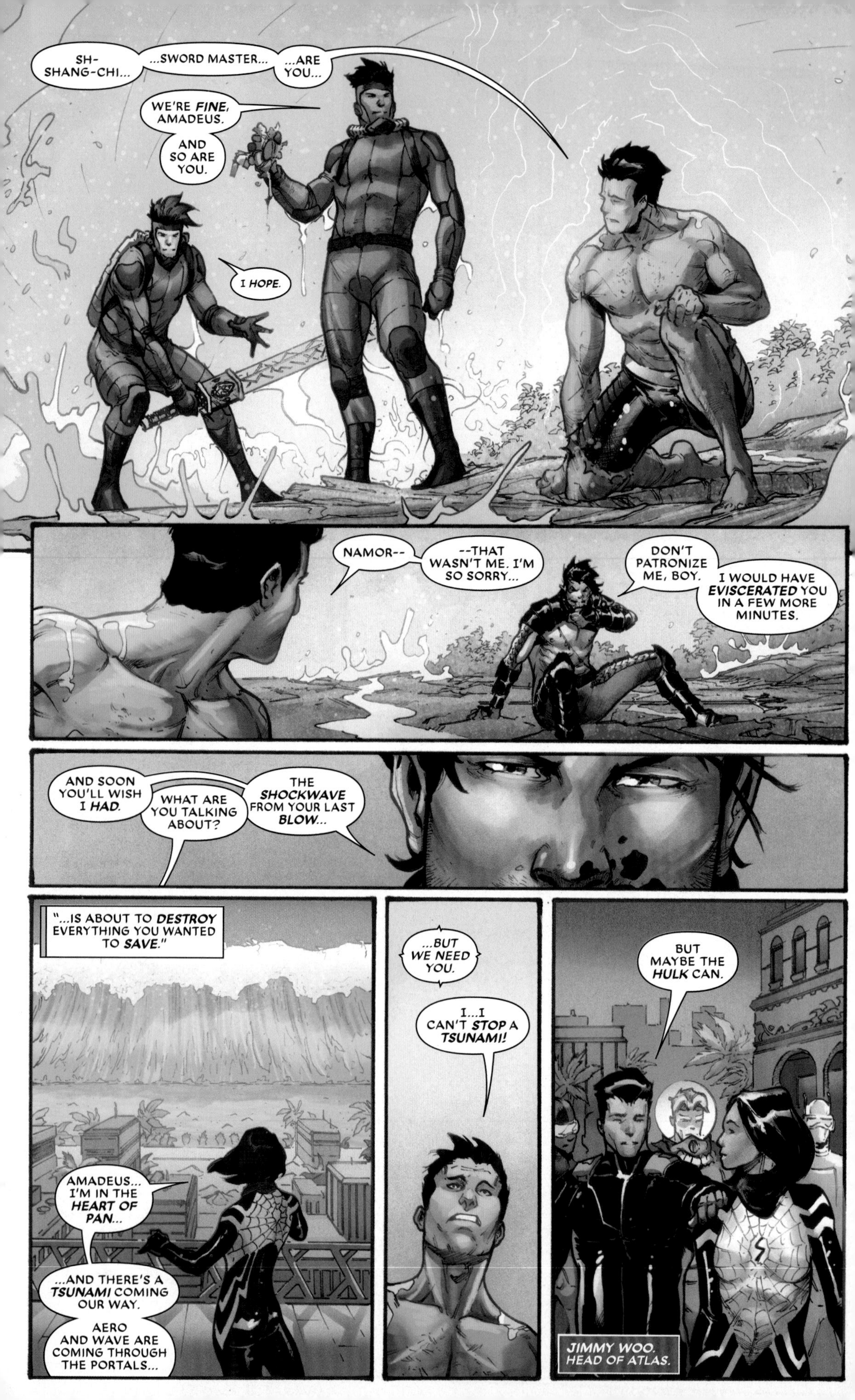
SH-
SHANG-CHI...
...SWORD MASTER...
...ARE
YOU...
WE'RE FINE,
AMADEUS.
AND
SO ARE
YOU.
I HOPE.
NAMOR--
--THAT
WASN'T ME. I'M
SO SORRY...
DON'T
PATRONIZE
ME, BOY.
I WOULD HAVE
EVISCERATED YOU
IN A FEW MORE
MINUTES.
AND SOON
YOU'LL WISH
I HAD.
WHAT ARE
YOU TALKING
ABOUT?
THE
SHOCKWAVE
FROM YOUR LAST
BLOW...
"...IS ABOUT TO DESTROY
EVERYTHING YOU WANTED
TO SAVE."
AMADEUS...
I'M IN THE
HEART OF
PAN...
...AND THERE'S A
TSUNAMI COMING
OUR WAY.
AERO
AND WAVE ARE
COMING THROUGH
THE PORTALS...
...BUT
WE NEED
YOU.
I...I
CAN'T STOP A
TSUNAMI!
BUT
MAYBE THE
HULK CAN.
JIMMY WOO.
HEAD OF ATLAS.

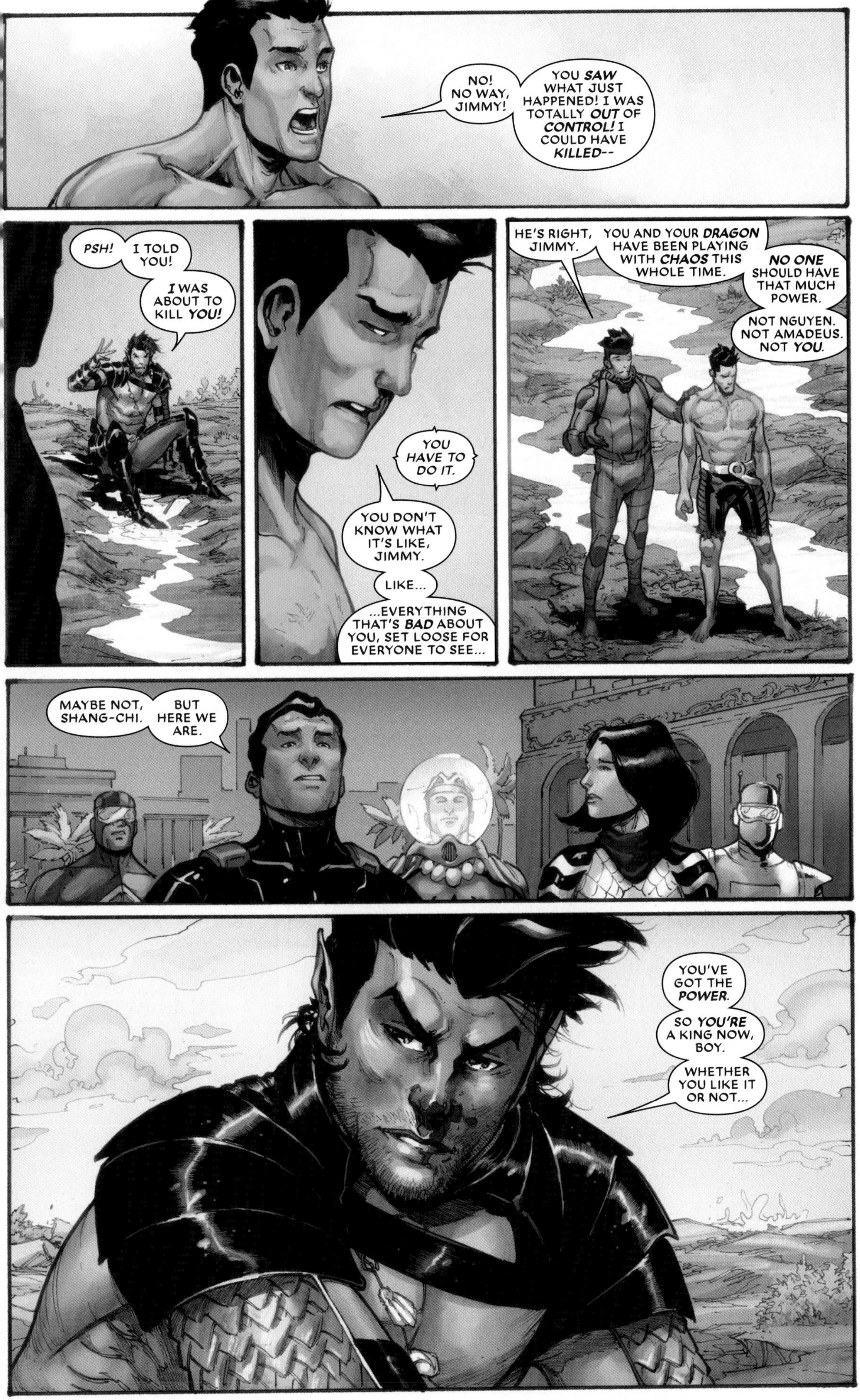
NO! NO WAY, JIMMY!
YOU SAW WHAT JUST HAPPENED! I WAS TOTALLY OUT OF CONTROL! I COULD HAVE KILLED--
PSH!
I TOLD YOU!
I WAS ABOUT TO KILL YOU!
YOU HAVE TO DO IT.
YOU DON'T KNOW WHAT IT'S LIKE, JIMMY.
LIKE...
...EVERYTHING THAT'S BAD ABOUT YOU, SET LOOSE FOR EVERYONE TO SEE...
HE'S RIGHT, JIMMY.
YOU AND YOUR DRAGON HAVE BEEN PLAYING WITH CHAOS THIS WHOLE TIME.
NO ONE SHOULD HAVE THAT MUCH POWER.
NOT NGUYEN. NOT AMADEUS. NOT YOU.
MAYBE NOT, SHANG-CHI.
BUT HERE WE ARE.
YOU'VE GOT THE POWER.
SO YOU'RE A KING NOW, BOY.
WHETHER YOU LIKE IT OR NOT...

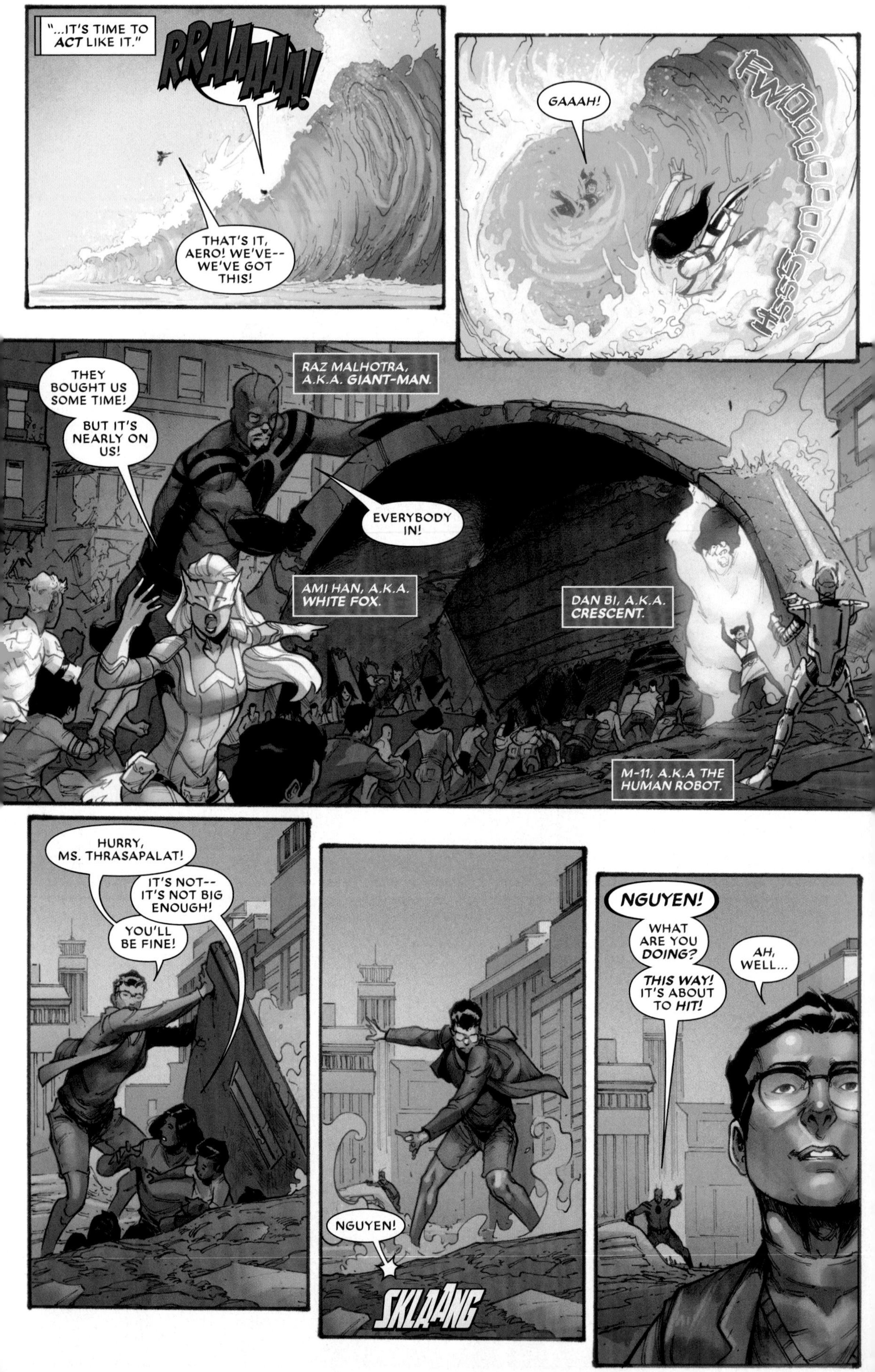
"...IT'S TIME TO ACT LIKE IT."
RRAAAAAA!
THAT'S IT, AERO! WE'VE-- WE'VE GOT THIS!
GAAAH!
FWOOOOOOOOSSSH
THEY BOUGHT US SOME TIME!
BUT IT'S NEARLY ON US!
RAZ MALHOTRA, A.K.A. GIANT-MAN.
EVERYBODY IN!
AMI HAN, A.K.A. WHITE FOX.
DAN BI, A.K.A. CRESCENT.
M-11, A.K.A THE HUMAN ROBOT.
HURRY, MS. THRASAPALAT!
IT'S NOT-- IT'S NOT BIG ENOUGH!
YOU'LL BE FINE!
NGUYEN!
SKLAANG
NGUYEN!
WHAT ARE YOU DOING?
THIS WAY! IT'S ABOUT TO HIT!
AH, WELL...

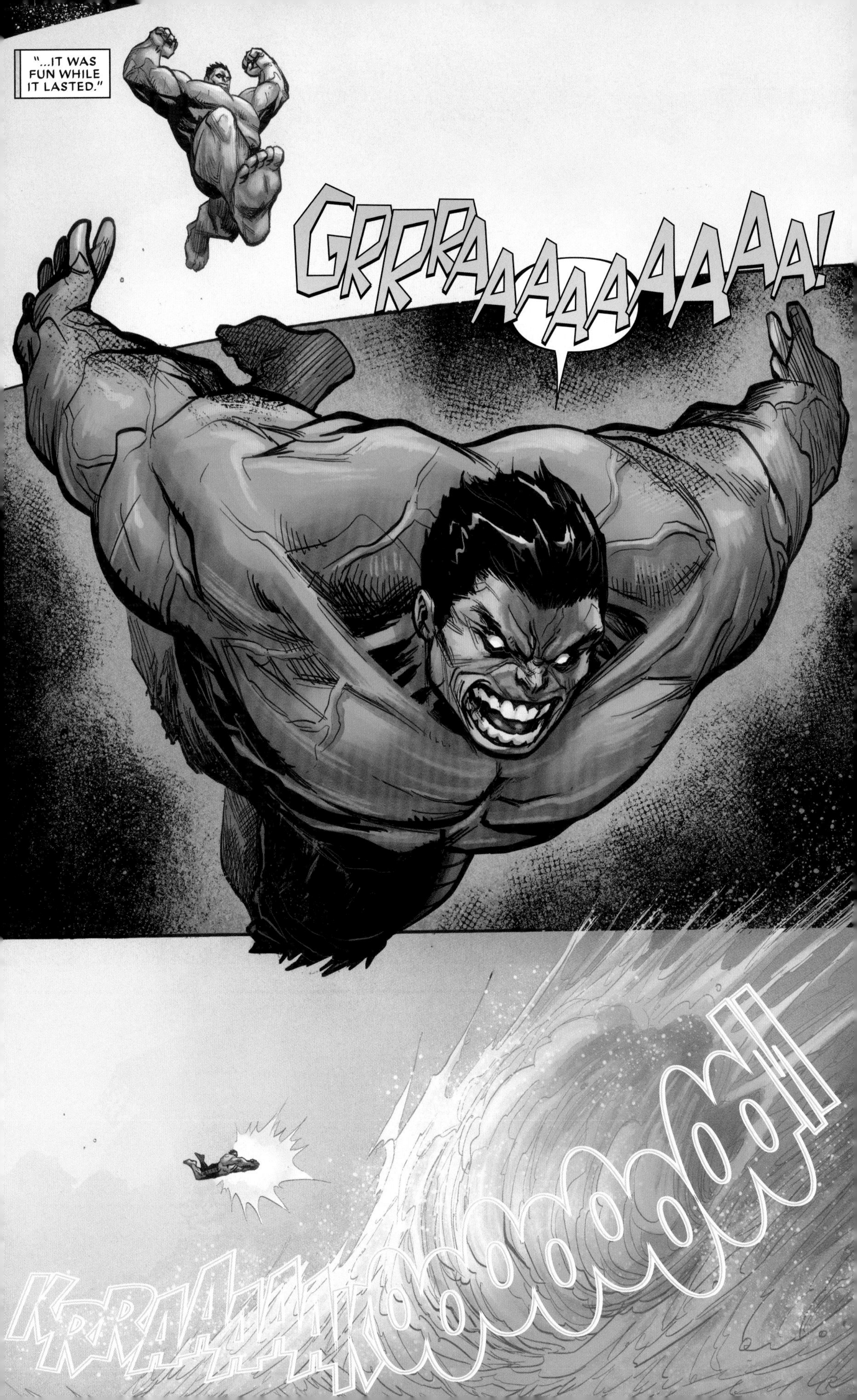
"...IT WAS FUN WHILE IT LASTED."
GRRRAAAAAAAAA!
KRRAAHHHKOOOOOOOOOM!

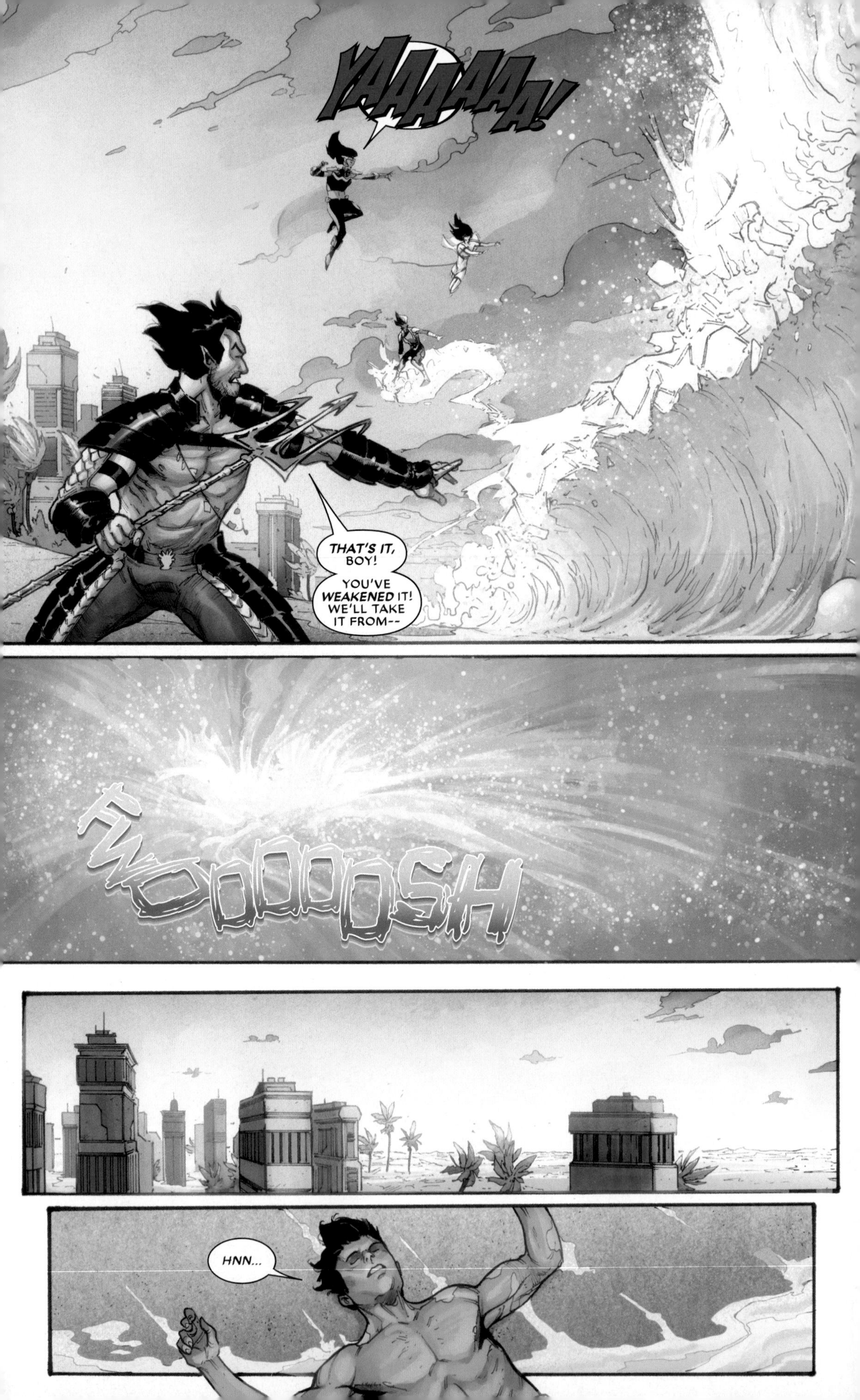
YAAAAAA!
THAT'S IT, BOY!
YOU'VE WEAKENED IT! WE'LL TAKE IT FROM--
FWOOOOOSH
HNN...

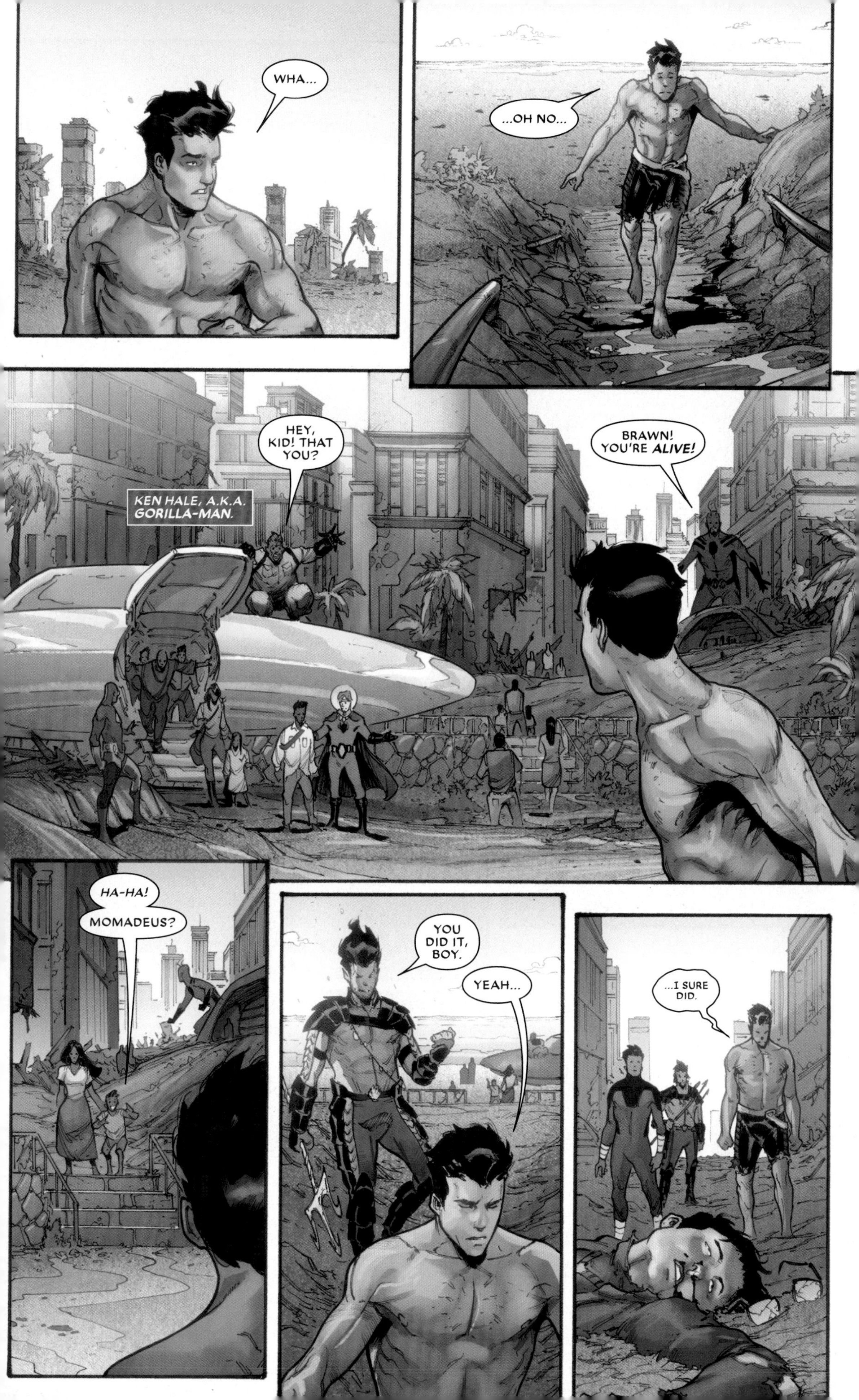
WHA...
...OH NO...
KEN HALE, A.K.A. GORILLA-MAN.
HEY, KID! THAT YOU?
BRAWN! YOU'RE *ALIVE!*
HA-HA!
MOMADEUS?
YOU DID IT, BOY.
YEAH...
...I SURE DID.

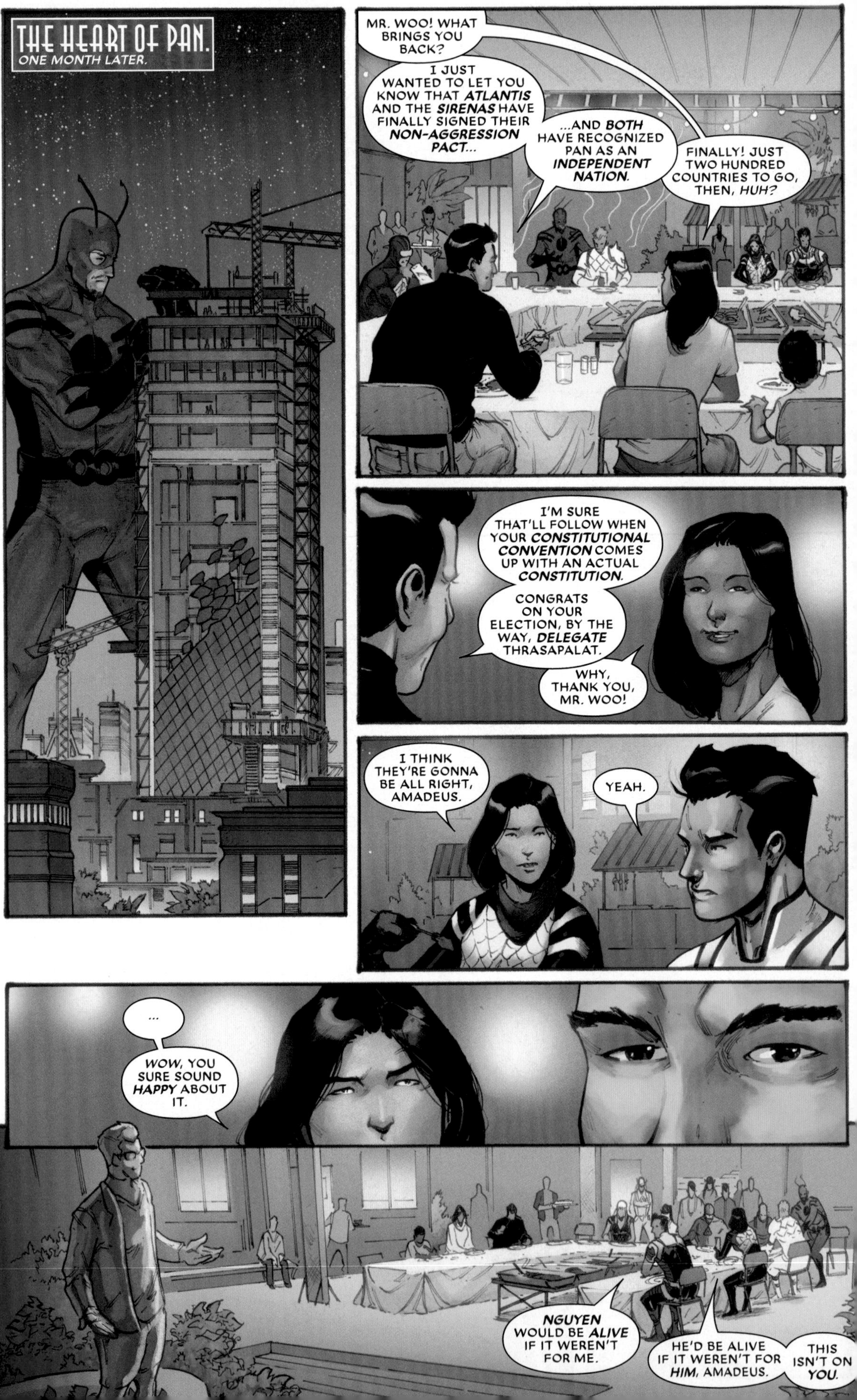
THE HEART OF PAN.
ONE MONTH LATER.
MR. WOO! WHAT BRINGS YOU BACK?
I JUST WANTED TO LET YOU KNOW THAT ATLANTIS AND THE SIRENAS HAVE FINALLY SIGNED THEIR NON-AGGRESSION PACT...
...AND BOTH HAVE RECOGNIZED PAN AS AN INDEPENDENT NATION.
FINALLY! JUST TWO HUNDRED COUNTRIES TO GO, THEN, HUH?
I'M SURE THAT'LL FOLLOW WHEN YOUR CONSTITUTIONAL CONVENTION COMES UP WITH AN ACTUAL CONSTITUTION.
CONGRATS ON YOUR ELECTION, BY THE WAY, DELEGATE THRASAPALAT.
WHY, THANK YOU, MR. WOO!
I THINK THEY'RE GONNA BE ALL RIGHT, AMADEUS.
YEAH.
...
WOW, YOU SURE SOUND HAPPY ABOUT IT.
NGUYEN WOULD BE ALIVE IF IT WEREN'T FOR ME.
HE'D BE ALIVE IF IT WEREN'T FOR HIM, AMADEUS.
THIS ISN'T ON YOU.

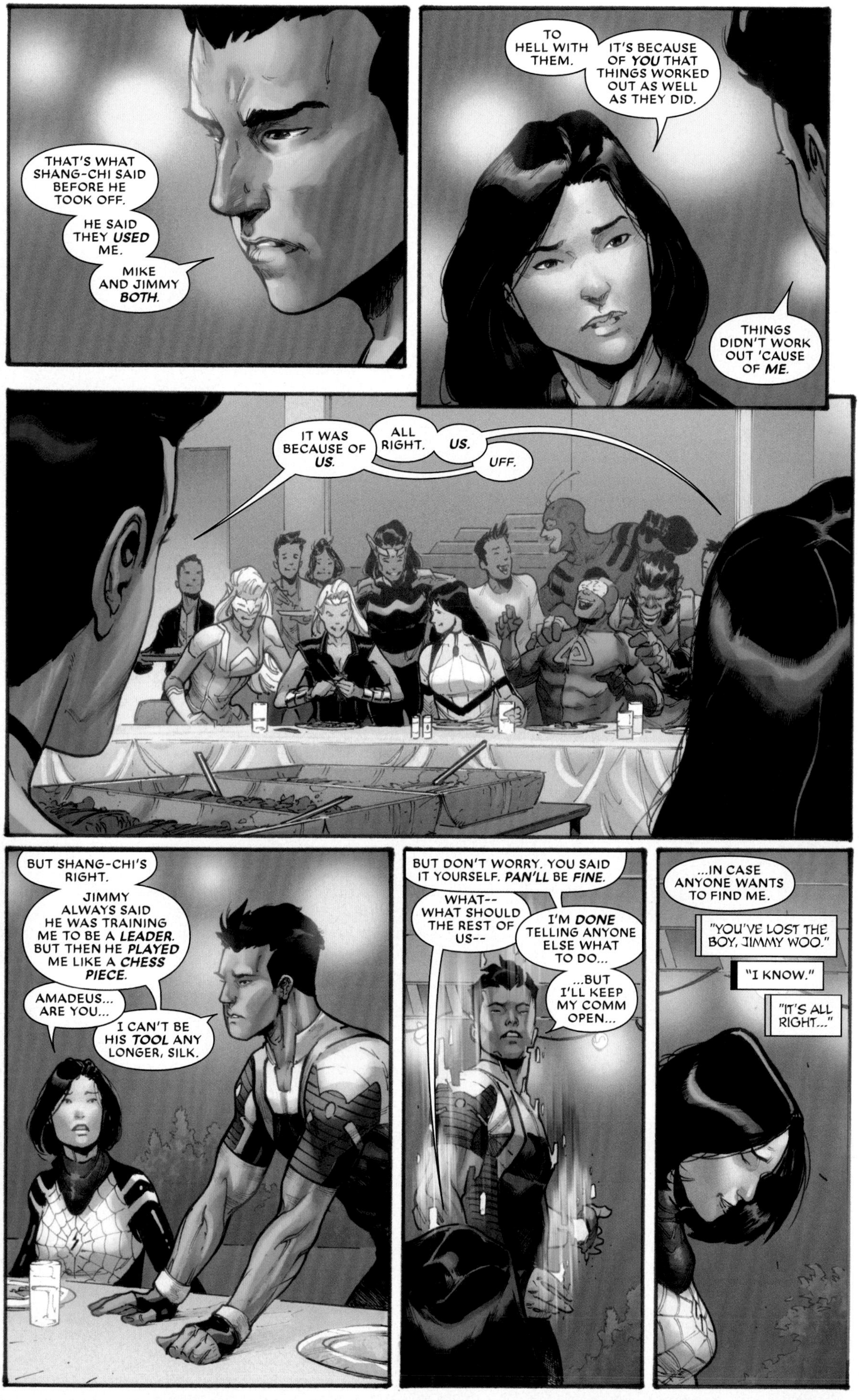
THAT'S WHAT SHANG-CHI SAID BEFORE HE TOOK OFF.
HE SAID THEY USED ME.
MIKE AND JIMMY BOTH.
TO HELL WITH THEM.
IT'S BECAUSE OF YOU THAT THINGS WORKED OUT AS WELL AS THEY DID.
THINGS DIDN'T WORK OUT 'CAUSE OF ME.
IT WAS BECAUSE OF US.
ALL RIGHT.
US.
UFF.
BUT SHANG-CHI'S RIGHT.
JIMMY ALWAYS SAID HE WAS TRAINING ME TO BE A LEADER. BUT THEN HE PLAYED ME LIKE A CHESS PIECE.
AMADEUS... ARE YOU...
I CAN'T BE HIS TOOL ANY LONGER, SILK.
BUT DON'T WORRY. YOU SAID IT YOURSELF. PAN'LL BE FINE.
WHAT-- WHAT SHOULD THE REST OF US--
I'M DONE TELLING ANYONE ELSE WHAT TO DO...
...BUT I'LL KEEP MY COMM OPEN...
...IN CASE ANYONE WANTS TO FIND ME.
"YOU'VE LOST THE BOY, JIMMY WOO."
"I KNOW."
"IT'S ALL RIGHT..."

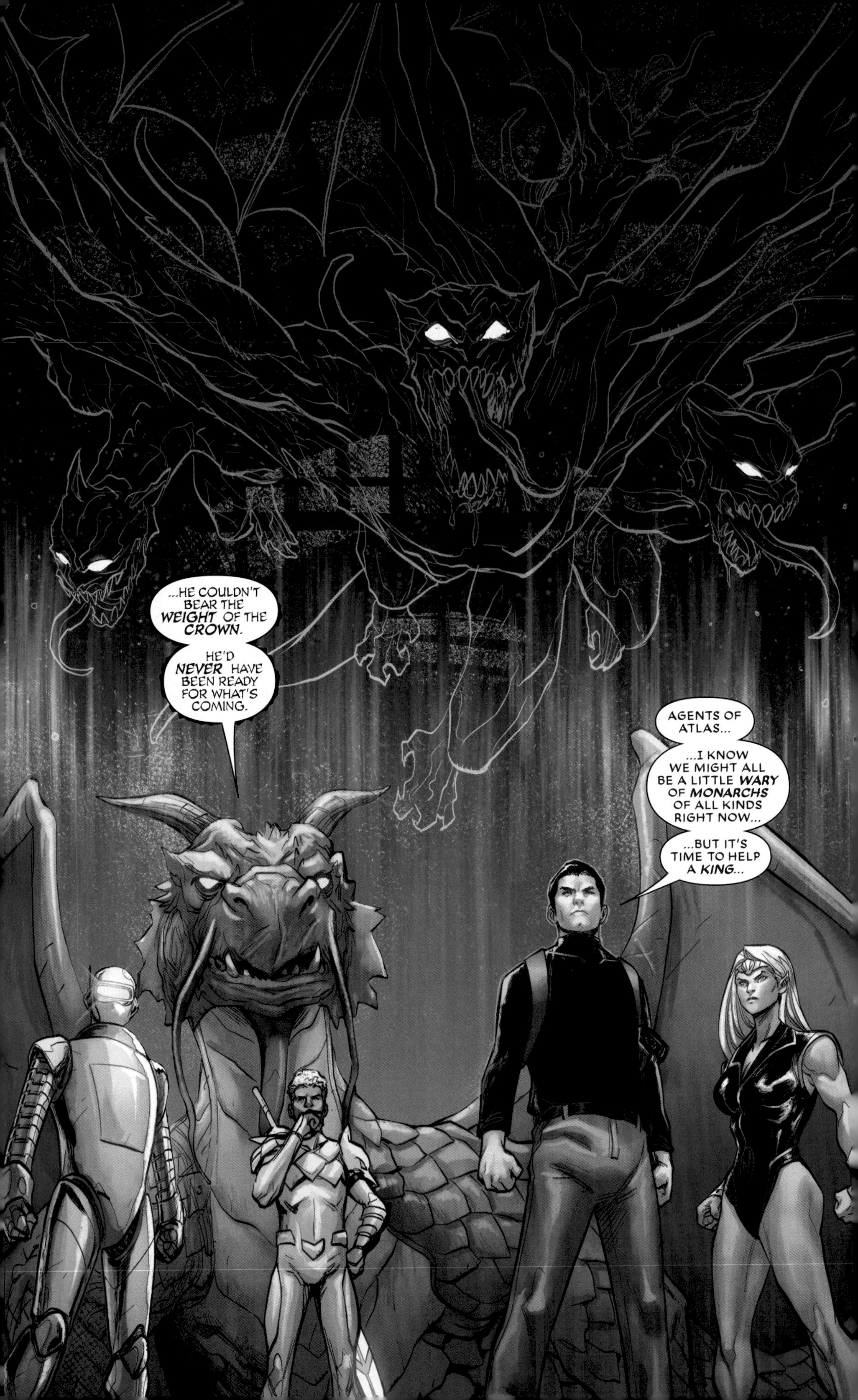

...HE COULDN'T BEAR THE *WEIGHT* OF THE *CROWN*.
HE'D *NEVER* HAVE BEEN READY FOR WHAT'S COMING.
AGENTS OF ATLAS...
...I KNOW WE MIGHT ALL BE A LITTLE *WARY* OF *MONARCHS* OF ALL KINDS RIGHT NOW...
...BUT IT'S TIME TO HELP A *KING*...

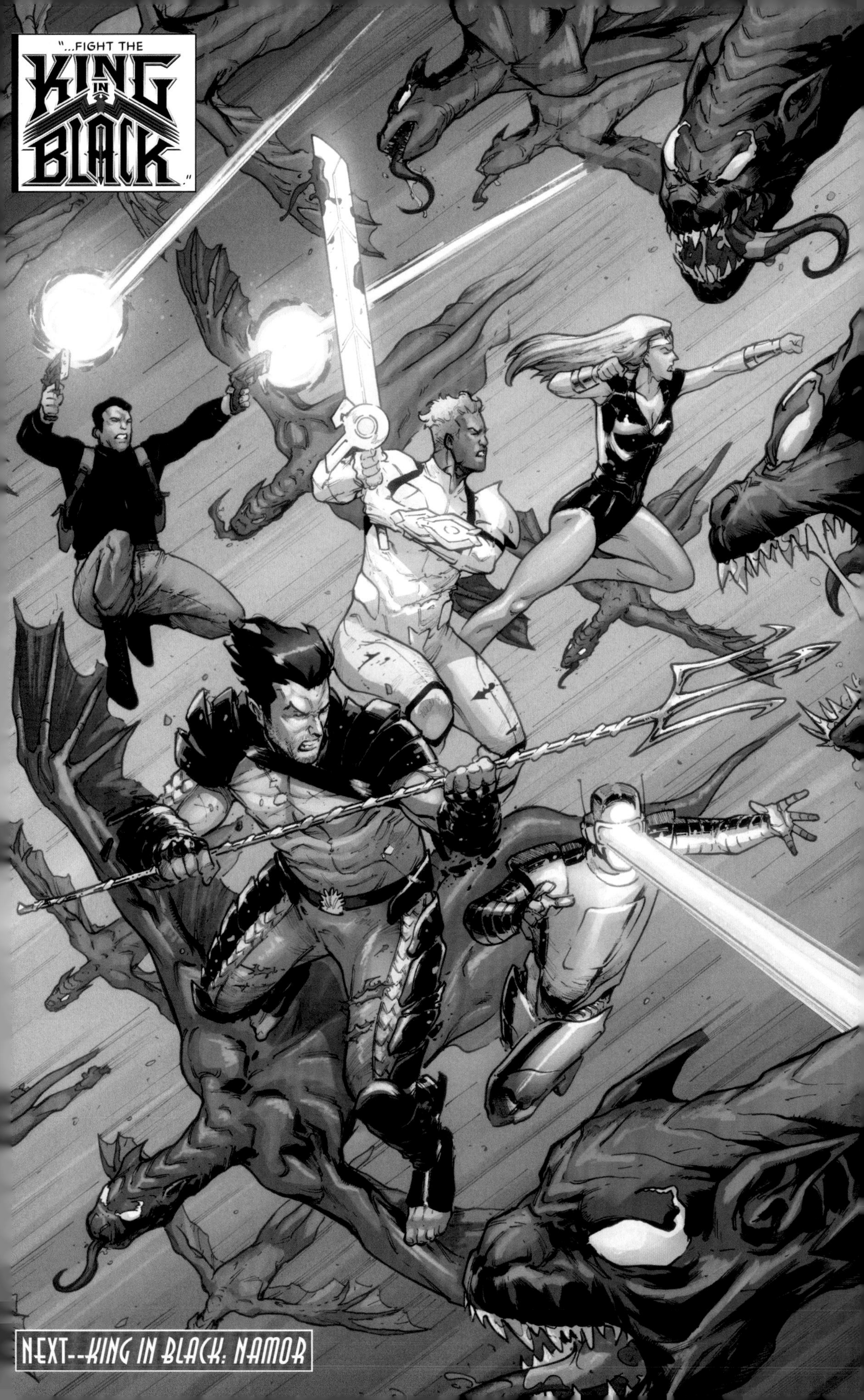
"...FIGHT THE
KING IN BLACK"
NEXT--KING IN BLACK: NAMOR

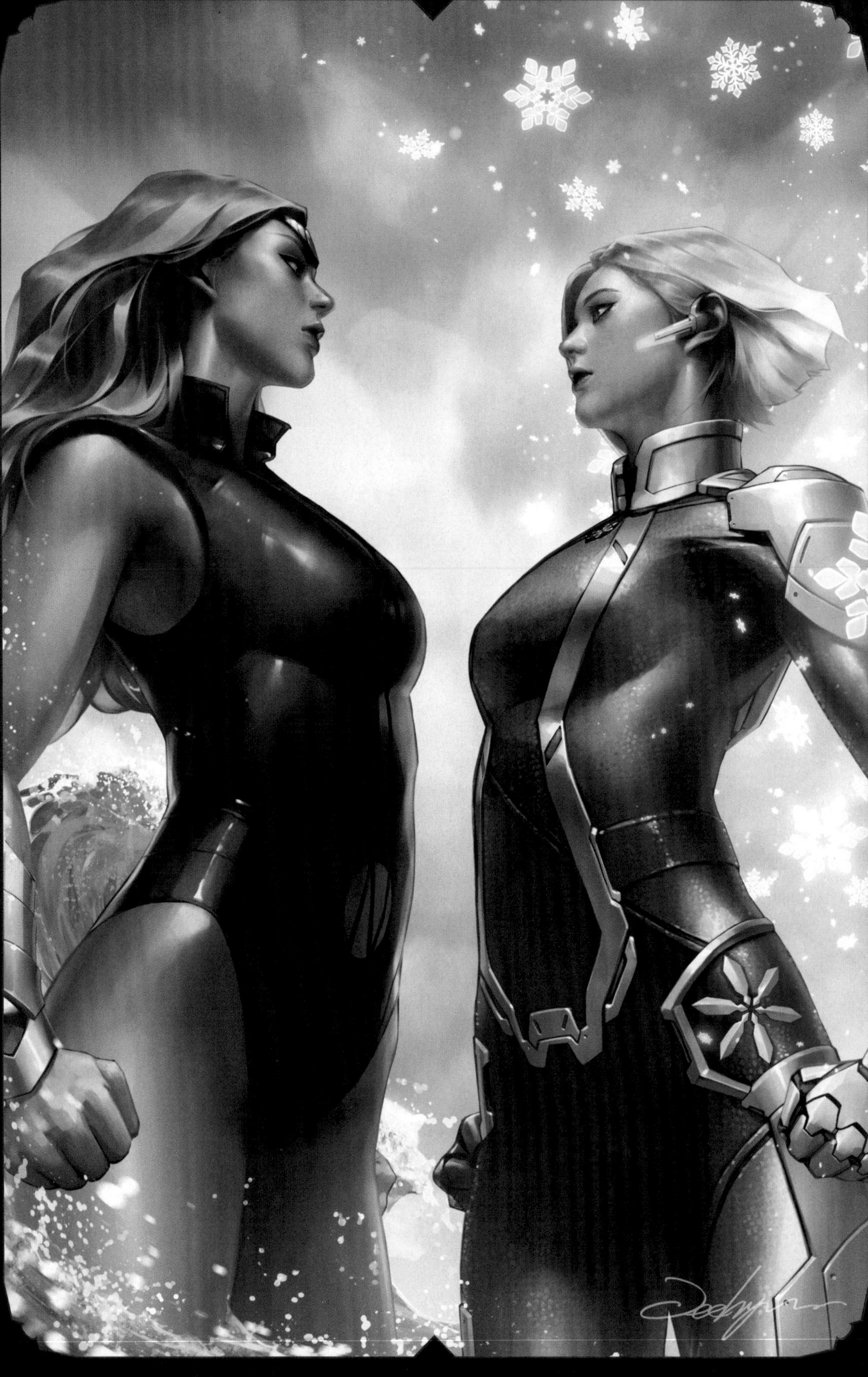

#1 VARIANT BY **JEEHYUNG LEE**

#1 HIDDEN GEM VARIANT BY
BILL EVERETT & **CHRIS SOTOMAYOR**

#1 VARIANT BY
RON LIM & **ISRAEL SILVA**

#1 CHINESE NEW YEAR VARIANT BY
GERARDO SANDOVAL & **ROMULO**

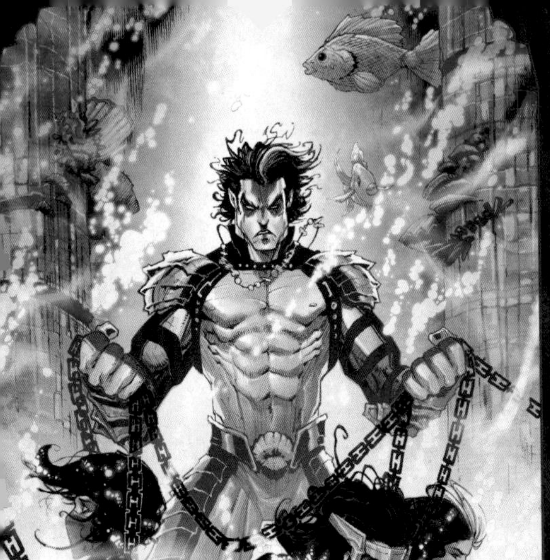

#2 VARIANT BY
GERARDO SANDOVAL & ROMULO FAJARDO JR.

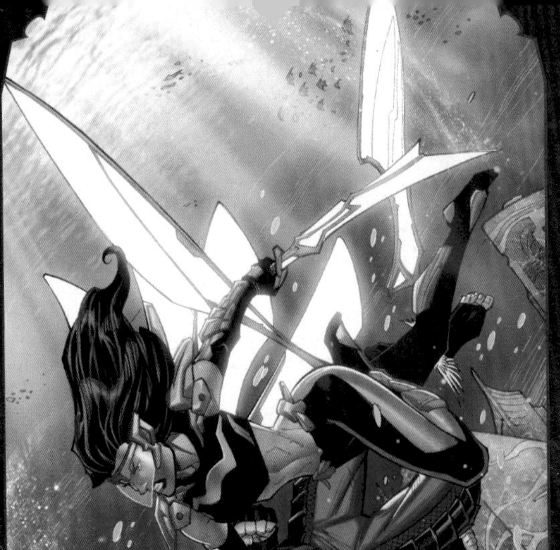

#2 VARIANT BY
RON LIM & ISRAEL SILVA

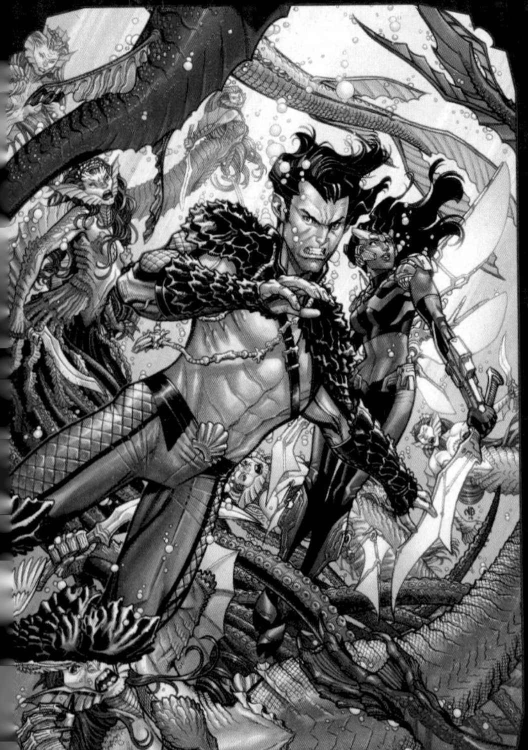

#3 VARIANT BY

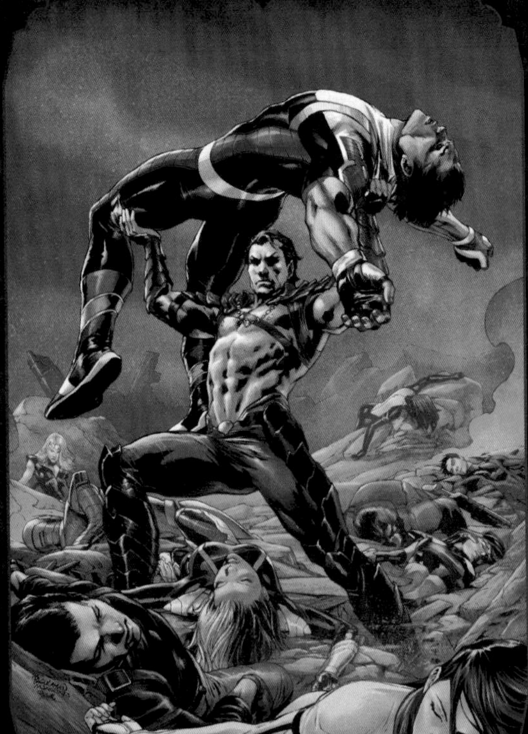

#5 VARIANT BY

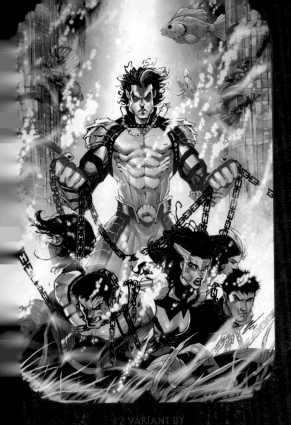

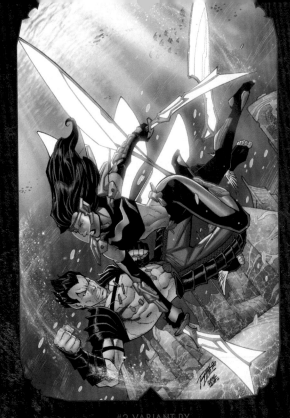